The New Public Safety

The New Public Safety

POLICE REFORM AND THE LURKING THREAT TO CIVIL LIBERTIES

Shawn E. Fields

UNIVERSITY OF CALIFORNIA PRESS

University of California Press
Oakland, California

Cataloging-in-Publication Data is on file at the Library of Congress.

ISBN 978-0-520-39599-2 (cloth : alk. paper)
ISBN 978-0-520-39600-5 (pbk. : alk. paper)
ISBN 978-0-520-39601-2 (ebook)

Manufactured in the United States of America

GPSR Authorized Representative: Easy Access System Europe,
Mustamäe tee 50, 10621 Tallinn, Estonia, gpsr.requests@easproject
.com

34 33 32 31 30 29 28 27 26 25
10 9 8 7 6 5 4 3 2 1

To my children
Who inspire me to do good

Contents

Contents

Acknowledgments

This book has been a multiyear labor of love that would not be possible without the love, support, and encouragement of many people. I benefited greatly from insights and productive conversations with brilliant scholars, including Don Dripps, Tony Ghiotto, Gustavo Ribeiro, Joanna Schwartz, Sean Scott, Erin Sheley, and Daniel Yeager. I am gratefully indebted to California Western School of Law for its institutional support, and especially to Susan Bisom-Rapp and Hannah Brenner Johnson for prioritizing the space needed to think about and wrestle with the ideas in this book. This book has also been made immeasurably better by the dedicated and talented publishers at University of California Press. I extend special thanks to Maura Roessner at UC Press, who believed in this project from the beginning and has supported it through all its twists and turns. And nothing I do would be possible without my wife, Noël, who selflessly gives of her time to support my writing, our family, and me. I dedicate this book to my beautiful, smart, impressively talented children, who are my reason for promoting a new public safety.

Introduction

THE UNINTENDED CONSEQUENCES
OF "DEFUND THE POLICE"

Santo de la Cruz called New York City's 311 help line seeking medical assistance for his son, Raul. Raul de la Cruz was homeless and had a history of mental illness, and on that particular morning he had begun acting erratically after showering at his father's house. Santo told the dispatcher that Raul was holding a kitchen knife and he was afraid Raul might hurt himself. Six police officers responded to the call and ordered Raul to drop the knife. The officers shouted commands in English, though Raul understood only Spanish. Raul kept his distance from the officers, neither lunging at nor threatening them. He also never made any movements to harm himself. It didn't matter. Twenty-eight seconds after arriving at the house, officers shot Raul six times.[1] He remained hospitalized for several weeks.

Officer Jeronimo Yanez of the St. Anthony Police Department outside Minneapolis pulled over thirty-two-year-old Philando Castile and his girlfriend for a traffic violation. Upon approaching the car, Yanez asked if Castile had any weapons in the car. Castile answered that he had a registered handgun for which he had a concealed-carry permit. Yanez ordered Castile three times not to "pull it out" before firing seven close-range shots at Castile, hitting him five times. Castile died twenty minutes later. The entire incident was captured on police dashcam video and Castile's girlfriend's Facebook livestream. Both videos show that Castile never reached for his firearm. Castile's four-year-old daughter watched the entire scene from the backseat of the car.[2]

Scott McKenna began suffering from a seizure in his home. His fourteen-year-old daughter called 911 and told the dispatcher his father was choking or having a seizure, but she wasn't sure. Two officers responded and ordered McKenna to stand up and put his pants on, which he could not do. Officers then handcuffed McKenna and pinned him to the ground, while one of the officers ransacked the bedroom and bathroom looking for evidence of drug use or other criminal activity despite the medical nature of the call. One officer on the scene later admitted that "we're always investigating for crimes" regardless of the emergency. The officers caused extensive property damage, and while McKenna survived the encounter he suffered broken bones and other life-altering injuries. All three of McKenna's young daughters were home and witnessed the incident.[3]

Ariell Brundige joined her boyfriend and a friend named Christopher Williams to buy what they thought was heroin from a drug dealer. Unfortunately, it turned out to be fentanyl, and Brundige overdosed. Williams immediately called 911 to seek medical attention, but instead police arrived ready to investigate the drug sale. As Brundige passed away, police focused on Williams, the man who had called 911 seeking help, and arrested him for manslaughter. At no point did officers provide aid to Brundige or attempt to reverse the overdose.[4]

These stories share certain similarities. In each case, police responded to a public safety event—a mental health disturbance, a traffic violation, a medical emergency, and a drug overdose—that did not involve the commission of a serious crime. In each case, police responded aggressively, using force first to resolve a nonviolent situation. Each case ended in unnecessary tragedy. And each case involved a public safety issue that did not require or inherently justify the presence of armed crime fighters trained primarily to use force and arrest criminals.

The decades-long conversation about whether, why, and how to reform policing in America burst into the nation's mainstream consciousness after the killing of Michael Brown in Ferguson, Missouri, in 2014, and again after George Floyd's murder in 2020. Most early reform conversations centered on how to better train officers to de-escalate situations, respond to welfare checks with more compassion and nuance, recognize implicit racial and intersectional bias, and stop targeting, arresting, and killing Black and Brown people at wildly disproportionate rates.

It hasn't worked. By the time of Floyd's murder, significant empirical evidence had shown that training programs to make police less violent and discriminatory had no meaningful impact on unlawful police violence or discriminatory enforcement. Training programs to make officers more capable of responding to the full panoply of noncriminal emergencies thrust upon them every day have had essentially no impact at all. In fact, as many as half of all people killed by American police had diagnosed disabilities, and at least 20 percent of all unarmed victims suffered from mental illness.[5] People with untreated mental illness are sixteen times more likely to be shot and killed by police, and that number doubles again for African Americans with mental illness.[6] Similar shocking statistics illustrate the disproportionate use of force—lethal and nonlethal—and tendency to arrest in situations involving medical emergencies, social welfare calls, homelessness issues, and nonviolent noncriminal traffic stops.

Not surprisingly, the reform conversation has stopped asking how to make police better all-purpose general responders to every public safety issue in society and has started asking why we make police respond to these issues at all. Ubiquitous rallying cries to "defund the police" in 2020 and beyond captured this sentiment, serving as a sort of umbrella term for various types of police reform advocacy all aimed at reducing the size, scope, and function of armed police in American society. These defund arguments come in many shapes and sizes. For example, total police "abolitionists" claim not to be surprised by the inability of police to reform, arguing that the entire system of policing in this country is rooted in oppression and exploitation and is designed to subjugate marginalized communities. They claim that the only solution is one that abolishes all police, root and branch, and replaces police with a radically reimagined public safety apparatus, one that places power in the hands of nongovernmental "communities of care," invests in social welfare first, and arrests and kills people last.

This "police abolition" sentiment sits within a larger abolition movement to dismantle the entire criminal legal system, including eliminating prisons and the prosecutors who fill them. Activists like Angela Davis, Mariame

Kaba, Ruth Wilson Gilmore, Andrea Ritchie, and Alex Vitale point to the inherent injustice infecting police at every level, but they lay the blame more broadly on a deeply flawed criminal legal system for which police are merely the frontline service providers. Criminal codes authorize severe punishment for nonviolent offenses. Prosecutors leverage their power against indigent defendants by overcharging them and threatening them with draconian sentences unless they waive their constitutional rights and plead guilty. Mandatory minimum sentences fuel a mass incarceration crisis defined by overcrowded prisons that do little more than exacerbate mental illness and leave people broken, penniless, and powerless upon reentry. Our society attaches so many collateral consequences to conviction—denial of housing aid, educational advancement, employment opportunities, and voting rights—that recidivism is all but inevitable. An unfair system disproportionately disadvantages poor communities and communities of color. These reformers see police as a tool in the larger exploitative criminal legal apparatus, a tool to be wholly dismantled and replaced.

A second set of reformers takes a more targeted approach, one that responds directly to the issues raised by the heartbreaking stories at the beginning of this introduction. Rather than abolishing all police and prisons and eliminating the criminal code, why not simply refocus the policing function on the things police are trained to do well—prevent and respond to violent crime—and let nonpolice experts in medical emergencies, mental health, substance abuse, homelessness, child welfare, and even traffic enforcement handle the rest? Alternately referred to as "disaggregating" or "unbundling" the policing function, these reformers seek to reduce (but not eliminate) the traditional armed police footprint in this country, in a way that reallocates resources efficiently and effectively to address myriad nonviolent public safety emergencies while retaining a small "crime-fighting" force to respond to violent crime. This approach, while more modest than total abolition, indirectly promotes some goals of that movement by removing the violent, carceral impulse of police from most public safety situations, which in turn reduces opportunities for arrest, unlawful force, and discriminatory treatment.

This approach also has the benefit of popular support. Ask any cross section of Americans whether they want to "defund the police" (as pollsters have done many times), and the overwhelming majority will say "no."[7] But phrase the question differently and ask if trained psychiatrists instead of police should respond to mental health disturbances, and an equal number of respondents will say "yes."[8] Indeed, dozens of cities large and small have funded pilot programs in recent years to allow nonpolice crisis interventionists, mental health counselors, homelessness outreach teams, and other "alternate responders" to address public safety issues without police involvement. And while still only an idea to date, the possibility of replacing police with civilian traffic monitors to enforce nonviolent laws on the nation's roadways has garnered increasing support, even among police.[9]

This unbundling of the police function—this "new public safety"—promises to radically redefine public safety. But it also poses significant and surprising risks to individual liberties. As academics, activists, and lawmakers explore alternatives to police, it also bears asking whether the constitutional guarantees regulating police conduct—laws preventing unreasonable searches, invasive seizures, and excessive force—would also regulate the actions of nonpolice alternate responders.[10] Surprisingly, the answer is often no. The US Supreme Court has emphasized in a long line of complicated and often contradictory cases that the "primary purpose" of these fundamental constitutional rights is to restrain criminal investigations by law enforcement. Outside that context, courts are reluctant to grant protections from government searches, seizures, and physical violence, and they are even more reluctant to strictly adhere to the probable-cause and warrant requirements that constrain police overreach.

Herein lies a major, unexplored challenge for this current police reform movement. By moving many public safety functions outside the criminal investigative sphere, reformers would also move much intrusive government conduct outside these traditional strictures and guardrails. The unintended consequences of this reduction in constitutional protections may subject—and in many cases, already has subjected—innocent people to unnecessary and harmful infringements of their privacy and liberty interests. This book examines two unintended consequences of this reduction in civil rights protections from alternate responder overreach, both of which highlight how the new public safety threatens to repeat many of the same violent, discriminatory, and overly punitive mistakes it is designed to solve.

The first unintended consequence involves the risk that alternate responders who regularly encounter illegal activity may effectively act as eyes and ears for police and prosecutors eager to use these responders' unconstrained access to arrest and imprison vulnerable citizens. To help illustrate the concern, a few hypothetical scenarios, adapted slightly from real-world situations, are instructive.

Hypothetical 1: A crisis counselor working with a city's homelessness outreach team has grown tired of the flow of drugs in a local homeless encampment and its deleterious effect on her clients. One day she snaps and barges into the encampment unannounced, ripping open tents and searching through unhoused persons' belongings until she finds illegal narcotics and related paraphernalia. She seizes and inventories them and turns them over to the police.

Hypothetical 2: A social worker for an impoverished family shows up unannounced to conduct a welfare check on the children. He finds that no one is home but the front door is unlocked. He enters the home without permission and, curious about how the family recently was able to purchase a new car, begins searching through drawers in the kitchen and bedroom. He quickly finds evidence of a counterfeiting operation, which he turns over to police.

Hypothetical 3: A sworn nonpolice civilian traffic enforcer stops a car for speeding. During the stop and with no reason to do so, he forces the driver out of the car, forcefully pins the driver to the ground, and pulls what is later determined to be an unregistered handgun from the driver's waistband. While the driver is pinned to the ground and in obvious pain, the traffic enforcer yells, "Tell me where you got this gun!" The driver reluctantly admits he bought it illegally from a pawnshop. The gun is turned over to the police; the driver suffers three broken ribs.

Serious breaches of constitutional guarantees appear to have taken place in each of these scenarios. The Fourth Amendment requires individualized suspicion of wrongdoing, either reasonable suspicion or probable cause, before engagement in the sorts of blatant searches and seizures conducted in these hypotheticals. No such suspicion existed here. The Fourth Amendment also prevents excessive force, which the traffic enforcer clearly applied. Had a police officer engaged in this conduct, these constitutional provisions almost certainly would have applied, thus allowing the victim to suppress the illegally obtained evidence (keep it out of court in any criminal case against him) and potentially to seek damages in a federal civil rights lawsuit.

But because the perpetrators in these scenarios were nonpolice alternate responders, with a primary purpose specifically divorced from criminal investigations, their actions may very well fall outside the Constitution's protections, at least under current court interpretation. Thus, the evidence in these hypotheticals, and in any future scenario involving an alternate responder and unsuspecting citizens, can be seized with brute force for any reason or no reason at all without any individualized suspicion or repercussion. This risk presents a potential end run around the US Constitution and other important civil liberties protections for "noncriminal" investigations by alternate responders. This potential loophole not only puts basic fundamental constitutional guarantees at risk in a world increasingly reliant on alternate responders but also risks frustrating the very noncarceral objectives behind replacing police with alternate responders.

One may read these scenarios and wonder whether someone trained and employed specifically to provide medical or mental health aid really would so willingly help police arrest their clients. Indeed, if they have chosen a profession designed in part as an alternative to incarceration, why assist in that criminal process? The answer is that many alternate response agencies have little choice but to cooperate with and assist police. While thousands of cities across the country employ "crisis intervention teams," or CITs, to triage various public safety emergencies, these teams often consist of a nonpolice expert who is required to co-respond with a uniformed officer who may or may not have received some level of CIT training herself. For those few alternate response programs allowed to respond independently of police, their mandate is limited to a small subset of calls where it is clear no weapon or criminal activity is involved. If either is identified by the responder, officers must be called to the scene. And even where law might authorize a completely independent nonpolice response, as in the case of psychologists assessing whether to hospitalize someone in crisis under an emergency psychiatric hold, police may ultimately be required to respond with force if the patient refuses to comply. In each of these situations, the responding nonpolice expert often will learn about some illegal activity and will be required to disclose that in debrief to the responding officer. This information will not have been collected pursuant to probable cause or a judicial warrant, because those requirements don't apply to alternate responders. And yet the officer can utilize that information to arrest and prosecute.

This risk that alternate responders will serve as the eyes and ears for police illustrates the second major unintended consequence of the new public safety: that a growing industry of emergency response nonpolice agents will continue to feed a problematic system of "soft policing" defined by forcibly removing undesirable citizens from the public square and into prison-like conditions of confinement in psychiatric wards, drug treatment centers, and dangerous temporary shelters. For many people experiencing an acute crisis, the presence of a medical professional instead of a police officer is a welcome sign. But for others, involuntary hospitalization by doctors empowered to forcibly medicate as an alternative to arrest and prosecution is no alternative at all. As one young Black woman with mental illness described, "Whether the cops or the EMTs come get me, I often can't tell whether I am in the jail or locked hospital ward. I guess one has slightly nicer sheets."[11] This alarmingly close connection between nonpolice alternate responders and the quasi-carceral systems within which they function provides another urgent reason to carefully examine how and with whom we replace police.

As its title implies, this book aims to do two things. First, it catalogs the evolving conversation around reimagining public safety without police and advocates for a significantly larger role for nonpolice alternate responders. Second, it provides the first-ever sustained evaluation of the risk this reimagined public safety poses to civil liberties and proposes legislative and judicial solutions to ensure the continued full protection of our civil and constitutional rights within this new public safety.

Here a few caveats are in order. First, despite the importance of the police and prison abolition movement in forcing Americans to reevaluate our relationship with police in recent years, the police reforms discussed in this book are not abolitionist in nature. Prison and police abolitionists envision a world with *no* police, *no* prosecutors, and *no* prisons. Thus, the unintended risk of criminal prosecution described in the hypotheticals above simply would not exist in a truly abolitionist world.

Indeed, some abolitionists might even point to the lurking threat to civil liberties posed by these so-called half measures at police reform as a further reason to dismantle the entire system. This point has value, and I return to it throughout the book by challenging the problematic quasi-policing nature of long-term psychiatric, drug treatment, social welfare, and temporary housing programs.

That said, the decision to focus directly on reforms aimed at reducing, but not eliminating, the police footprint stems from the urgent need to critically examine the new public safety as it exists today and as it is likely to evolve in the near future. Thousands of nonpolice crisis intervention teams, mental health responders, homeless outreach teams, and violence interruption units have been piloted or funded with reallocated police department funds. Many pilot programs launched after the 2020 police brutality protests, but others have existed for decades with relatively little scrutiny. And whether these disaggregation reforms are or are not more desirable than full-scale abolition, they are certainly more popular, politically palatable, and achievable. Either way, these reforms must be taken seriously. They have been and should be celebrated when they improve public safety, but they should also be critically examined when they do or threaten to violate fundamental civil liberties.

A second caveat is that this book's focus on civil liberties concentrates primarily on the threat to constitutional protections enshrined in the Fourth Amendment to the US Constitution. Along with the Fifth and Sixth Amendments, these protections are often referred to as the "criminal procedure amendments" because they apply primarily to criminal investigations and protect the rights of the accused. The most pressing reason for this focus involves the potential remedies available for government violations of these rights: the ability of a detained individual to challenge her detention and of a criminal defendant to prevent the use of unlawfully obtained evidence against her at her trial. The threat of an end run around these criminal investigative constraints leading to unjustified arrests and tainted prosecutions is the most significant lurking threat posed by the new public safety, at least to those individuals directly affected and facing the risk of jail time.

To be sure, there are other potentially valuable ways to reduce the threat of alternate responder overreach. Federal civil rights lawsuits, private state lawsuits for battery or false imprisonment, and adverse employment actions all might serve as valuable tools to restrain the unlawful impulses of nonpolice agents. I discuss each in turn. But none of them provide the suppression-of-evidence remedy most immediately valuable to those most directly and adversely affected by an alternate responder's unlawful seizure of criminal evidence. Moreover, none of these other tools possess the symbolic, expressive power of a court finding a violation of a fundamental constitutional right, the type of finding that often precedes necessary structural reforms.

Last, one might fairly wonder how widespread or serious the risks contemplated in this book really are, either currently or predictively into the future. After all, won't mental health experts, social workers, and substance abuse counselors be trained and oriented to provide more compassionate holistic care and be less likely to act violently or with any desire to collect evidence to use against their clients? That is a fair question. And certainly one would believe, as I do, that employing these trained experts will reduce many of the deleterious effects of an overzealous and overaggressive police force in this country. But we already know that replacing police with nonpolice alternate responders does not eliminate the perpetration of violence and infringement of fundamental liberties against innocent citizens. Throughout this book, I catalog many examples of emergency medical technicians, homeless outreach personnel, social workers, and crisis interventionists using what would be unlawful force, mandating what would be an unlawful detention, and procuring what would be tainted evidence against the very citizens these alternate responders were sworn to protect. Moreover, as these nonpolice agencies proliferate and constitute larger portions of municipal budgets relative to police departments, one may fairly assume at least some personnel overlap between former police officers and nonpolice public safety agents. This prediction, should it come to pass, may further entrench a carceral, criminal investigative mindset in organizations created in opposition to that approach.

At its core, this book both celebrates these sensible and much-needed police reforms and warns of the risks of uncritically replacing police with "Someone Else" charged with putting people in crisis "Somewhere Else."[12] Reducing the role of armed police as "jack of all trades" problem solvers and replacing them in at least some of these functions with trained non-police specialists benefits both police and the community they serve, promotes better access to social welfare resources, and saves lives. Chapters 1 and 2 explore why unbundling the policing function is so important and how this work is being done in cities and counties across the country.

Chapters 3 and 4 examine the darker side of nonpolice emergency response, both in practice and in theory. These chapters dive critically into the long and often regrettable history of soft policing by social workers who abuse clients, psychiatrists who hospitalize high-functioning patients in gulags, medical personnel who violently assault the infirm, and homeless "outreach" teams who sweep away entire communities without providing adequate alternatives. These individual actions are not isolated but often are dictated by programs that are billed as alternatives to arrest but that often lead to the same result: social welfare programs conditioning aid on arbitrary and invasive searches with threats of arrest for suspected fraud; long-term civil commitment that functions as a parallel prison system; agreements between doctors and law enforcement to turn over patients who test positive for drugs or, increasingly, who seek out illegal reproductive care. These chapters investigate alternate responder abuses through the lens of the laws that would protect these vulnerable victims if their perpetrators were police—the US Constitution's Fourth Amendment—but that fail to offer effective recourse against institutional soft policing. As we will see, alternative solutions like private lawsuits, tighter internal regulations, and adverse employment actions do not effectively fill the vacuum left by this gap in constitutional civil rights protection.

But the book ends on a hopeful note. Chapters 5 and 6 provide proposals for structural alternate responder reforms at the legislative, municipal, and judicial levels that retain the benefits of disaggregating the policing function while restraining the real and potential threats to civil liberties posed by nonpolice social welfare entities. One set of proposals includes model municipal legislation designed to preemptively address these risks by strictly limiting alternate responder authority and providing robust remedies for violations. These model rules have the added benefit of enjoying broad bipartisan support, making them achievable if packaged and communicated properly. The other set of proposals aims to undo much of the damage done by the US Supreme Court's unwillingness to apply the Bill of Rights' fundamental liberty and privacy protections to people abused by all government actors instead of just police. While prospects for this sort of rights expansion at the nation's highest court may be unlikely in the near term, much more receptive audiences exist both in the form of state courts interpreting their own respective constitutions and in the form of state citizens considering ballot initiatives to expand statewide protections against nonpolice abuse. These judicial reforms, which return the focus to the person harmed by government action rather than the subjective intent of or uniform worn by the government actor, accord with the original intent and design of the Fourth Amendment, have support across ideological lines, and promise to protect the rights of vulnerable Americans while allowing alternate responders to work toward meaningfully improving public safety in America.

1 Why Are Police Everything Everywhere All at Once?

In the surprise hit movie *Everything Everywhere All at Once*, a middle-aged Chinese American immigrant struggling with problems at home and work discovers that she is able to jump across multiple universes and multiple time periods. The film is a delightful, intentional mess. It incorporates many genres and film mediums—often simultaneously—including surreal comedy, science fiction, fantasy, absurdism, martial arts, and animation. The protagonist, Evelyn, jumps from one crazy universe to the next, including a universe where everyone has hot dogs for fingers and one where everyone is a rock with googly eyes. The movie goes so many places and spans so many dimensions so quickly while Evelyn becomes her own uber-competent superhero that it appears as if Evelyn truly is everything everywhere all at once. Yet for all the "swirls of genre anarchy" and "flights of science-fiction mumbo-jumbo," the film masterfully portrays a family trying to find meaning and light in a seemingly meaningless world.[1] With 266 awards out of 405 nominations, *Everything Everywhere All at Once* is estimated to be the most awarded film of all time.[2]

This fantasy of bending time and space and having just the right skill set to handle any situation in wildly different contexts is just that: fantasy. And yet it fairly describes what we expect from modern policing in the

United States. We rely on police officers—armed government agents trained almost exclusively to detect crime, arrest bad guys, and use force to do so—to travel the multiverse of public safety emergencies and solve a seemingly endless set of social problems that have nothing to do with crime and do not need force to solve. We ask police to be twenty-four-hour all-purpose general responders and resolve medical emergencies, mental health crises, substance abuse issues, homelessness, neighbor disputes, noise complaints, traffic infractions, and cats in trees. Professors Sylvester Amara Lamin and Consoler Teboh observed that police are asked to act as "veterinary surgeon, mental welfare officer, marriage guidance counselor, home-help to the infirm, welfare worker, friend, and confidant."[3] And these non-crime-fighting tasks constitute a substantial part of an officer's job. In many cities, as much as 90 percent of a cop's on-duty time is spent handling public safety issues not related to crime, while only an average of 4 percent of an officer's time is spent responding to violent crime.[4]

But unlike Evelyn, police do not possess Swiss army knife–like super-powers. No amount of training could adequately prepare one person to handle every public safety concern that arises in a given day. And in fact, police are particularly ill-suited to the task. Policing as an institution in the United States has a long and dismal record of using its immense power and discretion in discriminatory, unlawful, and unnecessarily violent ways. Much of American policing's history is defined by explicit commands to reinforce hierarchies along race, class, gender, and sexual orientation lines by criminalizing and disparately targeting vulnerable minority groups.[5] Contemporary efforts to redress these injustices through racial sensitivity, implicit bias, and procedural justice trainings have done little to change the racialized nature of policing.[6] And even if the structural inequities of policing could be trained away, the fact remains that the vast majority of a police cadet's short training focuses on using force to detect violent crime and catch the bad guys.[7]

In short, we ask a deeply flawed, deliberately violent, immensely powerful government institution to handle every social ill under the sun without providing it even a fraction of the training or tools necessary to do this impossible job. It should come as no surprise, then, that literally millions of Americans are arrested every year, most for nonviolent drug or "social disorder" offenses, and that as many as half of those millions suffer from mental health or substance use disorders for which a medical or mental health intervention would have been more appropriate.[8] It should also come as no surprise that half of all Americans who suffer violence at the hands of police (and 25 percent of those killed by police) suffer from mental illness, that a disproportionate number of these individuals are Black and Brown, and that most such violence arose from a nonviolent encounter like a traffic stop or welfare check.[9]

Something has to change. Even in today's deeply polarized political climate and even with as controversial a topic as police reform, large majorities of Americans across all demographic groups agree that some level of police reform is required.[10] But where do we begin to address this unique issue of asking police to be everything to everyone in our complex world of public health and safety? Princeton sociologist Patrick Sharkey says that any police reform movement should be guided by two questions: First, what do police actually do? Second, why does and why *should* the United States need armed police to do those things?[11] This chapter, and in some ways this entire book, attempt to answer these two questions.

WHAT DO POLICE DO ALL DAY?

Of all government institutions, including those tasked with various aspects of public safety, police are unique in that they are empowered not only to enforce criminal laws but to use force to do so. This uniqueness of police—the ability to use armed, deadly force to ensure compliance with criminal law—suggests that police are specialists who ought to be tasked with using that specialized skill set to respond to situations involving crime and the need to use force to ensure public safety. And in one sense, this does happen. Police alone are empowered to enforce criminal laws through investigations and arrests, and police alone are authorized to carry and use firearms and deadly force to do so.[12] No other government agency is given as much jurisdiction, discretion, and latitude over the use of force to ensure compliance with the law.[13]

But just because only police are authorized to use force does not mean police are authorized only to use force. In fact, most of what police officers do involves neither violence nor crime. Instead, policing in the United

States "tends to be a one-size-fits-all endeavor that . . . is an odd match, at best, for the actual problems the police are called out daily to address."[14] Police themselves recognize this reality. Former Dallas police chief and Chicago Police Department superintendent David Brown explained:

> We're asking cops to do too much in this country. . . . We are. Every societal failure, we put it off on the cops to solve. Not enough mental health funding, let the cops handle it. . . . Here in Dallas we got a loose dog problem; let's have the cops chase loose dogs. Schools fail, let's give it to the cops. . . . That's too much to ask. Policing was never meant to solve all those problems.[15]

The truth is, cops do remarkably little crime fighting. A "major theme of the earliest studies concerning urban officer workload involved dispelling the popular myth that police spend most of their time protecting the 'thin blue line' between law and order."[16] In Baltimore, "the most violent, the most addicted and the most abandoned city in [A]merica," according to then-mayor Martin O'Malley, regular patrol officers spent about 11 percent of their time dealing with crime.[17] Even that was split about fifty-fifty between serious crime and things like disorderly conduct, drug possession, drunkenness, and loitering.[18] One national study found that 50 to 90 percent of an officer's time is spent on social work functions, particularly in economically distressed areas.[19] Similar localized studies from New Orleans, Sacramento, and Montgomery County, Maryland, found that police spend only an average of 4 percent of their time on violent crimes, compared with roughly 50 percent on noncriminal disturbances and traffic accidents.[20] In smaller jurisdictions, the volume of time spent on crime, "defined comprehensively, can be way lower: 0.7 to 2.2% of a cop's shift."[21]

A sizable percentage of an officer's interpersonal "non-crime-fighting" time involves responding to and triaging issues stemming from mental illness. Well over half of all the nontraffic contacts police have with individuals involve someone with a diagnosed or presenting mental illness.[22] As many as 25 percent of those encounters end in arrest for a low-level offense when a medical or mental health intervention would have been more appropriate.[23] This reality itself is an uneasy fit for a crime-fighting force constituted and trained to enforce criminal laws. Why? Because of "the obvious (but seemingly elusive) point that mental illness is not a crime; it's a disease."[24] While it is of course true that mental illness can cause someone to commit a crime, most mental health disturbances to which police respond do not involve serious criminal behavior. Instead, they involve the kind of erratic behavior indicative of mental illness that a trained criminal investigator perceives first and foremost as suspicious behavior indicative of criminal activity. Indeed, most state police academies require eight hours or less of cadet training in how to identify and handle issues arising from mental illness.[25] Not surprisingly, then, "Stories abound of the police shooting and killing schizophrenic or mentally disabled people," including the homeless, for exhibiting atypical "suspicious" behavior during a mental health episode.[26]

Closely connected to mental illness triage is police's increasing role in addressing homelessness and the social ills related to America's affordable housing crisis. Nearly two-thirds of all unhoused persons in the United States suffer from mental illness, while 38 percent suffer from alcoholism and 26 percent experience drug addiction.[27] But rather than deploying substance abuse and mental health counselors to work with this population, most cities continue to rely on police to "adjudicate conflicts between people experiencing homelessness and people annoyed by those people's presence."[28] This reliance on police to resolve public safety issues concerning the unhoused has only increased with sharp rises in homeless populations, particularly in western states like California and Oregon. Recent court cases have thrust police into this role as "frontline workers for urban homeless," even though "officers aren't adequately trained to deal with the issues that those people are dealing with."[29]

In 2022, the Ninth Circuit Court of Appeals, the federal appellate court with jurisdiction over the western United States, held that states could not issue civil or criminal penalties against people for camping and sleeping in public where a lack of available shelter or affordable housing existed, reasoning that criminalizing involuntary homelessness amounted to cruel and unusual punishment.[30] The ruling stymied police-led efforts to destroy homeless encampments and arrest offenders in places like California, which has experienced double-digit percentage increases in homelessness year over year for a decade.[31] Two years later, the US Supreme Court reversed, holding in *City of Grants Pass v. Johnson* that states and cities could once again arrest individuals for engaging in "acts" related to being unhoused: sleeping, eating, drinking, sitting, and relieving oneself in public.[32] Within weeks of the decision, California governor Gavin Newsom issued an executive order directing the destruction of homeless encampments on state property and encouraged cities to do the same.[33] The order offered funding for services but relied critically on the power of police to destroy homes and force people to move under threat of arrest. These "sweeps" do not reduce homeless populations, nor do they address the underlying causes of houselessness. Nor, obviously, does an arrest and conviction for being houseless. And yet that remains the standard approach in even the most progressive jurisdictions.

Whether it is mental illness, addiction, homelessness, or some combination of the three, police have proven largely unequipped to deploy the skill sets needed to actually address these issues and improve the lives of those affected. This should not come as a surprise. As sociologist Bruce Western conceded, "Criminal justice is a poor instrument for social policy because at its core, it is a blaming institution."[34] It is not clear that the homeless, the mentally ill, and those addicted to drugs and alcohol are blameworthy in any classic sense. Thus, specialists with a monopoly on "force and law" seem to be particularly ill-suited to address these issues. And yet we continue to force police to do so.

But by far the greatest amount of noncriminal investigative time spent by police officers, as well as the most common contact between police and the public, involves traffic enforcement. Every year, approximately "50 million Americans come into contact with the police at least once," and "half of them are pulled over in a car that they're driving (19 million), or in which they are a passenger (6 million). Another 8 million are involved in a car accident."[35] But while most police interaction with civilians involves "driving around in cars talking to other people driving around in cars," there is no obvious connection between an officer "bedeck[ed] in cutting edge weaponry" and their functioning as a meter maid or traffic accident first responder.[36] This unnecessary marriage of nonviolent, noncriminal social infraction and violent "warrior cop" response predictably leads to unnecessary and tragic violent confrontation.[37] In fact, some police officers have responded to minor traffic infractions with what Salt Lake City district attorney Sam Gill calls "anticipatory killings," where officers "are primed with false narratives about the dangers of traffic stops and respond with over-aggression."[38] According to a *New York Times* investigative report, over four hundred unarmed passengers were killed by officers in a five-year period where neither drivers nor passengers were wielding a gun or knife, nor otherwise under pursuit for a violent crime. Only five officers were ever charged and convicted for these killings.[39]

POLICE AS REVENUE GENERATORS

Once we have a better understanding of *what* police do all day, the next natural question to ask is *why*. One answer: money. The singular reliance on police to enforce traffic laws and issue citations provides just one example of how state and local governments rely on police to generate revenue by regulating minor misconduct. A growing body of evidence "indicates that local police departments are increasingly being used to provide revenue for municipalities by imposing and collecting fees, fines, and asset forfeitures."[40] In the groundbreaking 2022 report *Revenue over Public Safety: How Perverse Financial Incentives Warp the Criminal Justice System*, researchers from the Brennan Center for Justice at NYU School of Law catalogued how cities lean on police to fill budget holes by fostering a culture of "more": write more tickets, make more arrests, incarcerate more people, and generate more city funds at every step.[41]

In addition to hefty traffic fines, many cities impose significant criminal fines for minor infractions and misdemeanors ranging from jaywalking and loitering to vandalism and drug possession. Criminal fees are imposed on defendants for the "privilege" of using the criminal justice system, including fees for indigent public defense, crime labs, and jail admission. Civil asset forfeiture laws allow police departments to seize and resell a suspect's assets and pocket the proceeds, including cash and cars, with no obligation to return the property even if the suspect is not convicted of a crime. And many cities contract with private community supervision companies to manage probation and parole, with fees charged to the people under supervision and split between the city and the private company.[42]

The revenue generated is far from trivial. In Georgia, ranked as the worst state in the country with laws that enable or encourage taxation through criminal citation, seventeen cities derive more than 25 percent of their budgets from traffic citation revenue alone.[43] When such revenue is combined with other criminal fines and fees, the total can make up a majority of a city's revenue. The city of Warwick, Georgia, derived 64 percent of its 2022 budget from criminal enforcement.[44] Similar fines and fees made up 73 percent of the budget of nearby Lenox, Georgia.[45] In Brookside, Alabama, where fines and forfeitures made up half of the city's revenues before litigation-spurred legislation capped the amount of money cities could derive from such sources, the local police department boosted the city's budget by 640 percent in just two years. Among other things, the department used those proceeds to purchase an armored vehicle nicknamed "The Tank" and a department K-9 named "Cash."[46]

Thousands of police departments generate this revenue by imposing quota systems on officers, tying performance metrics to quantitative data and requiring officers to issue a certain number of citations each day, week, or month. Examples of quotas disclosed by police include "twenty and one" (twenty tickets and one arrest per month); one speeding ticket per hour during a twelve-hour shift; eighteen tickets a shift; two to four warrants a week; and at least one hundred tickets a month.[47]

These fines and fees might prove less problematic if they were generated as a part of legitimate enforcement actions aimed at improving public safety. But often the opposite is true. Officers frustrated with these systems say they prevent officers from rendering nonenforcement assistance like mental health or substance abuse referrals, because those referrals cost the city money while arrests and citations make money. Quotas for low-level enforcement also disincentivize officers from spending time investigating more complex, potentially more serious crimes. One study found that officers with arrest and citation quotas have a lower clearance rate for violent crimes.[48] Quotas also encourage overpolicing of certain communities where minor infractions may be easier to identify and address, especially more impoverished and houseless communities; this decreases trust between police and those communities and further frustrates law enforcement investigations of more serious criminal activity.

Perversely, targeting poorer communities for nonviolent offenses and imposing the fines and fees associated with them makes communities less safe. In the fifteen states with the highest prison populations, 80 to 90 percent of all prisoners qualified for indigent defense.[49] Shockingly,

17 percent of respondents in one survey reported committing a crime—usually selling drugs—solely to pay off criminal fines and fees.[50] When poor people are burdened with thousands of dollars in fees for minor non-violent offenses, there may be no alternative.

Tom Barrett tried. A former pharmacist who fell into drug addiction and homelessness, he was arrested in Augusta, Georgia, for stealing a can of beer. He pleaded "no contest" and was sentenced to a $200 fine and a year of probation requiring him to wear an alcohol-monitoring bracelet. The bracelet, operated by Sentinel Offender Services, required a $50 start-up fee, a $39 monthly service fee, and a $12 daily usage fee. With no income or home and with an active addiction he was trying to control, Barrett donated plasma twice a month to pay the bracelet fees. With no money left over to buy food, Barrett began skipping meals, but his protein levels dropped so much that he became ineligible to donate plasma. When his debts to Sentinel grew to $1,000, the company sought a warrant for his arrest. And when Barrett was unable to pay, the judge put him in jail and charged him for the stay.[51] What Tom Barrett needed was a noncriminal response: a shelter, a recovery program, and mental health resources. What he got—what his hometown's citation quota system required—was a needless jail stay and crippling debt.

THE BROKEN THEORY OF BROKEN WINDOWS

Beyond the damning evidence that cities rely on police to fill public coffers to the detriment of public safety, ubiquitous police presence where not needed also is the natural consequence of a decades-long failed experiment with so-called broken windows policing. The theory, first articulated in 1982, posited that "if a window in a building is left unrepaired, all the rest of the windows will soon be broken."[52] By extension, petty criminal behavior and other minor social disturbances, left unchecked, will inevitably lead to more serious criminal activity. To ward off invasion of cities by criminal gangs, so the theory goes, police must aggressively enforce laws directed at minor social disorder, like littering or graffiti.

After decades of cities employing this strategy, study after study concludes that broken windows policing is incredibly expensive and has no measurable impact on levels of violent crime or overall safety. A major reason why this aggressive policing strategy does not work is precisely that so many of the people engaged in low-level petty social disturbances are struggling with mental illness, homelessness, and drug addiction, issues that cannot be addressed effectively with a badge and a gun, much less with handcuffs and expensive prison stays.[53] These underlying conditions often prevent people from engaging in the kind of cold, rational deterrence-based thinking upon which broken windows theory policing relies. In short, without the treatment needed to create a lasting positive impact on these low-level offenders' lives, we cannot expect any significant change in their "low-level offender" behavior patterns.

By criticizing broken windows policing, I am not saying we should ignore the broken window. Instead, we should recognize why the window was broken and try to address that root cause to prevent other windows from breaking. We ought to address the causes of minor social ills that broken windows policing has criminalized for so long: littering, vandalism, public intoxication, disorderly conduct. By doing so, we recognize these disturbances for what they often are: symptoms of a noncriminal public health and safety issue that would be better and more effectively addressed by a nonpolice public health and safety professional.

UBIQUITOUS POLICE, UBIQUITOUS DISCRIMINATION, UBIQUITOUS VIOLENCE

Whether by virtue of revenue generation incentives, broken windows enforcement strategies, or politically advantageous "tough on crime" policies, police are expected to be everywhere and address everything. And when given the opportunity to regulate every public disturbance in society, police have invariably used that "maximum policing" mandate in discriminatory and needlessly violent ways. It is beyond the scope of a book about the rise and risks of nonpolice entities to examine fully the centuries of discrimination and violence perpetrated by police entities. Dozens of others have covered these issues passionately and persuasively. But a brief discussion is warranted here, in part to underscore the urgent need for a new type of public safety that relies less on armed crime-fighting police.

Studies confirming the racially discriminatory impacts of policing are almost too numerous to count. Racial minorities, particularly Black individuals, are disproportionately targeted for adverse treatment at every step of the criminal investigative process. Black Americans are significantly more likely to be stopped and frisked, pulled over, searched without authorization, handcuffed, arrested, subjected to force, and killed by police officers.[54] For those who survive the police encounter, the adjudicative process ensures more disparate treatment: Black Americans are charged with more serious crimes than White Americans for identical conduct, are prosecuted and convicted at higher rates, and serve longer sentences for the same conduct.[55] Even when other variables, including poverty and the conduct of the suspect/defendant during the criminal legal process, are controlled for, the only salient distinguishing factor to explain this disparate treatment is race.[56]

Traffic stops are a particularly clear source of discriminatory treatment. In 2019, the Stanford Open Policing Project released the results of a study analyzing more than one hundred million traffic stops nationwide from 2011 to 2017. It found that "police stopped and searched Black and Latino drivers on the basis of less evidence than used in stopping white drivers, who are searched less often but are more likely to be found with illegal items."[57] A 2015 report by retired federal and state judges studying policing in San Francisco found significant "racial disparities regarding [San Francisco Police Department] stops, searches, and arrests [at traffic stops], especially for Black people."[58] In Chicago, a 2016 Police Accountability Task Force report found that "black and Hispanic drivers were searched approximately four times as often as white drivers."[59] Similarly, a 2015 analysis by the *New York Times* found that in Greensboro, North Carolina, police officers "used their discretion to search black drivers . . . more than twice as often as for white motorists."[60] This study also found that "officers were more likely to stop black drivers for no discernable reason. And they were more likely to use force if the driver was black, even when they did not encounter physical resistance."[61]

This focus on minority suspects, including minority drivers, is not the function of "smart policing." A study of over 4.4 million on-the-street stop and frisks in New York City between 2004 and 2012 found that, in addition to so unfairly targeting Black and Brown New Yorkers that a federal judge struck down the practice as unconstitutionally driven by race, the dragnet-style frisks were ineffective. Over 88 percent of all people stopped had committed no arrestable offense at all, and no racial or ethnic group was more likely than any other to have committed a crime.[62] Likewise, highway patrol officers speaking with me about this book admitted to using minor traffic violations as pretexts to search for more serious criminal activity but decried the practice as an inefficient waste of resources given the "terrible hit rate."[63]

But even compared to these discriminatory practices, no single policing issue garners more mainstream attention than police brutality. Like clockwork, video of a violent and often deadly police encounter with an unarmed citizen thrusts the issue into the spotlight year after year.[64] Violence is central to police work. It is inherent in a job where armed government agents are empowered to detain and arrest people against their will. Police make an arrest every three seconds in America, so perhaps it is not surprising that police turn to deadly violence almost three times a day.[65] Yet even in a country of 330 million people, ten million annual arrests and over one thousand annual deaths at the hands of police set the United States apart.[66] Police in America kill at a rate three to thirty times higher than other industrialized nations.[67] Arrest and incarceration rates far exceed those of other democratic countries.[68] And nonlethal uses of force by police in America often used to effectuate arrests exceed those of their counterparts in other industrialized nations.[69]

This ubiquitous violence is neither justified, necessary, nor the product of a few "bad apples."[70] At least "85,000 law enforcement officers across the [United States] have been investigated or disciplined for misconduct over the past decade," a number accounting for more than 10 percent of all uniformed police in the country.[71] Well over half of those investigations have involved claims of police brutality.[72] These epidemic levels of police violence are felt most acutely by the communities historically and explicitly targeted by law enforcement: communities of color (especially Black Americans), immigrants, women, and gender-nonconforming individuals.[73]

No adequate federal database of fatal police shootings exists, but several studies have catalogued the racialized nature of police killings. An August 2019 study by the National Academy of Sciences based on police-shooting databases found that between 2013 and 2018, Black men were two and a half times more likely than White men to be killed by police.[74] This disparate impact rises for unarmed citizens. A study from the University of California at Davis found that "the probability of being [Black, unarmed, and shot by police] is about 3.49 times the probability of being [White, unarmed, and shot by police] on average."[75] The risk of death for Black men at the hands of police is so great—approximately one in one thousand—that they are more like to die by cop than to die by drowning, fire or smoke inhalation, or a bicycle accident.[76] This disparity cannot be explained by greater justification for shooting Black individuals. An independent analysis of *Washington Post* data on police killings found that, "when factoring in threat level, Black Americans who are fatally shot by police are no more likely to be posing an imminent lethal threat to the officers at the moment they are killed than White Americans fatally shot by police."[77]

Disproportionate violence is not limited to fatal shootings. A Harvard study found that police officers are more likely to use their hands, push a suspect into a wall, use handcuffs, draw weapons, push a suspect onto the ground, point their weapon, and use pepper spray or a baton when interacting with Black individuals.[78] This study confirmed findings by the Center for Policing Equity, which found that "African Americans are far more likely than whites and other groups to be the victims of use of force by police, even when racial disparities in crime are taken into account."[79] This disproportionality in the use of force is particularly apparent in the use of restraints. A Stanford study of police practices in Oakland, California, found that, in a thirteen-month period, "2,890 African Americans were handcuffed but not arrested ... while only 193 whites were cuffed [and not arrested]. When Oakland officers pulled over a vehicle but didn't arrest anyone, 72 white people were handcuffed, while 1,466 African Americans were restrained."[80]

Disproportionate violence is not limited to Black men. In her powerful book *Invisible No More*, Andrea Ritchie catalogued how disproportionate police violence against the Black community is felt even more acutely by those at the intersections of race, gender, disability, sexual orientation, and gender identity.[81] Black women and girls face the double threat of racialized and sexualized violence.[82] Black people with neurodivergence or other mental health issues face the double threat of racialized violence and violence owing to an untrained officer's misinterpretation of symptoms of illness.[83] Black LGBTQIA+ people face the double threat of racialized violence and violence stemming from their suspicious "failure" to conform to heteronormative modes of presentation and behavior.[84] Police failure to distinguish between nonviolent, neurodivergent, gender-nonconforming behavior and criminally suspicious behavior remains one of the largest threats to nonconforming and mentally ill individuals in this country. We must have a different approach.

A SYSTEM THAT CAN'T BE REFORMED?

To many critics, the violence and discrimination present in modern policing are not the function of bad policy or training but inherent features of an institution designed to reinforce hierarchies along racial, gender, and class lines. Where police reform advocates "think that if we improved police we would escape its violence," abolitionists posit that "the only way to stop the violence of policing is to make the cops obsolete."[85] As Ohio State law professor Amna Akbar explained in her article "An Abolitionist Horizon for (Police) Reform," these total abolitionists view the existence of modern police as "rooted in histories of enslavement and conquest," with the current "scale, power, and violence of police becom[ing] defining pieces of architecture within our political economy."[86] Modern municipal policing traces its roots directly to southern slave patrols charged with violently enforcing the enslavement of humans and restricting the movement of persons based on skin color alone.[87] Historians have long connected these slave patrols to the rise of the Ku Klux Klan and other vigilante and domestic terror groups, with the ranks of these groups often simultaneously filling the ranks of sheriff's departments in the South and throughout the country.[88] To Akbar and other abolitionists, this history replays itself today through racialized policing and mass incarceration: "Police are a regressive and violent force in a historical power struggle over the distribution of land, labor, and resources, and their power has historical, material, and ideological bases."[89]

Not surprisingly, those who view police discrimination as a feature of rather than a bug in the system also tend to advocate total abolition. For example, prison abolitionists Angela Davis and Ruth Wilson Gilmore view

American prisons as deliberately created "tools of White supremacy" and the police who enforce laws that fill those prisons as the facilitators to address a range of "social ills," including racial equality, homelessness, immigration, and gender nonconformity.[90] Likewise, in *The End of Policing*, Alex Vitale argues that police reform as conventionally understood is doomed to fail precisely because "policing is fundamentally a tool of social control to facilitate our exploitation."[91] "The origins and function of the police are intimately tied to the management of inequalities of race and class," so "a kinder, gentler, and more diverse war on the poor is still a war on the poor."[92] Thus, in answering the question "Why are police everywhere?" abolitionists answer that it is by design to reinforce structural inequality. To them, the answer to the question "What do we do about it?" is total elimination of all police and prisons.

WHAT ABOUT VIOLENT CRIME?

While abolitionist proposals gain scholarly traction, the notion of removing all police officers from the street remains broadly unpopular in mainstream society. A 2020 Gallup survey conducted during the height of the George Floyd protests found that a large majority of respondents agreed that police should undergo major changes, but "just 15% of Americans support getting rid of the police."[93] There remained relatively little enthusiasm specifically in Black communities for abolishing the police, with only 22 percent of African American respondents in favor.[94] And although the same poll found overwhelming support for redirecting some government funds away from law enforcement to other forms of community investment, little appetite existed for ending policing altogether.[95]

To date, the total abolition movement remains an outlier in part because of the lack of substantive response to literature evidencing a positive relationship between police presence and decreases in violent crime. If we are talking narrowly about reducing violent crime, police presence works. One study analyzing the effects of post-9/11 "high alert" days in Washington, D.C., when more police were deployed to certain areas, found that violent crime decreased significantly on those days.[96] A study analyzing the effects of University of Pennsylvania campus police deployments to certain defined zones in Philadelphia found that the increased police presence correlated with declines in violent crime rates up to 60 percent.[97] Another study reviewed data sets from 1960 to 2010 and found that every \$1 spent on extra policing generated approximately \$1.63 in social benefits, primarily by reducing murders.[98] In other words, for all the social harms that armed officers currently inflict on society—overpolicing minority neighborhoods, targeting poor and marginalized populations for nonviolent activity, using unnecessary and unlawful force—police create a net social benefit in the narrow category of preventing and responding to violent crime. But their creation of a net social benefit does not mean that policing should not change at all. Instead, the findings suggest that by removing the opportunities to inflict mass social harm and refocusing police efforts on the things police do well—responding to and preventing violent crime—society will experience greater net social benefits. Indeed, given that police constitute by far the largest line item on virtually every major American city's budget, we ought to demand a greater return on investment.

These findings that police benefit society in the area of violent crime response are not trumpeted only by propolice activists. Professor Sharkey, a supporter of limited police defunding proposals, observes that "those who argue the police have no role in maintaining safe streets are arguing against lots of strong evidence."[99] The failure of abolitionists to provide "a detailed vision about what [police-less] empowered communities are going to do about violent crime" remains a sticking point for those skeptical about a proposed "post-police world."[100] One critical review of Vitale's book observed that *The End of Policing* "didn't contain an answer to the question about what a huge reduction in the number of police would mean for violent crime."[101] In truth, entirely "abolishing police departments tomorrow would not abolish violence or vaporize the guns that accompany so much of it."[102]

Even self-styled abolitionists often advocate for less than a total dismantling of the existing police state. In a powerful 2020 *New York Times* editorial, activist Mariame Kaba bluntly declared in her title, "Yes, We Mean Literally Abolish the Police."[103] The editorial persuasively articulated the ills of current policing and tied today's problems to policing's tainted history: "There is not a single era in United States history in which the police were not a force of violence against black people. So when you see a police officer pressing his knee into a black man's neck until he dies, that's the logical result of policing in America. He is doing what he sees as his job."[104] Yet despite the seeming nonnegotiable stance in her title, Kaba ultimately settles on demanding only that society "cut the number of police in half and cut their budget in half."[105] While this proposal can fairly be read as an intermediate step along the way to "making police obsolete," Kaba nonetheless does not suggest a concrete replacement for responding to truly violent crimes.[106]

What Kaba, Vitale, and others convincingly argue, however, is that very little of an officer's actual time is spent "catching the bad guys."[107] Vitale references the "big myth" that police officers "chase bank robbers [and] catch serial killers," when in reality police spend most of their time "responding to noise complaints, issuing traffic citations, and dealing with other noncriminal issues."[108] Kaba accurately observes that "police officers spend a lot of time . . . as de facto untrained community mental health providers."[109] They are surely correct that it would be better to actually solve America's housing and mental health problems rather than use police as violent Band-Aids.

AN EMERGING SOLUTION: UNBUNDLE THE POLICE

Instead of eliminating police entirely, the police reform movement has begun reshaping public safety in America by removing certain functions from police departments, thereby "unbundl[ing] the police."[110] Asking police to wear many ill-fitting civil servant hats often serves no one's interests. Institutionally, police "regard it as their duty to find criminals and prevent or solve crimes."[111] Radically reshaping the institution to force some uniformed officers into professional roles already filled by people in those professions—psychologist, substance abuse counselor, homeless advocate—neither redresses the serious problems endemic in policing nor makes much practical sense. Many departments have tried this approach by instituting crisis intervention training for officers and deploying those "CIT-trained officers" to noncriminal disturbances, without any measurable impact.[112] Thrusting noncriminal social welfare services onto police instead often increases the harm to society, because officers respond to nuanced public safety issues with the blunt instrument of the criminal law.[113] And that harm reinforces existing social inequities. As Yale law professor Monica Bell observes, "Routing rehabilitation and social services through the police could perversely widen the carceral net and reify the 'culture of control'" over poor, Black, and other marginalized communities.[114] Police, by their nature, are often "more punitive and less empathetic than the average civil servant," even when empathy and nonviolent, noncriminal solutions are required.[115] More training for more cops with more guns will not solve this problem.

Instead, the solution increasingly advocated is to "unbundle this holy mess."[116] While different commentators use different terminology—*defund, disaggregate, disentangle, unbundle*—the basic concept remains the same: remove from policing the social work, traffic, homelessness, mental health, and other noncriminal functions currently assigned to officers and redirect funding to nonpolice agencies better trained and equipped to respond to these social problems. Many city councils have approved experimental programs reallocating funds to nonpolice alternate response agencies to both triage these issues in the short term and provide long-term treatment that police departments are not designed or equipped to provide.[117]

These proposals respect the continuing role for traditional law enforcement in preventing and responding to violent crime, and no alternate response agencies to date pose any meaningful threat to the comparatively outsized budgets of police departments in cities and towns across the country. But a natural consequence of large-scale police disaggregation may one day be a somewhat smaller and less funded policing footprint in America. If it improves public safety, then we should welcome the change. We turn now to how governments have experimented with reallocating public safety resources and how these programs might expand in the future to address society's many complex public health and safety needs.

2 The New Public Safety

Samuel Mason had been arrested over fifty times by Anne Arundel County, Maryland, police, mostly for minor disturbances related to his diagnosed schizophrenia. In his words, "I got a problem, I think people are after me. I got in trouble some when I was off my meds." The arrests stopped, however, when someone called 911 about Mason's erratic behavior and the dispatcher rerouted the call from a police hotline to the county's "warm line," a call center focused on mental health issues. One of the county's Crisis Intervention Teams responded, a rapid response emergency unit consisting of a uniformed police officer and an independently licensed behavioral health clinician. The unit connected Mason with appropriate mental health resources, including a clinician to assist him with medication refills. Mason later credited the CIT with saving his life more than once: "I would be dead by my hand or someone else's" without their help.[1]

This type of holistic, compassionate approach to a nonviolent emergency reflects the new direction of public safety in America today. Thousands of towns and cities across the country have adopted or are experimenting with crisis response teams similar to the one in Anne Arundel County, voted the "International Crisis Intervention Team of the Year in 2021."[2] Rather than serving as competition to and potential replacement for police, these CITs often complement police by serving as a trusted voice where trust in police has been lost. Indeed, as one member of the Anne Arundel CIT explained, their job in part is to "help people have faith in the police again."[3]

Faith in the policing institution has been shattered, and understandably so. Contrast Samuel Mason's experience with Victoria Lee's experience in Fort Lee, New Jersey. On July 28, 2024, Lee's brother Chris called 911 requesting help for a mental health crisis stemming from her bipolar disorder. In that call, Chris emphasized that his sister was not violent, that she was experiencing a mental health episode, and that he was requesting only an ambulance to take her to the hospital. When the dispatcher told him a police officer would accompany the medics, Chris requested that police not come. The dispatcher denied the request. Chris then called 911 a second time trying to cancel the call and explaining that his sister, despite holding a small foldable knife, was not a threat. Within minutes, however, multiple officers arrived at the residence and began breaking down the door. Video footage shows a discussion about whether the officers should "go lethal" or "less lethal" upon entering. Two officers can be heard deciding to "go lethal" just before barging through the door. Five seconds after opening the door, and without any indication in the video that Lee was threatening herself or anyone else, officers shot her dead.[4]

It is tragic that Victoria Lee's brother attempted to cancel getting needed help for his sister out of fear of the police. It is equally tragic, and telling, that he was right. Police training, which primes officers to view unusual actions suspiciously, to assume violence, and to respond in kind, is particularly ill-suited to handling a mental health crisis like Victoria Lee's. Or Sonya Massey's. Chris Lee's fateful 911 call came only three weeks after Sonya Massey's mother called 911 seeking mental health services for her daughter. When deputy Sean Grayson arrived at the home, he missed a number of clues that experts say would have alerted him to the presence of a mental health issue, including an unusually messy living area, Massey's difficulty understanding basic questions, and her statement that "I took my medicine" in response to a question about whether she felt well. Grayson also allowed Massey to walk by a pot of boiling water several feet from him, and rather than try to de-escalate the situation when she claimed to "rebuke you in the name of Jesus" he immediately pointed his gun at her and yelled, "You better fucking not or I swear to fucking God I'll shoot you in the fucking face!" He then stepped toward her, further escalating the encounter, shot her in the head, and refused to provide medical attention even after realizing she was still alive.[5] She died a few minutes later.

There has to be a better way. Alternate responders provide that better way. These nonpolice trained experts—emergency medical technicians, mental health counselors, crisis interventionists, substance abuse professionals, social workers, homelessness outreach advocates, violence interrupters, and civilian traffic enforcers—provide a much-needed overhaul of government public safety services. An array of public health and safety issues exist outside violent criminal conduct, and these professionals have and provide the tools necessary to effectively address these issues and allow police to focus on serious criminals. They also can reduce the risk of senseless violence experienced by Victoria Lee, Sonya Massey, Linden Cameron, Daniel Prude, Steven Kissack, and so many more who needed help and services instead of handcuffs and bullets.[6]

CAHOOTS: THE ORIGINAL ALTERNATE RESPONDERS

Decades before George Floyd's murder spurred calls to defund the police, the small college town of Eugene, Oregon, began what was then a radical experiment with removing police from some areas of emergency response. In 1989, the Eugene Police Department partnered with the White Bird Clinic, a mental health crisis intervention initiative created as an "alternative for those who didn't trust cops," to create a new mobile crisis response team designed to address lower-risk emergency calls involving mental illness, homelessness, and related issues.[7] This response team was called Crisis Assistance Helping Out on the Streets, or CAHOOTS, a name chosen by the White Bird Clinic to reflect the fact that the clinic "was now 'in cahoots' with the police."[8] CAHOOTS is believed to be the earliest nonpolice mobile crisis team of its kind in the United States.

CAHOOTS "provides immediate stabilization in case[s] of urgent medical need or psychological crisis," and each response team is staffed with a medic (a nurse or an EMT) and a crisis worker with significant mental health experience.[9] CAHOOTS team members respond to immediate health and safety issues, de-escalate crises, and help to formulate a plan involving the delivery of medical, mental health, and other welfare services, including finding a bed in a homeless shelter or transportation to a health care facility. CAHOOTS operated from the Eugene Police Department until 2023, when it transitioned to oversight with Eugene's fire department. It responds to a different number not available to police, which allows it to provide services without police response or interference, though calls from 911 dispatch can also be routed to CAHOOTS if they fit within its mandate.[10] CAHOOTS does not handle requests involving violence, weapons, serious crimes, or similarly dangerous situations.

The level of impact CAHOOTS has on public safety in Eugene is an area of some debate. In a given year, CAHOOTS responds to anywhere from 13 to 20 percent of all emergency calls made to the Eugene Police Department.[11] But a large percentage of these calls are specific requests for CAHOOTS service to which police would not normally respond. While this fact alone suggests a positive impact on the community—the ability to seek help where police likely would offer none—it appears that the number of calls to which police would have responded if not for CAHOOTS (the "true divert rate") is closer to 5 to 8 percent. Regardless, CAHOOTS has proven remarkably successful at resolving public health and safety emergencies nonviolently. CAHOOTS personnel do not carry firearms or other weapons, and calls handled by CAHOOTS require police backup only about 2 percent of the time, a remarkably low percentage given the over twenty-one thousand calls to which the agency responded in 2023.[12] The cost savings are also impressive. CAHOOTS operates on a budget just under $1 million, while the Eugene Police Department budget exceeds $60 million.[13]

But perhaps CAHOOTS's largest impact is felt outside Eugene. After the massive protests against police abuse in 2020, hundreds of cities in the United States requested information from CAHOOTS as they considered experimenting with similar alternate responders. In 2021, federal legislation directed up to $1 billion to cover 85 percent of the expenses of similar mobile crisis teams around the country.[14] By 2024, most US states had multiple cities implementing such programs or had begun offering them statewide. The National Alliance on Mental Illness reports that as many as 2,700 local jurisdictions have created mental health CITs to respond to emergencies that previously were handled solely by police.[15] Many of these CITs, including teams in Denver, Portland, Atlanta, and Charlotte, specifically sought out guidance from CAHOOTS in crafting their own programs.

The goal of these programs is clear. Far too many mentally ill individuals in the United States have been detained, arrested, injured, and killed by armed officers interpreting bizarre or abnormal behavior as criminal or violent behavior and responding the way they were trained: with force.[16] Officers trained to ferret out criminal behavior often enter a mental health emergency with a jaundiced eye, interpreting anything out of the ordinary as suspicious. Trained clinicians, on the other hand, approach identical situations with a different mindset; an approach focused on de-escalation, validation, and empathy; and a far superior set of skills and training to more accurately interpret bizarre behavior for what it is—a mental health disturbance.

MODELS OF RESPONSE: TRAINED POLICE, CO-RESPONDERS, AND INDEPENDENT AGENCIES

The ways in which cities deploy alternate response services vary significantly. With many local governments still experimenting with pilot programs since 2020, agencies are still collecting data on how best to deliver alternate response services. The method of service delivery is critically important both for ensuring that people can seek and receive the help they need without fear of arrest or police violence and for determining whether the rights that normally attach to police-led investigations might (or might not) attach to these alternate response encounters.

Broadly speaking, three models of alternative response have emerged in recent years. The first model, often referred to as the "Memphis model," involves police officers with specialized crisis intervention training responding to emergency calls and utilizing that training to find a solution other than investigation and arrest. The second model, often called the "co-responder" model, involves uniformed police officers and trained nonpolice professionals "co-responding" to calls, much like the Anne Arundel County

Police CIT described at the beginning of this chapter. The third model, which I call the "independent agency" model, involves groups like CAHOOTS responding directly to emergency calls without direct police involvement unless specifically requested by the agency.

Trained Police

The most modest and least transformative "alternate responder" model does not involve an alternate response from a police officer at all. Instead, uniformed police officers attend specialized crisis intervention trainings where they receive programming on how to identify and respond to mental health and other noncriminal disturbances, utilize non–law enforcement tactics to resolve situations despite the presence of low-level criminal activity, and facilitate transfers to relevant medical and mental health resources. This model was developed in Memphis, Tennessee, following a 1987 incident in which police responded to a 911 call by DeWayne Robinson's mother about her son's self-harm related to mental health and drug use issues. When police arrived, Robinson "lunged" at officers but did not appear threatening. Officers shot him multiple times and killed him. Community organizers, city officials, the University of Memphis, and the Memphis Police Department collaboratively organized the Memphis PD's Crisis Intervention Team, with the stated goal of reducing violence during encounters between police and people with mental illness.[17]

Officer CIT training has expanded across the country, including in both large cities and smaller towns and counties. For example, the Atlanta Police Department is one of many departments in Georgia that sends officers to that state's Public Safety Training Center for a forty-hour course in CIT training offered by the Georgia chapter of the National Alliance on Mental Illness and focused on "people with mental illness and brain disorders."[18] Videos of Atlanta PD officers employing CIT tactics have been posted online by the department, including one of officers successfully talking a mentally ill and intoxicated man out from behind the wheel of a car and onto a stretcher to receive services at a local hospital.[19] Smaller cities, like Durham, North Carolina, staff intervention team response units with police officers who receive training in "responses and best practices" and sometimes with nonpolice personnel as well.[20]

Improving awareness among police officers of how to handle mental illness certainly is a step in the right direction. But there exists little evidence that CIT-trained officers alone reduce arrests, officer injuries, citizen injuries, or overall police use of force.[21] If measured solely by the number of people "diverted" from jails to hospitals, these CIT-trained officers appear to create a small benefit to the community. Studies have shown that CIT training increases the number of prebooking diversions from jails to hospitals and psychiatric facilities. And CIT appears to have beneficial officer-level outcomes, including officer satisfaction and self-perception of a reduction in use of force. But no study has yet shown a meaningful correlation between CIT-trained officer response and reductions in crime, arrests, or homelessness.

Another major obstacle to officer-led CIT response is the significant drop in the number of officers who voluntarily participate in these trainings. In the New York Police Department, the country's largest department, the number of officers receiving CIT training dropped precipitously from 2020 to 2022, to the point that two-thirds of active-duty officers remain untrained.[22] That drop, combined with New York City mayor Eric Adams's directive to officers to more aggressively force mentally ill homeless people into involuntary psychiatric treatment, has weakened that city's ability to provide tailored, nonviolent mental health services to its more than eighty-eight thousand unhoused residents.[23] It is why savvy New York City residents like Peggy Herrera, who called 911 for her son experiencing a mental breakdown, specifically told the dispatcher she "need[ed] an ambulance to show up—not the police. My son has issues. Mental issues. And I will not let anyone in unless EMT is there because . . . police . . . are not trained to deal with EDP [emotionally disturbed person] situations."[24] Despite her plea, officers arrived first. Within minutes she had been arrested for obstructing officer's entry into her home, and her son was arrested for obstruction and strapped to a gurney for trying to intervene.[25]

Co-responders

An increasingly popular approach, the "co-responder model," allows a nonpolice expert to embed with a police department and respond in tandem with officers to address noncriminal issues within the scope of that alternate responder's expertise. An increasing number of police departments have directly hired, paid, and housed mental health clinicians, medically trained nurses and paramedics, homeless outreach advocates, and other crisis interventionists. These alternate responders often ride along with police, either taking the lead when responding to a call or deferring to the officer and jumping in when requested.

Cities have long experimented with this approach. In the 1980s, the Los Angeles Police Department became the first major department to create an embedded Mental Evaluation Unit (MEU) to respond to mental health calls, but the unit was composed entirely of uniformed officers with specialized mental health training. After several high-profile incidents involving MEU officers violently accosting mentally ill individuals and placing them in the Los Angeles County Jail—referred to by many as the "largest mental health hospital in the country"—the LAPD changed course and created the Systemwide Mental Assessment Response Team (SMART). SMART consists of a mental health clinician and a sworn officer, with both officials serving as co-responders to mental health calls that meet certain criteria.[26]

Following that lead, in 2014 New York City piloted a program putting members of the nation's largest police force and social workers together in subways. In its first few months, social workers succeeded in placing 388 individuals into shelters and long-term outpatient treatment, compared with only 63 the entire previous year.[27] Following the program's initial success, Mayor Bill de Blasio announced plans to centralize mental health services in an effort to avoid criminal enforcement, explaining that "for people who are sick, we will offer healthcare, not handcuffs."[28]

Beyond triaging urgent medical, housing, or mental health emergencies, many police departments have folded in social workers addressing intractable issues and connecting individuals with appropriate long-term resources. The social work function represents a "prime example of what a reimagined policing agency leaning heavily on specialists might look like," and there exists "a long history" of such collaboration.[29] This co-responder model where social workers are housed inside police departments has borne fruit in some jurisdictions. In Lumberton, North Carolina, the Lumberton Police Department found that "intervention by social workers has virtually eliminated repeat calls from chronic problem homes."[30] Dallas, Houston, and San Antonio have adopted similar co-responder models in recent years, with social workers riding along with police and connecting crisis victims to long-term housing, health care, childcare, and substance abuse programs.[31]

But for all of this promising interagency collaboration, the question remains "whether the police are needed at all. When the police are involved, enforcement always is a possibility; without them there, it is much less so (though the police always can be called, of course)."[32] For example, a hopeful initiative in Martinsburg, West Virginia, a community ravaged by the opioid epidemic, "pairs police, mental health, and substance abuse professionals to reach out to kids whose parents are struggling with addiction; the idea is to offer a whole suite of services to help the kids now and avoid another generation of addiction and drug abuse down the line."[33] Such a program can truly work only with a commitment from police not to reflexively enforce criminal drug laws against parents and further erode family bonds, something that may prove difficult to do for those trained in force and law. Programs like this also suffer from low voluntary participation rates without commitments not to arrest, something that may prove hard to provide.

Indeed, the presence of uniformed officers reinforces fears of an enforcement response among would-be callers, even if the officers have no intention of making arrests. That lack of trust makes it more difficult for nonpolice personnel to form the relationships necessary to triage urgent issues and to begin longer-term service delivery. Reluctance is heightened in communities already fearful of police. Social workers in particular, who rely on long-term trusting relationships with their clients to be effective, express deep concern about co-responding with police. In response to the National Association of Social Workers' proposal to increase co-response collaboration with law enforcement, one social worker explained that

> this alliance of police and social work can be harmful in communities of color. If we're already fearing the police and then we're also going to fear those who are supposed to be helping us because they're connected to the police. . . . Social workers cannot build trust with people if we respond to a crisis accompanied by police. Police come armed with tasers, guns, and batons, prepared to deploy violence and punishment. Social workers show up with a willingness to listen, engage, and help heal.[34]

Independent Agencies

Since 2020, more cities and counties have begun experimenting with eliminating the police entirely from certain categories of calls, often citing CAHOOTS as inspiration.[35] Independent agency response challenges outdated notions that only police can respond to every public safety emergency on a 24/7 basis. Many of these programs have even begun investing in alternative dispatch infrastructure to ensure that calls can be routed somewhere other than police departments.

In Denver, for example, the city piloted a program called the Support Team Assistance Response (STAR) on June 1, 2020, just days after George Floyd's murder. The pilot program, based explicitly on CAHOOTS and designated to last six months, provided a mobile crisis response for community members experiencing problems related to mental health, depression, poverty, homelessness, or substance abuse issues. The STAR response consists of two health care staff (typically a mental health clinician and a paramedic in a specially equipped van) who provide rapid, on-site support to individuals in crisis and direct them to further appropriate care.[36]

Interestingly, the initial pilot program operated in eight Denver precincts designated as "displacement-vulnerable," where rapidly gentrifying neighborhoods posed housing and minor social disturbance risks for poorer community members being pushed out. Recent studies have shown the wisdom of this focused strategy, illustrating how neighborhoods undergoing periods of rapid demographic change experience a higher level of noncriminal "social disputes" between people from different backgrounds who are unfamiliar with one another. Lacking the connection and cohesion to deal with minor disagreements informally, residents in these neighborhoods turn to the "formal social control" mechanism of a police response.[37] STAR focused its efforts in these precincts to replace the Denver Police Department's practice of "rabble management"— enforcement actions against overwhelmingly nonviolent neighborhood disputes, mental illness, homelessness, and addiction. STAR personnel responded to a dedicated line routed directly to them and dispatched services if the incident involved calls for assistance, intoxication, suicide threat, welfare checks, indecent exposure, trespass of an unwanted person, and syringe disposal.[38] In six months, STAR responded to 748 calls, none of which required police assistance or a response to a criminal offense.[39] A study of this pilot program found a 34 percent reduction in reports of minor crime to police, a corresponding reduction in arrests, and no detectable increase in more serious crimes. The program was so successful, it has become a permanent agency within the Denver municipal government.[40]

In contrast with STAR's compassionate, albeit limited, approach to addressing public safety, New York City mayor Eric Adams operationalized his predecessor's long-promised independent response agency with an aggressive mandate to force noncriminal health and safety issues off the streets. Beginning in June 2021, the Behavioral Health Emergency Assistance Response Division (B-HEARD) deployed teams of emergency medical technicians and social workers to precincts in Harlem to address cases where violence or self-harm did not appear imminent. The program suffered from early funding, staffing, and dispatch problems, but Mayor Adams promised to expand the program citywide and expand its mandate to include clearing homeless encampments and involuntarily hospitalizing many of the city's tens of thousands of unhoused residents even if they posed no threat to other people.[41] In November 2022, Adams announced a major push to force people into treatment who "were a danger to themselves, even if they posed no risk of harm to others," claiming a "moral obligation" to do so.[42] The city now averages 143 involuntary hospitalizations of unhoused individuals per week.[43] These contrasting experiences between Denver's STAR program and New York City's B-HEARD program reflect the reality that even fully independent agencies can act as aggressive, "soft policing" arms of the state depending on their mandate and how local governments seek to utilize them.

RESPONDING TO THE "CRIME" OF HOMELESSNESS

Behind Mayor Adams's aggressive policy, and similar policies in California and elsewhere, is the growing recognition of the overlapping risks of mental illness, alcohol and drug addiction, and houselessness. Often, assisting an unhoused person to come in from the streets involves providing not only shelter but also wraparound services for outpatient mental health appointments, prescription refills, medical care, and addiction recovery programs. But as the epidemic of homelessness in America has grown in size since the pandemic, it has also grown more complex and can no longer be treated simply as a drug or mental health problem.

The U.S. Department of Housing and Urban Development reported in late 2023 that the number of homeless individuals nationwide had grown 12 percent in a single year to 653,000, the largest number on record.[44] Much of this increase was attributable to people experiencing homelessness for the first time and citing the unaffordable cost of housing as COVID-19 rent subsidies ended and housing prices skyrocketed. Large increases in migrant populations also put a strain on the availability of housing in cities and rural areas alike. One-quarter of the entire homeless population is concentrated in New York and Los Angeles, the nation's two largest cities, while Seattle, San Diego, and Denver each also recorded more than ten thousand homeless residents, more than 1 percent of their total populations.[45] Homelessness also increased by double digits in rural areas and among Black and Latinx residents, who continue to make up nearly two-thirds of the entire unhoused population.[46]

Co-responder models have become popular in dealing with these intractable homelessness issues, particularly in Sunbelt states where populations have exploded. Co-responder models in Sarasota, Florida, and Houston, Texas, deploy police as backup to homeless outreach teams liaising with the unhoused with the goal of providing needed social services and offering shelter.[47] The Community Connection Center in Salt Lake City, Utah, "relies on police, social workers, and homeless advocates working together to triage short-term intervention."[48] HELP Honolulu coordinates police and social workers responding to homelessness in a unique way, allowing police to put on street clothes and get a better perspective on "what the social service side is doing. . . . Now they can understand the issues and address the larger problems rather than just saying, 'Move it along.'"[49]

Most such teams, often referred to as homelessness outreach or "HOT" teams, follow a strict co-responder model, with uniformed officers approaching unhoused individuals in homeless encampments alongside a nonpolice homeless response advocate. As of 2024, 76 percent of the HOT teams in the nation's one hundred largest cities involved the police, with 59 percent of these teams designed to issue and enforce civil and criminal infractions for crimes related to houselessness—sleeping, drinking, urinating, and defecating outside.[50] Nearly half of these teams state as a primary objective the removal of encampments, often by destroying and disposing of an unhoused person's tents and personal belongings. Major cities, including New York City, San Francisco, Los Angeles, and Portland, utilize this co-responder "enforce and sweep" model, whereby uniformed officers and HOT team personnel enter large encampments, cite unhoused individuals for illegal housing violations, forcibly remove belongings from the street, offer mental health or other services as needed, offer shelter options as available, remain in place until the cited individuals leave the area, and then fence it off.[51]

San Diego County provides a helpful illustration in contrasts between this predominant co-responder approach and an alternative independent agency approach. The city of San Diego, with the nation's fourth-highest homeless population at over ten thousand unhoused residents, employs an embedded HOT team with the San Diego Police Department and conducts routine sweeps of encampments through a model of "progressive enforcement."[52] As SDPD's website explains, this model "is compassionate yet firm," authorizing police to offer housing and other services prior to arresting individuals for camping on public property, possessing illegal lodging, or encroaching on private property.[53] The model also allows diversion programs for alcohol and drug users and those with mental health issues. Progressive enforcement models attempt to strike a balance between assisting the unhoused and maintaining clean and safe streets, but as structured they appear in practice to rely primarily on the power to arrest and prosecute. San Diego possesses a woefully inadequate supply of shelter housing, and wait lists often extend for months. So any offer of shelter in exchange for removing one's current habitation, even if illegal, is often illusory.[54] Moreover, in the year since the city passed its "unsafe camping ordinance" preventing sleeping outside anywhere on public property, arrests of the unhoused have increased while the actual homeless population has remained flat.[55] Rather than improving public safety by reducing homelessness and helping those in crisis, this model has succeeded only in shuffling homeless populations around the city and placating the most vocal home and business owners:

While encampments are much less noticeable in some areas—such as downtown, in the city's main park, and around certain schools—they're just as prevalent, if not more so, near freeways and along the banks of the San Diego River. The city's homeless shelters are full, often with no beds for people who want to avoid a citation. There's no evidence the city's overall homeless population has decreased in the eight months since enforcement started.[56]

In contrast to "progressive enforcement," nearby La Mesa, California, a small city east of San Diego, has adopted what it calls a "progressive engagement model." Established in 2020, the city's Homeless Outreach and Mobile Engagement (HOME) program employs social workers, mental health counselors, and substance abuse counselors who respond to a dedicated phone number and community app. They also can respond to calls routed from the La Mesa Police Department to HOME if the issue involves activities associated with homelessness. In unanimously adopting the plan, the city council expressly noted the influence of CAHOOTS on the structure of HOME, and in its four years of operation city reports indicate that a large percentage of La Mesa's unhoused community has found permanent shelter.[57] Meanwhile, the fiscal savings to the La Mesa Police Department in not responding consistently to repeat calls about the same individuals has far outpaced the cost to the city of the HOME program.[58]

In some ways, the success of HOME, CAHOOTS, STAR, and other independent agencies should not come as a surprise. One set of nonpolice actors have successfully responded for decades to medical and other health crises: emergency medical technicians (EMTs). These paramedics act as roving emergency rooms, ready to triage noncriminal health and safety emergencies on the spot. But while these medically trained personnel can respond without the need for law enforcement, they are almost always joined eventually by a police presence, at least in situations reported through 911.[59] In virtually all jurisdictions, police either have the option or are required to respond to "all but the most patently unnecessary" 911 calls, even where no criminal activity is reported.[60] The presence of armed, nonmedically trained officers at a health emergency seems curious, and many argue that their presence can be counterproductive and even dangerous.[61] And in cases where emergencies have resulted from drug use or minor disputes, the risk of an unnecessary and unhelpful carceral response to a medical issue only increases.

Both EMT and homeless outreach response provide examples where it bears asking whether co-responder models are doing more harm than good. There exists little reason for a uniformed, armed officer to respond to every emergency medical crisis, and doing so seems just as likely to frustrate medical service delivery as it is to provide any net benefit to the patient or the alternate responder. Likewise, HOT team co-response models relying overwhelmingly on police to cite and arrest impoverished people for the "crime" of being unable to afford to sleep indoors do nothing to actually reduce or address the root causes of homelessness. Independent agency responses like those in Eugene and La Mesa provide hopeful templates for a better approach.

ADDRESSING VIOLENCE WITHOUT POLICE?

While most alternate responders seek to supplement or replace police in nonviolent situations, an emerging alternate response approach called violence interruption has received praise—and funding—for attempting to reduce organized violent crime without a law enforcement response. "Violence interrupters," as the name implies, train to step into and de-escalate potentially volatile and violent encounters. Violence interruption was conceived by Gary Slutkin in Chicago in the 1990s as a public health response to shootings.[62] Slutkin posited that violence "spreads like a disease," with individuals and organized gangs alike retaliating in a never-ending cycle, but that interrupters could step in to end the cycle.[63]

Historically, nonpolice entities like Cure Violence and Advance Peace have recruited members of local communities with a history of violence and gang activity to serve as interrupters.[64] By allowing those with personal knowledge and history of the issues plaguing communities, these experienced mediators attempt to de-escalate interpersonal conflict with a combination of positive motivation and cautionary "Do as I say, not as I did" rhetoric. As with other policing alternatives, violence interrupters around the country have worked both in tandem with officers on the beat and alone as replacements for traditional police response.[65] Often, violence interrupters encourage gang members to lay down their arms and pursue nonviolent conflict resolution, supporting their pitch with a veiled threat of arrest from police if they do not voluntarily participate.

In the short term, the goal of violence interruption is to curb violence. Long term, interrupters hope to bring peace as a value to communities plagued by violence, an enticing idea to reformers looking for ways to reduce violent crime without the need for "armed officers capable of their own violence."[66] This decades-old concept received new life in 2020 as policymakers sought alternatives to traditional policing.[67] President Biden even directed federal funding toward interrupter pilot projects, describing the approach as an "evidence-based model,"[68] despite inconsistent efficacy findings.[69] But like many alternate responders, violence interrupters increasingly rely on co-response with police to implore gang members and others to heed their "last chance" before police and prosecutors step in. This continued presence of law enforcement has limited the voluntary participation of individuals distrustful of the true motives of police and the alternate responders who work with them.

TRAFFIC WITHOUT THE POLICE?

The most radical, and potentially transformative, public safety proposal to replace police involves traffic enforcement. Police have no inherent role in traffic enforcement, where virtually all illegal conduct involves nonviolent infractions. Yet traffic stops represent by far the most frequent interaction between police and citizens.[70] And as discussed in chapter 1, they also are rife with problems. Motorists of color are disproportionately stopped by police for traffic violations and "disproportionately questioned, frisked, searched, cited, and arrested during traffic stops."[71] Many of these stops are pretextual, serving as a fishing expedition for police to find minor criminal activity and funnel people into the criminal legal system.[72] Even without finding independent evidence of criminality, officers often fall back on "lawful order statutes" authorizing them to arrest motorists "whenever they view the actions of motorists as merely disobedient."[73]

To redress these injustices, reformers have begun theorizing ways to replace police with a separate civilian agency tasked specifically with traffic enforcement. The United Kingdom has long separated armed police from unarmed traffic enforcers, and at least one US jurisdiction—Berkeley, California—attempted to experiment with this approach before being blocked by the California legislature.[74] But to date, the idea remains mostly theoretical, with the most thorough and serious treatment coming from University of Arizona law professor Jordan Blair Woods in his article "Traffic without the Police." Drawing on experiences from the UK New Zealand, and elsewhere, Professor Woods posits that states could create "traffic agencies" staffed with "traffic monitors," that traffic agencies "would operate wholly independently of the police," and that "traffic monitors would enforce traffic laws through in-person traffic stops" while monitoring certain automated aspects of traffic enforcement.[75]

Professor Woods attempts to limit the reach and authority of traffic agencies through positive law municipal regulations, explaining that "traffic monitors would be strictly limited to traffic-law enforcement, not criminal investigations."[76] Traffic monitors also would not be vested with typical police powers to detain, search, or arrest, but if a traffic monitor uncovers evidence of a serious felony offense (such as a motorist driving under the influence or driving a stolen vehicle), they could "contact police dispatch through a specialized channel" to assist with the more serious offense.[77] Perhaps recognizing the difficulties entailed with such a radical public safety transformation, Professor Woods cautions that "a true normative commitment to removing police from traffic enforcement would mean that traffic monitors could not serve as eyes for the police (or as mere substitutes that stand in place of the police)."[78]

NO "SOFT POLICE"

It is this concern—that alternate responders will serve as eyes and ears for the police, and thus "simply subject vulnerable people to cops by a different name"—that represents perhaps the most fundamental structural hurdle for police reformers as the rise of nonpolice response goes from reality to pilot programs to permanent reality.[79] Memphis model and co-responder model alternate response programs retain direct police involvement and thus continue to pose risks of unhelpful law enforcement actions carried out with unnecessary violence. They also do little to ease distrust. Independent agencies like CAHOOTS, STAR, and B-HEARD liaise with and in important ways rely on police presence. And many "violence interruption programs also work in collaboration with, or at least with the threat of, police intervention to varying degrees."[80]

Indeed, some police abolitionists express skepticism about whether these "reforms" constitute meaningful change at all when the "authority figures who make up the 'soft police'—including medical professionals, social workers, and government bureaucrats—engage in policing in their own right, and are often entangled with traditional [criminal] law."[81] In their book No More Police, Mariama Kaba and Andrea Ritchie explain that "police" and "policing" are not the same thing, that one can remove police while retaining policing, and that the "state's police power is also located in the social welfare and medical systems offered as 'alternatives' to policing."[82] Kaba and Ritchie claim that "the impulse to replace every police function with an institutional alternative can actually undermine movements to defund police and invest in community safety:

> Calls for "alternatives" to police are often rooted in this "common sense" presumption that we need to continue to control currently criminalized people and populations by placing them "Somewhere Else." This, in turn, requires having "Someone Else"—if not police—to put them there. At the height of the 2020 Uprisings, this instinct quickly surfaced in an insistence that defund organizers immediately and convincingly answer an avalanche of questions: If we defund police, who will answer calls about noise complaints? Conflicts? People with unmet mental health needs? Who will get unhoused people off the streets and subways? Who will issue traffic tickets? What will we do about drug users and dealers?[83]

Kaba, Ritchie, and others generally believe that those questions have been answered unsatisfactorily and that the alternate response programs described in this chapter and elsewhere simply constitute policing by a different name. In one respect, they have a point. Many of the mental health services offered by even independent agencies and pitched as an "alternative" to police response end with the involuntary detention and psychiatric commitment of individuals in a prison-like institution where doctors retain the right to forcibly medicate and physically coerce compliance.[84] Likewise, substance abuse counselors offer drug diversion programs as an alternative to, but operate with the threat of, criminal punishment. Patients must acquiesce to entry into drug treatment centers where they are subjected to strict regulation of their movements and bodily integrity, forced medication, physical restraints, and lost privacy and confidentiality, not to mention rampant emotional, physical, and sexual abuse. Social welfare programs require recipients to open their private lives to intrusive examination by social workers to root out evidence of criminal fraud, with the ever-present threat of arrest. Even basic medical care often intertwines with law enforcement and forms of soft policing, with doctors referring to law enforcement pregnant mothers who test positive for drugs and, more recently, those seeking or suspected of receiving abortions or other illegal reproductive care. In other words, defunding the police too often means "funding the soft social police" operating within very similar "forms of surveillance, confinement, containment, and control."[85]

The abolitionist impulse, then, is to eliminate both the police and the soft police, to abolish as inherently illegitimate all government-funded public safety and social welfare programs that use involuntary incursions into one's liberty or privacy. I disagree. First, surveillance, confinement, and control are legitimate and often necessary objectives when the ones being surveilled, confined, and controlled are violent criminals for whom a law enforcement response is preferable. Moreover, there exist limited situations where some level of involuntary restriction is necessary to promote public health and safety. When a severely mentally ill unhoused individual cannot care for himself and is at risk of death in subzero temperatures, involuntary commitment in a treatment facility may be the only alternative. When someone seeks sanctuary in a government-funded shelter, including domestic violence shelters, strict curfews and visitor limitations are necessary to protect residents from outside harm. These restrictions, while uncomfortable, often are preferable from a public safety standpoint to the alternatives of either criminal arrest or simply doing nothing.

Nonetheless, criticisms of alternate responders as soft police are valid and merit serious attention. We rely far too frequently on these quasi-punitive, involuntary social welfare programs to simply "sweep away" the unhoused and lock up the mentally ill through government actions that both deeply invade the liberty, privacy, and bodily integrity rights of citizens and fail to provide meaningful help to those being put "somewhere else." And we do so in large part with the help of a legal structure that permits nonpolice alternate responders to infringe upon the rights of the people they serve with relative impunity. Any government action depriving people of their freedom of movement or subjecting them to forced medication ought to be tightly regulated and justified only upon a showing of exceeding necessity. But unlike police, whose conduct is closely circumscribed by probable-cause and warrant requirements before they search, arrest, or interrogate criminal suspects, few such restrictions apply to alternate responders before they search, detain, commit, or even medicate noncriminal patients and clients.

Herein lies the unintended consequence of replacing police with nonpolice alternate responders. Failure to carefully regulate the activities of these soft police poses a significant lurking threat to the constitutional rights of vulnerable people—including the mentally ill, addicted, and unhoused—who rely on these responders for a compassionate and noncriminal alternative to police violence. Many of those important rights—to be free from unreasonable searches, seizures, and excessive violence—traditionally apply only when police are involved in a criminal investigation. Where police are not involved, or where police are responding not in an enforcement capacity but in a "community caretaking" capacity, these rights may not apply. This threat has potentially disastrous consequences for those affected, because it is these rights protected in the Constitution that restrain unlawful police investigations and prevent the introduction of illegally obtained evidence in a criminal prosecution. If police in their co-response capacity or independent alternate responders in their capacity find and turn over evidence or secure involuntary incriminating statements, whether intentionally or not, the very risk of arrest and prosecution that the new public safety seeks to avoid becomes real once again. This threat is magnified for the exact community alternate responders seek to protect, given the prevalence of illegal drug use and illegal housing activities in these communities.

This lurking threat to civil liberties illuminates three distinct yet overlapping concerns about alternate responders acting as "soft police" stand-ins for traditional law enforcement. The first is the broad societal critique of alternate responders serving as tools of a larger system of government control and exploitation. The second involves the relative legal impunity enjoyed by alternate responders when they interact with the public and invade their liberty and privacy interests while funneling them into these quasi-carceral social welfare programs. The third involves the threat that alternative responders could use this impunity, intentionally or not, to serve as eyes and ears for police and funnel vulnerable people into the very carceral net that the new public safety is designed to avoid. In the chapters that follow, we will explore how each of these three concerns has been and continues to be realized with the help of a lax legal infrastructure unprepared for the type of mass structural police reform our communities so desperately need.

3 Search and Seizure without Police

Krysta Sutterfield was having a bad day. She had recently received some unsettling news, and in venting her frustrations with her therapist she allegedly quipped, "I guess I'll go home and blow my brains out."[1] Despite recording no history of suicidal ideation, Sutterfield's therapist called police to check on her. Police initially could not find her. Two hours later, when Sutterfield became aware police were staked out in front of her house, she called her therapist to confirm that she was fine and requested that she call off the police "welfare check." The therapist did so, but police refused to back down. Instead, they completed a Statement of Emergency Detention by Law Enforcement Officer, a form authorizing police to forcibly detain and commit for psychiatric evaluation someone they believe might be a danger to themselves. The form requires no probable cause or judicial approval. Nine hours later, after Sutterfield arrived home and denied police entry, two officers broke down her front door, handcuffed her, searched the entire house, seized her firearms, and committed her for a four-day mental health evaluation.[2]

This story may appear routine. And in many ways it is. Police regularly conduct welfare checks at the request of medical professionals. But underneath the surface lurks a troubling reality: police needed neither a warrant, probable cause, nor anything other than a single hearsay statement from a doctor in a confidential therapy appointment to barge into someone's home, search it top to bottom, seize her firearms, and commit her to a hospital, where she received forced medical treatment and forced medication. And even that one hearsay statement was later contradicted by the therapist and Sutterfield herself. Yet the Seventh Circuit Court of Appeals upheld this action as lawful because police, activated by an alternate responder, were acting in a noncriminal "community caretaking" capacity and relying upon the "exigent circumstances" requiring emergency aid.[3]

Utilizing nonpolice public safety experts as an alternative to traditional police can improve outcomes for people experiencing crisis. But lurking in all of these nonpolice interactions remains the potential for a law enforcement response, either because of the presence of a co-responding police officer, the existence of police oversight over independent agencies, the threat of a "soft police" decision to place a citizen somewhere else against their will, or, as in the case of Krysta Sutterfield, the decision of a nonpolice actor to mobilize police for crisis response.

This potential raises important issues about the rights people possess— or don't possess—when they are being policed by nonpolice entities. Much of the concern about alternate responders promoting public safety through containment and confinement stems from the lack of choice individuals have in the matter. They are placed involuntarily in an ambulance, a psychiatric hospital, a drug treatment center, a housing shelter. And unlike in many criminal investigations led by police, people involuntarily confined in these nonpolice situations often have no rights to prevent or challenge their detention. These fundamental liberty deprivations, secured without equally fundamental rights to resist them, pose a serious threat to the freedoms of vulnerable communities as the "someone elses" of alternate responders expand their reach.

When police respond to public safety threats with traditional law enforcement, they often rely on similar containment and confinement tools of detention, arrest, force, and imprisonment. But their ability to do so is tightly regulated and restricted by virtue of constitutional rights that we all have to be free from certain types of government intrusion. Police can search our persons and our belongings only if they have probable cause (and often a warrant) that we have committed a crime. Likewise, they can seize us involuntarily only if they have reasonable suspicion about our criminal activities and can arrest us only upon probable cause. And they can seek certain information from us, including incriminating statements made by us, only after informing us of our rights to remain silent and to seek the advice of an attorney. And those rights, once invoked, must be respected by police.

But these rules largely do not apply in the alternate responder context. Put another way, our rights to be free from unreasonable searches and seizures, excessive force, and forced interrogations largely do not exist when a CIT worker, mental health counselor, or other alternate responder interacts with us, because those interactions fall outside what the US Supreme Court considers the "primary purpose" of these rights: to protect us from overzealous criminal investigations by police.[4] Because alternate responders exist as an *alternative* to criminal investigation by police, these rights and their restrictions on government action either do not apply at all or apply with far less force.

This reality—that lurking behind an otherwise positive moment in police reform lies the potential loss of fundamental constitutional rights—is important for a number of reasons. First, the ability to sue public officials for civil rights violations to seek both compensation for past harms done and changes to future government conduct is contingent upon the application of a constitutional right. If no such right applies, these important vehicles for redress and positive change cease to exist. Second, without protection from unreasonable searches and seizures, vulnerable people lose the ability to challenge their involuntary confinement in often-squalid, dangerous, and prison-like conditions in psychiatric wards, drug treatment centers, and temporary shelters. While the resources offered at these institutions can provide much-needed relief to those in crisis, any significant restriction on one's liberty and freedom of movement by the government without sufficient protective guardrails raises alarms about abuse—alarms that have been borne out time and again.

Third, and perhaps most concerning, without the protections of these rights articulated in the Constitution's Fourth Amendment, any criminal evidence discovered by alternate responders can be freely turned over to police and prosecutors regardless of how that evidence was found. In a traditional police investigation, much evidence seized in violation of the

Fourth Amendment's probable-cause and warrant requirements must be suppressed, meaning it cannot be used against the defendant in a criminal trial. The purpose of this "exclusionary rule" is to deter overzealous police misconduct and protect people from prosecutions based on the government's ill-gotten gains.[5] The risks of this kind of end run around these rights by alternate responders are particularly high given the types of situations to which they most commonly respond: erratic behavior driven by mental illness that often involves criminal disorderly conduct or weapons possession; illegal drug use and overdoses from those illegal drugs; and homelessness, which inherently involves activities criminalized in many jurisdictions. And even if alternate responders want to avoid a criminal response to these crises, many responders operate within a system where police either must respond with them or must be notified of any "serious" criminal activity. In short, utilizing nonpolice agents to address public safety issues but requiring them to coordinate with and provide information to the police may have the unintended consequence of increasing the risk of an arrest and prosecution devoid of fundamental protections for the criminally accused.

To take just one example, consider the debate over pending legislation in California that would extend the power to place someone under an emergency psychiatric hold beyond just police to government-designated psychiatrists, psychologists, clinical social workers, licensed marriage and family therapists, and clinical counselors. Granting mental health experts in addition to police the ability to respond to mental health crises makes good sense. As bill sponsor Sen. Aisha Wahab remarked, the problem with the current system of so-called 5150 holds in California "is that the individuals that are actually trained in the science, in this profession, in this industry, are not empowered enough to make the best decision for the people they work with the most."[6] These professionals can respond to a crisis, assess the immediate-term and root cause issues, and counsel the patient on the best course of action to protect themselves and others.

But offering mental health resources and forcing someone into treatment against their will are two different things. In Senate testimony, Disability Rights California advocate Debra Roth observed, "We don't see how [alternate responders] are going to transport a person who does not want to go to the hospital, to the hospital. And we think law enforcement is going to get called, and that's how it will play out in real-time."[7] And once the alternate responder calls law enforcement for backup, the risk of arrest increases, particularly when the officer arrives and begins grilling the mental health expert about what danger the person poses, whether they are armed or on drugs, and what the person may have said during intake. These facts, once voluntarily disclosed bits of information to an alternate responder, now become evidence for a criminal prosecution.

Even the most "independent" alternate response agencies are required by law to involve police under relatively vague guidelines. CAHOOTS's current contract with the City of Eugene requires CAHOOTS personnel to "summon a Police Officer when a dangerous situation appears to exist," without defining "dangerous situation" or differentiating between dangerous medical or mental health emergencies and dangerous situations involving firearms or physical violence.[8] CAHOOTS is also required to notify dispatchers "to have Police Officers respond, and [shall] stand by to assist officers as necessary" if someone appears mentally ill or intoxicated but is "unwilling to be transported to a treatment center."[9] This fallback reliance on police to facilitate involuntary transfers in cases of mental health or intoxication crisis highlights the limits of alternate responders to truly separate themselves from police; the requirement that alternate responders assist police after gathering potentially incriminating evidence increases the risk of an unhelpful carceral response.

It is fair to ask at this point whether this concern is real. How likely is it that someone who works as a mental health crisis counselor or homeless outreach interventionist would voluntarily turn over evidence to police when their whole job is defined by trying to avoid police involvement? With many such independent response agencies still in their infancy, it frankly is too hard to predict with any certainty how widespread the issue will become. One would hope these alternate responders would take the "high road" and seek police involvement only as a last resort. But in this chapter and the next, we will examine plenty of existing, real-world examples of alternate responders taking the "low road" and using their power to turn over physical evidence to police, force confessions that are later used against citizens, seize and involuntarily detain people for days or weeks at a time, and use excessive violence in doing so. These concerns do not mean we should abolish all "soft police" and start from scratch. But they do mean we need to particularly address not just whom we replace police with but what rules we write to govern their behavior.

THE FOURTH AMENDMENT'S "PRIMARY PURPOSE"

Any discussion of civil rights in the context of policing and public safety has to begin with the Fourth Amendment to the US Constitution. The Fourth Amendment is the primary source of legal regulation for and restraint on police investigative activity.[10] But whether and to what extent the amendment applies to nonpolice officials providing noncriminal public safety services has proven to be a source of immense confusion and contradiction.

The Fourth Amendment is a mere fifty-four words long. It reads: "The right of the people to be secure in their persons, houses, papers, and effects, against unreasonable searches and seizures, shall not be violated, and no Warrants shall issue, but upon probable cause, supported by Oath or affirmation, and particularly describing the place to be searched, and the persons or things to be seized." While this single sentence describes whom the amendment protects (the people), what it protects (their persons, houses, papers, and effects), and what it prohibits (unreasonable searches and seizures), it does not describe whose conduct it restrains. All people? Only government officials? Only certain government officials, like police? The text, and much of the amendment's history, are silent on this question.

But the Supreme Court has not remained silent, stating that it is reluctant to apply the amendment to the actions of government officials when "the challenged conduct falls outside the area to which the Fourth Amendment most commonly and traditionally applies—law enforcement."[11] Courts do so in recognition of the long-held view that the "primary purpose of the Fourth Amendment [is] to prohibit unreasonable intrusions in the course of criminal investigations."[12] And when the Court has considered the application of the amendment to noncriminal investigations, "it has been careful to observe that the application of the amendment is limited."[13]

In a typical criminal investigation, where police pursue criminal evidence or suspects of a completed or in-progress crime, traditional Fourth

Amendment restrictions apply. Questions about whether a police officer's rummaging through a bedroom constitutes a "search" or whether hand-cuffing a suspect constitutes a "seizure" are routinely taken for granted, and the inquiry moves to the reasonableness of those actions as required by the amendment. Warrants, supported by probable cause, are "presumptively required."[14] Where an exception to the warrant clause exists, probable cause nonetheless "remains the touchstone in criminal investigations."[15] And even where probable cause is not required, a search or seizure that takes place as part of a criminal investigation "is ordinarily unreasonable [and therefore constitutionally impermissible] in the absence of *individualized* [reasonable] suspicion of wrongdoing."[16] In short, the full force of the Fourth Amendment's restrictions on government action applies presumptively in police investigations.

However, outside criminal investigations where police are not present, the Fourth Amendment routinely does not apply, even if the conduct of a government official would otherwise be considered a search or seizure. And in the limited circumstances where the amendment's protections do apply outside criminal investigations, individualized suspicion of wrong-doing is rarely required before authorizing intrusive searches; warrants and probable cause are "typically treated as irrelevant."[17] Suspicionless, broad, and often incredibly intrusive searches and seizures are frequently permitted in the noncriminal realm. Thus, the line between a "traditional criminal investigation [by police] and a search or seizure designed primarily to serve non-criminal [public safety] goals is a line of considerable constitutional importance."[18] It is also "thin and, quite arguably, arbitrary."[19]

For example, the Supreme Court has held that the Fourth Amendment *does* apply to housing inspectors seeking to enter dwellings for evidence of code violations, firefighters seeking to enter homes to investigate fire causes, federal employers subjecting train conductors to random drug tests, and school officials searching backpacks for drugs and weapons.[20] But the Court has also held at various times that the amendment *does not* apply to medical personnel invasively searching a patient's body for criminal evidence, psychiatrists evaluating the mental fitness of a criminal suspect, and social workers entering homes unannounced to investigate potential fraud. In reaching these seemingly contradictory rulings, the

Court has consistently drawn a line between nonpolice conduct subjectively "designed to elicit a benefit for the government in an investigative" capacity and conduct subjectively motivated by noninvestigative ends.[21] Determining whether an alternate responder's intrusions are subjectively motivated by a desire to assist in an investigation has proven incredibly difficult, especially when police are present to influence the alternate responder's conduct or an active criminal investigation is taking place alongside a nonpolice co-responder's activities.

MEDICAL RESPONSE

One set of nonpolice government workers who consistently seem immune from Fourth Amendment scrutiny are medical and mental health personnel. In a series of cases involving extremely invasive and often wholly unjustified procedures, government doctors, EMTs, and psychiatrists have been exempt from the Fourth Amendment precisely because they could articulate a subjective medical purpose for their actions even when they knew their actions would support a criminal arrest and prosecution.

For example, in *United States v. Attson*, the Ninth Circuit found that the Fourth Amendment did not apply to a government-employed doctor who took an involuntary blood sample from a criminal suspect and conducted a blood alcohol analysis on it, "because the physician had acted for medical reasons and did not possess the requisite intent to engage in a search or seizure under the Fourth Amendment."[22] Although evidence existed that police directed the doctor to take and analyze the blood sample, the fact that the doctor "offered specific medical reasons for taking the blood sample" immunized him from Fourth Amendment scrutiny, which prevented the defendant from suppressing the results of the involuntary blood test at his criminal trial.[23]

Attson, widely followed as a "leading" case by other circuits,[24] suggests that an alternate responder's awareness that the results of her invasive search will be used for criminal investigatory purposes will not implicate the Fourth Amendment, even if that search was directed by police. Only a purposeful, subjective intent to "elicit a benefit" in that criminal investigation will do. Relying on this case, courts have refused to apply the Fourth

Amendment to doctors visually inspecting a criminal suspect at the request of police looking for evidence tying the patient to an altercation, technicians performing X-rays at the behest of police to identify foreign bodies suspected to be balloons of drugs, and nurses drawing blood over a patient's express objection at the request of police investigating a DUI. In none of these cases did police have probable cause or a warrant; instead, they used medical personnel to get around those requirements.

In one particularly gruesome example, prisoner Matthew Perez was suspected of having received contraband from his girlfriend during a visit at Salinas Valley State Prison in California. When Perez refused a police officer's request to submit to X-rays, multiple officers dragged him to a hospital emergency room, strapped him to a gurney, and told a technician to perform X-rays and CT scans. A doctor reviewed the scans and saw "five foreign bodies" that were unobstructed in the anal cavity and would "come out on their own."[25] Despite finding no medical reason to force the objects out, the doctor prescribed a laxative after police aggressively insisted they obtain the evidence. A nurse then forcibly poured seven full cups of laxative down Perez's throat over the course of ten minutes, and when Perez said he could take no more two officers strapped him down and forcibly poured the laxative down Perez's throat until he began coughing and choking. When that did not work, two officers and a nurse stripped Perez naked and administered enemas, without lubrication, in front of multiple male and female police officers. Despite these allegations, the court dismissed Perez's claim against the doctor that these actions constituted either an unreasonable search or an unreasonable seizure, because there was no evidence the doctor "acted for an investigative rather than medical purpose."[26]

This narrow requirement that nonpolice personnel subjectively harbor an intent to assist a criminal investigation most clearly immunizes alternate responders like doctors and EMTs providing medical emergency care. For these professionals, because their overriding concern is with providing medical care, any secondary benefit their activities provide to a criminal investigation will not trigger Fourth Amendment scrutiny. Courts have regularly found that the Fourth Amendment does not apply to "paramedics answering a 911 emergency request for help," because they do so "to render aid" instead of assist in a criminal investigation, even if they ultimately do assist that investigation.[27]

And in fact, medical personnel regularly participate in the search and seizure of evidence, later turned over to the police for prosecution, without being subjected to Fourth Amendment scrutiny. Indeed, medical "treatment often leads directly back to criminalization and punishment":

> For instance, medical providers frequently participate in the profiling and criminalization of pregnant people who use drugs or who experience adverse pregnancy outcomes that are presumed to be the result of self-managed abortions. Medical and public health professionals produce evidence and testify in prosecutions based on self-managed abortion care, HIV criminalization, drug use and overdose, and self-managed gender-affirming care. Hospital staff call the cops on undocumented migrants and "noncompliant" patients. Health care systems refuse treatment or collude with police to punish people in the sex trade.[28]

Adora Perez fell into this treatment-turned-criminalization trap. After going into labor, she went to the hospital for medical assistance. Shortly after arrival, she delivered a stillborn son named Hades. While still grieving her loss, the doctors who assisted her were calling the cops to report on her use of methamphetamine during pregnancy. Six months later, Perez had been convicted of manslaughter and sentenced to eleven years in prison.[29] Two years later, nineteen-year-old Brittany Poolaw suffered a miscarriage and sought medical treatment at the hospital. When she disclosed to doctors that she had used marijuana and methamphetamine during the pregnancy, doctors referred her to prosecutors, who arrested her for first-degree manslaughter. After spending a year and a half in jail because she was unable to post the $20,000 bond, she was convicted and sentenced to four years in prison.[30] In neither case did doctors secure consent to disclose this confidential medical information, yet the information they provided to prosecutors helped secure convictions without any Fourth Amendment scrutiny.

In addition to traditional homicide laws, many states criminalize "fetal assault" through so-called chemical endangerment laws, making it a serious felony to consume drugs during pregnancy. During the height of the opioid epidemic, when drug-related birth defects increased five-fold from 2004 to 2014, half of all states passed versions of laws classifying drug use during pregnancy as child abuse.[31] These laws illustrate what the

American College of Obstetricians and Gynecologists defines as the criminalization of pregnancy: "the punishing or penalizing of individuals for actions that are interpreted as harmful to their own pregnancies, including enforcement of laws that punish actions during pregnancy that would not otherwise be criminal or punishable."[32] These laws have a chilling effect on women's health, as demonstrated by one Tennessee woman who gave birth on the side of the road to avoid going to the hospital and being slapped with a fetal assault charge.[33] International human rights organizations, as well as the National Organization on Fetal Alcohol Syndrome, have called for the repeal of these laws, while the American Medical Association called for "non-punitive public health approaches to treatment [that] result in better outcomes for both moms and babies."[34]

These laws function because doctors are all too willing to participate in criminal investigation and enforcement yet are not bound or restrained by the Fourth Amendment given their primary purpose of delivering medical care. While the Supreme Court ruled in 2000 that hospital policies requiring doctors to drug-test all pregnant patients without consent and refer all positive tests to police for arrest triggered Fourth Amendment scrutiny because the program was "indistinguishable from the general interest in crime control," this case does not prevent individual doctors in individual cases from unilaterally providing evidence to police to assist with a criminal investigation.[35]

Following the Supreme Court's 2022 decision in *Dobbs v. Jackson Women's Health Organization* eliminating constitutional protections for abortion, public health experts warned that criminalized pregnancy prosecutions would increase. In the decade prior to *Dobbs*, dozens of women were prosecuted for crimes related to self-managed abortion, including mishandling of human remains, concealment of a birth, practicing medicine without a license, child abuse and assault, and murder.[36] These prosecutions relied on critical evidence gathered and provided by doctors assisting these women with complications arising from their self-managed care. And this was before total or near-total abortion bans were passed in half the states in the country. These prosecutions will only increase, and the penalties will become more severe, as evidenced by fetal personhood laws like Georgia's Living Infants Fairness and Equality (LIFE) Act, which bans abortion after six weeks and defines "unborn children" as persons, paving the way for "a woman who obtains or self-manages an abortion after six weeks [to] be charged with murder."[37]

Unlike in the pregnancy context, where criminalization is on the rise, a growing practice of providing nonpunitive health care treatment to those who overdose on drugs has softened some of the hard edges of soft medical policing. A 1975 federal law prohibits doctors from directly disclosing drug use to police, a restriction seen as necessary to foster honest communication for purposes of diagnosis and treatment. And a growing number of states have passed "Good Samaritan" laws shielding people from prosecution if they call 911 to report a drug overdose. But when EMTs and police co-respond to an overdose, police often arrive with a naturally punitive impulse to investigate and arrest for illegal drug use or sale. While EMTs and police are trained to treat "overdose events first and foremost as health emergencies," important information obtained by medical professionals on the scene often ends up shared with police and leads to an arrest.[38]

THE "SPECIAL NEEDS" FOURTH AMENDMENT

As with the case of medical personnel, the Fourth Amendment's protections against unreasonable search and seizure do not apply in many noncriminal contexts. But even when they do, courts employ a relaxed standard to justify broad, suspicionless searches and seizures when a noncriminal "special need" warrants the intrusion. This new class of so-called special needs searches does not require a warrant, probable cause, or even individualized suspicion that the person being searched has done anything wrong. Instead, broad, intrusive government searches need only be "reasonable under the circumstances"; these searches require only a balancing test in which "the need to search [is weighed] against the invasion which the search entails."[39] This standard is far weaker than a requirement that police develop probable cause of wrongdoing and submit that evidence to a judge to secure a warrant before initiating any search.

For some special needs searches, such as baggage screenings by Transportation Security Administration (TSA) officials at an airport, the special needs standard seems rational and obvious. The need to ensure that bombs, firearms, or other weapons stay off airplanes outweighs any inconvenience of a suspicionless search, and people desiring to avoid such intrusions can choose to avoid airplanes. But many far more intrusive administrative searches seem far less justifiable and yet have been upheld as reasonable by courts. These searches—including some revealing intimate family details discovered in the sanctity of the home—require neither a warrant, probable cause, nor suspicion. And many of them are conducted by alternate responders.

For example, in *Wyman v. James*, the Supreme Court upheld a system of welfare case worker "home visits" that required welfare recipients to admit a government worker into their home for interview and inspection or lose eligibility for benefits.[40] Because the purpose of the visits—to determine if any fraud or other legal or administrative violations required the termination of welfare benefits—was noncriminal in nature, visits needed only to be "reasonable" and did not at all have to be limited to people suspected of wrongdoing. This case, which is still good law, is troubling on several levels. First, it subjects every single recipient of government benefits (not just welfare but Social Security Disability, unemployment benefits, and even Medicare) to the possibility of random search by a government official. Second, it strikes a concerning balance between the need to investigate for possible entitlement violations and deeply intrusive searches into a person's home, long deemed one's "castle" that received special privacy protection under the Constitution. Third, it seems to ignore the practical reality that home visits by social workers and others are closely tied to and could easily uncover evidence of criminal activity, risking the seizure and use of evidence in a criminal prosecution without any traditional Fourth Amendment scrutiny.

Wyman has been extended to other social welfare home inspections, including child welfare, custody, and general wellness checks on welfare recipients residing both in homes and in unhoused environments.[41] Indeed, so long as the purpose of the invasion is noncriminal in nature, searches of probationers' homes, government offices, and government employees' blood and urine are permitted under the Fourth Amendment without any individualized suspicion of wrongdoing; the scheme itself must only be reasonable under the circumstances, even if the searches do or are likely to uncover evidence of criminal activity such as drug use or fraud.[42]

These suspicionless searches can intrude deeply into the sanctity of the home, long regarded by the Supreme Court as a place that "is first among equals" in Fourth Amendment protection.[43] State and local investigators have relied on *Wyman* to justifying unannounced, suspicionless searches of homes financed by low-income residents with Section 8 housing vouchers.[44] Perhaps most notoriously, for a quarter century the County of San Diego, California, implemented "Project 100%," a mandatory part of San Diego's public assistance program that required applicants eligible for any government cash assistance to consent to a warrantless and extended "home walkthrough" or face denial of aid. Over three thousand such suspicionless home visits took place, many of which resulted in criminal prosecution based on evidence seized by workers and turned over to police. The Ninth Circuit upheld these searches as reasonable. Even though "investigators ma[de] referrals for criminal investigation ... if they discover[ed] evidence of contraband" during their searches, the court reasoned that this "is a routine and expected fact of life and a consequence no greater than that which necessarily ensues upon any other discovery by a citizen of criminal conduct."[45]

Except it isn't. Sure, private citizens who discover criminal evidence are free to provide it to the police. But typically these citizens are not government workers threatening to take away vital, lifesaving money unless they can search people's homes for that evidence. Moreover, the government cannot enter a home and conduct an invasive search for evidence without probable cause of criminal activity and a warrant granted by a judge authorizing that search. But because welfare fraud investigators, and not police, entered the homes and found the evidence, these protections did not apply. Despite regular refrains from lower courts that "there is no 'social worker' exception to the Fourth Amendment," the reality is that any application of the amendment to even the most invasive social worker activities relies upon a threadbare finding of an administrative "special need" to justify bureaucratic enforcement of a social soft policing regime.[46] These sorts of oppressive invasions highlight the worst of soft policing: "When administrative rule violations are criminalized as welfare fraud, the soft policing of social benefit agencies funnel[s] people towards more explicit police violence."[47]

The invasive administration of these programs also does not benefit the public or public safety. In twenty-five years of Project 100%, far more taxpayer money was spent investigating welfare fraud than was paid out to purportedly fraudulent recipients. Instead, this soft policing simply intimidated and scared people for no reason. Investigators referred recipients for benefits termination and prosecution based on "evidence" that single women were relying on unreported sources of additional income—an extra toothbrush, a pair of boxer shorts, an extra-large T-shirt. The searches were intrusive and humiliating, with investigators "often comb[ing] through every nook and cranny of a home, including laundry bins, cupboards, trash cans, bedrooms and bathrooms, as well as deeply personal items such as letters from a former spouse."[48] These searches, more comprehensive and invasive than many warrant-authorized searches, led many recipients to simply end participation in the program, further placing them on the financial margins and at risk of homelessness. In short, "P100" cost more money than it saved, prosecuted vulnerable people for no good reason, and drove needy families away from seeking out crucial government benefits.

THE TRAGEDY OF SPECIAL NEEDS AND INVOLUNTARY CIVIL COMMITMENT

Among the most invasive public health and safety actions taken by government actors involve involuntary psychiatric holds, both by in-field first responders triaging potential emergencies and by psychiatrists conducting longer-term evaluations. Nearly every state allows nonpolice psychiatrists to authorize short-term involuntary psychiatric holds, and every state provides a process for long-term involuntary civil commitment in a psychiatric institution.[49] But rather than recognizing these significant liberty deprivations for their quasi-punitive nature and utilizing traditional Fourth Amendment protections, courts also view psychiatric holds as a "special need."

Each state's psychiatric hold statutes differ slightly with respect to the standards and processes governing commitment decisions and who is allowed to authorize such holds. But it is possible "to generalize criteria for involuntary treatment into one sentence, from which all other detail springs: states have the authority to intervene and provide involuntary care if an individual poses a danger to self or to other people."[50] The underlying principle behind these holds is that individual or public benefits of managing someone's mental health needs supersede that person's rights to refuse psychiatric care in certain narrow circumstances.

However, those narrow circumstances are growing ever wider. A showing of imminent danger to self or danger to others was once the norm for psychiatric holds, but now only a few states require it. An increasing number of states permit involuntary treatment and forced medication merely on a finding of foreseeability that one might not be able to care for oneself in the future due to mental illness. This far broader definition of harm, described alternately as "grave disability" or "psychiatric deterioration," sweeps in a far larger set of erratic but not dangerous behaviors and casts an ever-widening net for people subject to forced hospitalization.[51]

Courts have routinely considered the process of determining whether to subject someone to an involuntary psychiatric hold as a special need under the Fourth Amendment, even when these holds require significant invasions of privacy and liberty. For example, police arrived at Ruchla Zinger's home to place her into a psychiatric hospital in response to her doctor's application for involuntary civil commitment. The application vaguely referenced her danger to herself related to a mental illness arising in part from her experience as a Holocaust survivor during World War II. When Zinger refused to allow police into her home, officers forcibly broke down the door and pinned the sixty-four-year-old woman to the ground, where she died of cardiorespiratory arrest.[52]

Despite the lack of significant evidence of Zinger's imminent risk of harm, the lack of any observable information by police to suggest Zinger needed treatment, and the lack of probable cause or a warrant, the First Circuit Court of Appeals upheld the officers' actions as reasonable under the special needs doctrine. In doing so, the court ignored decades of precedent confirming that a person's private home is "first among equals" among Fourth Amendment protections, holding instead that "the City policy, as evidenced by the actual conduct of its police officers, falls squarely within a recognized class of systemic special need searches which are conducted without warrants in furtherance of important administrative purposes."[53]

As Northwestern University law professor Jamelia Morgan observed in her article "Psychiatric Holds and the Fourth Amendment," there are significant problems with analyzing involuntary commitment procedures as a special need.[54] Most special needs searches are justified as an exception to the Fourth Amendment's traditional requirement, because of their limited nature. They include discrete subpopulations in discrete locations subjected to limited suspicionless searches—airline passengers in an airport, children in a school, motorists at a sobriety checkpoint. But the mentally ill are not a discrete subpopulation in a discrete sensitive location justifying reduced privacy expectations. As with Ruchla Zinger, many mentally ill patients experience crisis in the privacy of their own homes, and they are subjected to far more invasive restrictions on their freedoms when being committed to a hospital than someone passing through a TSA scanner or a sobriety checkpoint.

Moreover, special needs reasonableness is far too relaxed a standard for such a significant restriction on freedom, particularly given that researchers have demonstrated how courts treat the special needs standard as akin to "rational basis review," the lowest possible standard of judicial review of government conduct.[55] Under rational basis review, courts will uphold as reasonable any government action so long as there was some minimal possible justification for the action. Thus, practically speaking, officers and alternate responders alike are allowed to impose forced hospitalization and medication on little more than a possible justification.

For example, in *May v. City of Nahunta*, an officer received statements of two EMTs who said of a patient that she was "a little combative to herself and was upset . . . clasping her fists and vigorously . . . scruffing and hitting herself in the head."[56] The officer went to May's home and observed that her hair was "all over her head in disarray." Based on this threadbare "evidence" of risk, the officer forcibly committed May. She stayed for only two hours before the treating nurse released her, confirming that there was no need for her to be there. The Eleventh Circuit upheld the forcible entry and commitment, expressing a reluctance to "second guess an officer's decision on these facts to transport a person to the hospital and evaluate possible mental-health concerns."[57] In other words, better safe than sorry.

There are at least two serious problems with this "better safe than sorry" approach. First, it unlocks the potential for broad criminal investigations by police and alternate responders on merely theoretical justifications. Courts have regularly recognized the ability for government actors to conduct broad, suspicionless searches as a regular part of a mental health seizure, analogizing it to an officer's ability to conduct broad, suspicionless searches for evidence "incident to a lawful arrest."[58] Thus, after placing someone in a psychiatric hold pursuant to a minimal special needs showing, mental health responders and police are free to search automatically for evidence of criminal activity.

Second, erring on the side of "safety" in authorizing psychiatric holds ignores the significant invasions suffered by, and harm done to, the people placed in hospitals against their will. Most government-run psychiatric hospitals operate under prison-like restrictions, with the use of tie-down bed restraints and chemical sedation the norm. Nurses in these hospitals have reported that safety-based practices and strict application of rules and regulations in psychiatric hospitals take priority over providing therapeutic care, priorities "rooted in fear and stigmatization [of] . . . mentally ill people as dangerous and unstable."[59] Because of security concerns, psychiatric hospitals install video surveillance cameras in patients' rooms to record their movements, with one study concluding that "safety is not merely a consideration or goal, but the highest value."[60] Personnel in these hospitals report keeping patients' rooms forced open at all hours and refusing patient requests to dress or use the bathroom in private. Two patients forced involuntarily into temporary psychiatric treatment explained how little privacy exists in these institutions:

> They sent me in the last available room, kept the lights on (and didn't let me turn them off), left my door open, and turned off the heating in my room. I sat there cold, tired, and afraid for several hours until the people from the next shift arrived.
> They watched me as I got undressed and watched me as I dressed in these awful scrubs. . . . I was never left alone and I felt humiliated. I had no sense of privacy at all, I wanted to see the doctor and get out that night. . . . As a rape survivor, this was horrifying to me.[61]

Not surprisingly, involuntary psychiatric "hospitalization was found to induce significant fear, which eventually acted as a deterrent to seeking future mental healthcare services."[62] Rather than promoting healing and improved public health outcomes, many psychiatric hospitals have become secured holding cells in a soft policing structure putting people somewhere else. According to one report noting the lack of privacy and the common practice of forced chemical sedation in these facilities, "People forced into psychiatry are overwhelmingly innocent people, very few are criminals, yet these law abiding people lose more human rights than even a convicted criminal loses in a super-max prison. Those targeted for forced psychiatry lose the right to own their own body. [It] is often described by many survivors of it, as being experienced as a kind of biological rape."[63]

And yet the scope of involuntary commitment continues to grow. Two of the country's most populated states increasingly rely on "someone else" to put the mentally ill "somewhere else" without any meaningful legal restrictions on these expanded programs. "California Governor Gavin Newsom's CARE Court and New York City Mayor Eric Adams's involuntary hospitalization policy exemplify the trend of moving beyond existing standards of dangerousness under civil commitment laws and towards the use of preventative detention as a way of removing individuals who 'appear to be mentally ill' or are unable to care for themselves."[64] California's CARE Court program in particular (Community Assistance, Recovery, and Empowerment) has devoted hundreds of millions of dollars to creating an entirely new court system devoted solely to placing more mentally ill Californians in involuntary psychiatric treatment with the promise of long-term care and long-term housing. Those promises, based on current funding and housing shortages, appear likely to remain unfulfilled while more people with mental illness become ensnared in yet another system of court hearings and forced confinement.

These quasi-punitive functions ought to be subject to the same legal standards as traditional punitive law enforcement actions. Disability and mental health rights advocates explain that these "medicalized carceral spaces" often are indistinguishable from prison cells. As one woman explained, "After a [mental health episode], whether the cops or the EMTs come get me, I often can't tell whether I am in the jail or locked hospital ward. I guess one has slightly nicer sheets."[65] Another woman described being confined by "handcuffs or Haldol" (a powerful psychiatric drug) for most of her life.[66] As involuntary civil commitment takes on more characteristics of traditional criminal arrest, treating it as a noncriminal special need appears less and less justifiable.

"COMMUNITY CARETAKING"

Related to the Fourth Amendment exception for special needs searches is what courts have called the "community caretaking" exception. When a police officer acts "totally divorced from the detection, investigation, or acquisition of evidence relating to the violation of a criminal statute," she acts in her capacity as a community caretaker and need not possess probable cause or a warrant to intrusively invade people's privacy and, if necessary, use force to seize them "for their own good." The problem with this exception is that police are routinely called to respond to noncriminal disturbances that may include or evolve into criminal activity:

> Police departments dispatch thousands of welfare checks per year in response to a variety of requests submitted by the community. These calls are unpredictable and require talented and flexible responses. Some callers report that their neighbor's home is being burgled, others worry about unresponsive grandparents, others call to report "sketchy" or sick-looking individuals in the community. . . . Police officers are "a jack-of-all emergencies," who are "expected to aid those in distress, combat actual hazards, prevent potential hazards from materializing, and provide an infinite variety of services to preserve and protect community safety." Courts describe this function as "community caretaking."[67]

Not surprisingly, this doctrine can be applied as malleably and as infinitely as the malleable and infinite number of public health and safety emergencies that exist. That creates significant civil liberties risks, since a doctrine with such broad application also removes invasive police conduct from normal probable-cause and warrant requirements. For example, in *Tinius v. Carrol Cnty. Sheriff Dept.*, officers observed a man walking along the highway in the middle of winter without a coat. After suspecting the man might be intoxicated, officers handcuffed him and took him to the hospital, where they held him down while medical staff obtained a urine sample through a painful and physically forced catheterization. The officers and medical staff then agreed to transfer the man to a psychiatric facility. At no point was the man suspected of any crimes, nor did he give his consent to the detainment and forced catheterization. On appeal, the court absolved the officers, finding they "were exercising their community caretaking functions when they transported Tinius to the hospital and later restrained him" and that the officers' actions neither violated the Fourth Amendment nor created the basis for a tort claim for battery or false imprisonment.[68]

Police were similarly found to be engaged in "community caretaking" when they observed Jose Gallegos crying and talking to himself just after 1 a.m. in Colorado Springs, Colorado. An officer walked up and grabbed Gallegos by the arm, but Gallegos jerked free and demanded to be "left the fuck alone." Police responded by arresting Gallegos for interfering with an officer, placing him in an arm bar, and forcing him face down on the pavement in the middle of a public street. Just then, a car approached and attempted to brake but ran over Gallegos before speeding away. Gallegos suffered significant injuries, but the police were absolved of liability for acting "reasonably under the circumstances" given their role as community caretakers.[69]

These kinds of violent police responses to mental health emergencies clearly support the use of alternate responders in these kinds of situations. Yet not surprisingly, if police can engage in such intrusive and physically assaultive activity and evade Fourth Amendment scrutiny as "community caretakers," the same troubling exception likely would apply to alternate responders. And it does.

COMMUNITY CARETAKING BY DESTROYING COMMUNITIES: HOMELESS ENCAMPMENT "SWEEPS"

Among the many things authorized by the community caretaking exception is the ability for police and others to seize personal property "in the name of protecting the community." This power depends solely on "the authority of police to seize and remove from the streets vehicles [or other property] impeding traffic or threatening public safety and convenience."[70] As one court observed, this portion of the "community caretaking exception to the warrant requirement is an issue that disproportionately affects homeless individuals because, unlike those with homes in which to store their belongings, the homeless are more likely to carry the majority of their personal belongings with them at any given time."[71] That reality is becoming more prevalent in the new public safety as states increasingly rely on the progressive enforcement model of homeless encampment sweeps and citations to "solve" the homelessness crisis plaguing many cities.

When a city considers a tent encampment to be a nuisance—"most commonly due to complaints from nearby homeowners, business owners, and other power brokers in the city"—it is then "swept."[72] Notices of an impending sweep are posted a few hours or days before the planned action, and then a combination of police and nonpolice sanitation workers and HOT personnel "escort those living in the tents away, fence off the area, and ... begin throwing everything into" the trash.[73] Brooke Carrillo experienced a recent sweep in San Francisco, where she was given "15 minutes to get what you want. ... They ended up taking my birth certificate, my Social Security card, my mother's necklace that her mother gave her, the only pictures of my brother and dad, both of who are no longer here. I felt like my own life went into the trash." Carrillo saw sanitation workers throw away a friend's parent's ashes, expensive family heirlooms, and life-saving expensive medications. "I felt alone, worthless, and that I was going to die by my own hands, or just by being out here with nothing. It makes you feel like you don't matter."[74]

THE "MIXED MOTIVES" OF ALTERNATE RESPONDERS

Much of the discussion of when and how the Fourth Amendment applies depends on the subjective motivations of the alternate responder. While this line between criminal and noncriminal is critical, it can be especially difficult to draw when government actors have multiple reasons for conducting an investigation. As one officer responding to a seizure-induced medical emergency admitted, police are "always investigating for crimes" even if other reasons led them to the interaction.[75] So-called mixed-motive investigations animated by both criminal and noncriminal purposes represent difficult line-drawing problems for the Court.

For example, in *New York v. Burger*,[76] police officers entered a junkyard without probable cause or individualized suspicion and asked to inspect the business license and "police book," a record of automobiles and parts on the premises.[77] A New York law required junkyards to maintain these records and authorized limited inspections of the police book as a matter of administrative oversight. When the owner conceded he had neither the license nor the book, the officers proceeded to search the junkyard for hours looking for stolen vehicles and other contraband, found several stolen vehicles, and arrested the owner.[78] Once the junkyard owner admitted he was in violation of New York regulations, the "administrative search" had ended; any further investigation into the junkyard itself "took on the obvious cast of a police effort to undercover evidence of criminal activity."[79] However, the Court upheld the search of the junkyard and the seizure of the stolen vehicles as part of an administrative "special needs" search, reasoning that the administrative regulations themselves were not intended for criminal purposes, even though the officers relying on those regulations clearly had criminal investigative intent.[80]

This case has troubling applications to alternate responders. Social workers investigating administrative welfare fraud operate with a noncriminal administrative programmatic purpose, though they may also uncover evidence of criminal conduct, either intentionally or accidentally. Likewise, psychiatrists evaluating patients for short-term involuntary holds have a primary noncriminal purpose but may also be motivated in part to determine whether a potentially dangerous mentally ill patient is also engaged in criminal activity. HOT teams sweeping encampments also operate under noncriminal "community caretaking" protocols, though many such alternate responders expressly note that a secondary purpose of the sweeps is issuing criminal citations for illegal camping.

Noncriminal regulations removing alternate responders from Fourth Amendment scrutiny despite their obvious criminal investigative intent apply with particular force to civilian traffic enforcement. Much like the administrative regulations in *Burger*, traffic monitor proposals contemplate administrative regulations empowering traffic monitors to issue vehicle-related citations but not to investigate crimes or gather evidence for criminal prosecutions. The objective of these proposals is specifically nonpenal, even if evidence of criminal wrongdoing may be uncovered during a traffic stop. Because the traffic agency itself has a stated noncriminal purpose and prescribes different noninvestigative methods of addressing criminal roadway behavior, traditional Fourth Amendment requirements of individualized suspicion, probable cause, and warrants will not apply even if during the course of a traffic stop the line between criminal and noncriminal intent blurs.

Take one example. A traffic monitor, pursuant to regulation, pulls over a vehicle for failing to signal before changing lanes. During the stop, the monitor exceeds her administrative regulatory authority and searches the vehicle and occupants. During the search, the monitor finds evidence of illegal drug and firearm possession, which is later used in a criminal prosecution. Under *Burger*, because the administrative purpose of the stop was noncriminal, the "mixed motive" of the traffic monitor would be irrelevant in determining whether to apply the Fourth Amendment to the search; it simply would not apply at all.

One obvious response to this concern is to simply make it illegal for traffic monitors to conduct searches or gather evidence. Indeed, many existing alternate responder regulations limit powers in precisely this way, including regulations governing CAHOOTS and STAR. The governing contract between CAHOOTS and the City of Eugene affirmatively prohibits CAHOOTS personnel from searching for criminal evidence or effectuating any arrest-like seizures; discovery of criminal activity or violent conduct necessitating a law enforcement response requires CAHOOTS to call police for backup rather than pursuing their own search, seizure, and arrest activities.

Surprisingly, however, even regulations prohibiting alternate responders from investigating or seizing evidence of a crime does not solve the Fourth Amendment problem. As the Supreme Court explained in *Virginia v. Moore*, a government actor's violation of a state law or city regulation will not invalidate a search or seizure for Fourth Amendment purposes if that activity was otherwise constitutional.[81] In *Moore*, an officer pulled over a motorist for a minor driving offense, which under Virginia law authorized the officer only to issue a citation. Ignoring this restriction, the officer arrested the driver and conducted a search of the car incident to the arrest, which turned up evidence later used in a criminal prosecution. A unanimous Court upheld the search, finding the arrest and subsequent search to be reasonable and thus permissible under the Fourth Amendment, regardless of whatever state law restrictions may have otherwise prevented the search.[82] *Moore* thus stands for the remarkable proposition that a search or seizure can be actually illegal and yet still constitutionally reasonable!

Thus, criminal evidence seized by a traffic monitor (or social worker, or HOT member, or psychiatrist) in violation of state or local law preventing such searches may nonetheless be introduced in a criminal prosecution so long as the search was independently justified under the Fourth Amendment. And given that regulations governing alternate responders have a primary noncriminal purpose, any alternate responder action resulting in the discovery of criminal evidence likely will be deemed constitutional, whether or not that action violated state or local law. Indeed, if we are to take *Burger* at face value, it should not matter that an *individual* rogue alternate responder had criminal investigative motives. The *programmatic* purpose of the traffic agency, psychiatric hold process, and drug diversion program is noncriminal. While the defendant may have civil legal recourse for violation of state or local law, after *Moore's* rejection of these "subconstitutional" safeguards, such recourse will do little to protect the defendant in a criminal trial.[83]

SOCIAL WORKERS AND THE INEVITABILITY OF MIXED MOTIVES

The nature of social work regularly implicates mixed criminal and noncriminal motives. Social workers address long-term welfare issues often closely related to criminal activity—drug use, child abuse, domestic violence—that blurs the line between penal and nonpenal motives for these individuals. This close relation to criminal activity also helps explain social workers' long close working relationship with police, as well as the distrust many marginalized communities have of these alternate responders.[84] Social workers enter family residences to conduct child welfare visits, mediate domestic disputes, and provide drug abuse counseling. But under *Burger*, a social worker who begins a home visit and searches the home for noncriminal purposes may very well seize evidence of a crime (and later report it to police) without probable cause or a warrant because that desire to support a criminal arrest was secondary to the primary purpose of delivering social services.

The lack of trust created by this close connection to police and criminal investigation threatens to erode the effectiveness of all alternate responders, not just social workers, even in the absence of criminal activity. Police officers regularly describe widespread lack of trust from the community as a primary reason why they cannot effectively respond to noncriminal public welfare calls.[85] Much of this distrust stems from community fear—particularly from Black and Latinx communities—that armed officers may arrest or inflict unlawful force during the course of providing "welfare" to these individuals.[86] But that distrust also stems from a recognition that officers always have the ability and desire to "ferret out crime," find evidence, and arrest criminals.[87] If the actors replacing police have even greater powers to discover and respond to crime without the bother of Fourth Amendment restrictions, one wonders how alternate responders like social workers who rely on a foundation of trust can make the kinds of inroads police reformers promise. As one social worker union explained in an open letter challenging increased police co-response collaboration, "If all we do is replace police with social workers without eliminating the carceral aspects of social work, we will simply subject vulnerable people to cops by a different name."[88] This soft policing poses real risks for vulnerable people subject to the new public safety, risks that are exacerbated by courts' refusal to apply the Fourth Amendment's strictures and guardrails to these punitive alternate responder practices.

4 Brutality without Police

Andrew Douglass had been living in a tent on a sidewalk in San Francisco's Tenderloin neighborhood for months, but he was only one day away from securing housing. He had an appointment the next morning with his street medicine case manager, who would meet him at his tent to help him move into a low-income housing unit with wraparound medical and mental health services. But instead, San Francisco Public Works crews entered Douglass's tent, dismantled it, and threw it away while Douglass frantically packed his few belongings into plastic bags. During the chaos, Douglass lost his ID card, which is necessary to gain entry to the city's low-income housing, as well as his required and expensive epilepsy medication. Douglass also missed his appointment.[1]

Many long-term homeless people like Douglass eventually find their way off the streets not through case managers but through inpatient psychiatric evaluation, either voluntary or involuntary. But the risks inside the hospitals are often greater than the risks on the street. One such patient anonymously reported that therapists and nurses constantly encouraged her to have sex with them, with one "psych nurse scanning me with the contraband wand . . . and saying to me he wanted to spank my ass with it."[2] Others, including children and adolescents, reported being strapped face down to their beds every day for hours at a time and injected in the buttocks with "booty juice," a powerful antipsychotic sedative rendering patients disoriented and unconscious for hours.[3]

The government's unjustified destruction of one's belongings and horrific physical violence against someone in custody ordinarily would constitute an "unreasonable seizure" and an act of "excessive force" giving victims the right to seek protection under the Constitution—at least, that is, when the perpetrator of this abuse is a police officer carrying out his law enforcement duties. But for those abused by city workers destroying encampments, psychiatric hospital workers forcibly medicating and harassing patients, and any number of alternate responders, these constitutional protections against government brutality often do not apply.

Among the many ills attributed to police in America, none dominates the reform conversation like police brutality. Shocking videos of violence seared into our collective consciousness, together with shameful statistics confirming the sheer scope and racially disparate impact of police use of force, command our attention and spur urgent calls to action. It is this epidemic of police violence, more than anything else, that has accelerated the pace of public safety reform. Much of that reform has come in the form of removing police from the equation in many situations and replacing them with unarmed alternate responders.

And the presence of alternate responders appears to have a positive impact. Since programs around the country allow alternate responders to take a large percentage of 911 calls previously routed to police and virtually none of those calls have required police backup, preliminary studies suggest that arrest rates decrease when alternate responders are involved, as do rates of violence.[4] As expected, alternate responders train not to use violence themselves. But nonpolice brutality still occurs, both from individual overzealous actors and as a result of the structural denials of bodily integrity woven into involuntary psychiatric treatment, homeless encampment "sweeps," and other forms of soft policing. Acts of unjustified violence committed by EMTs frustrated with drug-addicted individuals, homelessness outreach personnel's forcible destruction of an unhoused person's property, and psychiatrists' forcible restraint and chemical sedation of patients are just some of the routine uses of physical violence by alternate responders serving in their soft policing capacity.

While removing police to reduce police violence makes good sense as a matter of policy, it does not automatically improve legal protections for those who are harmed. In fact, the opposite is often true. Courts routinely decline to apply constitutional protections in cases of shocking physical abuse unless the victim is being arrested or is the subject of a criminal investigation. Moreover, the Supreme Court's narrow definition of *seizure* excludes violent dispersal tactics designed to compel citizens to leave an area, a legal loophole particularly relevant to HOT teams increasingly called upon to disperse and relocate unhoused persons. And the Constitution's only other source of protection from government brutality, the Due Process Clause, has proven woefully inadequate to address even the most unjustified government abuses, including sexual violence by police and nonpolice alike.

THE LAW OF EXCESSIVE FORCE

Officer Elton Hymon responded to a 911 call about a burglary taking place. When he arrived on the scene, he was met by a neighbor who claimed to have heard glass breaking next door. Hymon investigated, and he saw a young skinny Black boy running across the yard. Hymon told the boy to stop, but he kept running and began climbing a fence to get away. Hymon, who later acknowledged the boy was not armed and posed no danger, shot him in the back of the head and killed him. Edward Garner was fifteen years old and 110 pounds at the time of his death. He was carrying a wallet with ten dollars inside it.

The Supreme Court ruled that Officer Hymon's use of deadly force violated the Fourth Amendment's protection against unreasonable seizures, observing that "it is not better that all felony suspects die than that they escape."[5] Four years later, the Court extended this rationale to all claims of excessive force against police officers, not just deadly force. Thus, an officer's use of handcuffs, tasers, batons, fists, or knees to the neck would be analyzed under the Fourth Amendment as a potentially unreasonable seizure. The Court explained in the landmark case *Graham v. Connor* that "determining whether the force used to effect a particular seizure is 'reasonable' under the Fourth Amendment requires a careful balancing of . . .

the individual's Fourth Amendment interests against the countervailing governmental interest at stake."[6]

Scholars and commentators have criticized various aspects of this test since it was articulated over three decades ago, pointing to its vagueness as promoting unjustified deference toward police, its requirement only that officers use force that is "reasonable" rather than force that is "necessary," and the Court's refusal to consider seemingly important factors like an officer's attempts at de-escalation or an officer's actions that exacerbated a situation. But for all the faults of this standard, at least one exists to restrain police violence. This same standard almost never applies at all to alternate responders outside police criminal investigations.

Frankly, this makes little sense. If anything, uses of force ought to be scrutinized more forcefully and authorized less frequently with alternate responders. Excessive force law as applied to police is informed by the reality that police are expected to confront potentially violent criminals and situations and are authorized and expected to use force when doing so; indeed, police have a "monopoly" on lawful violence for this very reason.[7] Alternate responders have no such authority or mandate; they are not a part of the monopoly of lawful violence. In fact, their mandate is inapposite to police violence. Medical first responders, mental health professionals, and social workers all follow a code of professional ethics centered on doing no harm to patients and clients. Their primary goal centers on individual patient well-being, not public safety through law enforcement. It should follow, then, that *no* amount of physical force is objectively reasonable when compared to the police need to use force when subduing and arresting criminal suspects. At a minimum, one might imagine a far more tightly defined standard for what qualifies as "objectively reasonable" use of force in the nonpolice alternate responder context.

In theory, then, excessive force law should protect citizens against nonpolice brutality more than it currently does against police brutality. I say "in theory," because currently excessive force law largely *does not* apply to nonpolice brutality at all. Rather than more tightly regulating acts of violence committed by nonpolice actors, existing law confirms that these actors operate almost entirely free of any unreasonable seizure restraints.

Why does this matter? If someone physically assaults you, can't you just sue on any number of state law tort claims, including assault, battery, and false imprisonment? Sure. And in fact, most plaintiffs who bring constitutional claims of excessive force also bring private tort claims. But as we will see, only constitutional civil rights claims offer the financial incentive of attorneys' fees for the prevailing party and the legal vehicle to bring about sorely needed institutional change within government agencies. Moreover, as with Fourth Amendment search law, evidence unlawfully obtained as a result of an unreasonable seizure may be excluded from evidence in a future criminal trial, an important remedy not available in a private lawsuit. But these important remedies often are not available against alternate responders, who operate largely outside these restraints.

VIOLENCE OUTSIDE CRIMINAL INVESTIGATIONS

As with search and seizure law, the "primary purpose of the Fourth Amendment's [excessive force provisions is] to prohibit unreasonable intrusions in the course of criminal investigations."[8] However, while courts regularly address whether a nonpolice actor's search or seizure constitutes a "special needs search" or falls within the "community caretaking" exception, comparatively few cases have addressed specifically when and to what extent the law of excessive force applies outside police criminal investigations. The few cases considering this issue typically concern police sexual misconduct and overly aggressive medical personnel. In these cases, courts ask two questions before applying the Fourth Amendment. First, did the perpetrator commit a violent act during the course of an investigation?[9] Second, was the perpetrator subjectively motivated to carry out some formal governmental objective when using physical force?[10] If the answer to either question is "no," courts rarely find the existence of a Fourth Amendment seizure.

Noninvestigative Brutality: Sexual Misconduct

As Justice Anthony Kennedy once argued, "any invasion of a person's personal security" ought to trigger the Fourth Amendment, including not just "a serious assault . . . [but] any offensive touching."[11] But "the vast majority of courts only apply [excessive force doctrine] to cases involving arrestees, suspects, or other investigative settings" involving police officers.[12] Drawing the line between investigative and noninvestigative brutality occurs most frequently in cases involving police sexual misconduct. If an officer sexually assaults someone during the course of an active criminal investigation, the Fourth Amendment will apply. But if an on-duty police officer "sexually assaults a person in her home, in a noninvestigative setting," the Fourth Amendment "generally does not" apply.[13]

For example, in *United States v. Langer*, an officer who pulled over female drivers, detained them on the side of the road, and pushed them against the car while forcibly kissing them was found to have committed a "severe infraction of the Fourth Amendment" because the assaults occurred during the course of a traffic stop investigation.[14] But in *Poe v. Leonard*, the Second Circuit held that an on-duty officer who surreptitiously videotaped women undressing in a closed room did not commit a Fourth Amendment violation because this behavior "occurred outside of a criminal investigation or other form of governmental investigation or activity" and was instead "for personal reasons."[15] These contrasting cases highlight the arbitrary distinction between investigative and noninvestigative activity. The officer in *Langer* was engaged in "investigative activity" only to the extent that he used the pretext of a traffic stop to perpetrate sexual violence, even though sexual violence can never serve a legitimate investigative function.

This arbitrary line drawing was on full display in *Montanez v. City of Syracuse*, where a Syracuse police officer responded to a 911 call from a woman claiming that her sister had kidnapped her daughter and taken her from New York to Alabama.[16] The responding officer arrived at the woman's apartment, made lewd remarks about her appearance, and then raped her. The court admitted that Officer Chester Thompson "was in Plaintiff's apartment in response to a 911 call, and thus on police business," but nevertheless declined to find expressly that the Fourth Amendment applied.[17] The court concluded that because "there is no evidence that Thompson sexually assaulted Plaintiff during the course of an arrest or seizure or that Plaintiff was under suspicion of criminal activity," a clear Fourth Amendment violation had not been alleged.[18] While the plaintiff ultimately withdrew her Fourth Amendment claim voluntarily and settled her private tort law claims with the city for $500,000, the court's reluctance to find that the Fourth Amendment applied at all is telling.

The implications of these cases in the alternate responder context are troubling and far-reaching. If the Fourth Amendment does not apply to a rape by a police officer when responding to a 911 call solely because the victim was not a criminal suspect or arrestee, one can scarcely imagine when the amendment would apply to nonpolice actors. Indeed, the very purpose of a nonpolice alternate responder is to authorize a government actor to respond to *noncriminal* activity with a *noninvestigative, noncarceral* response to a public safety concern. Alternate responders generally have no power to investigate criminal activity or make arrests as a result of their role as alternatives to criminal enforcement; thus, any potential target of their nonpolice violence by extension will not be a "suspect" or "arrestee" as understood in *Montanez*.

Physical Violence during Medical Emergencies

This reasoning has particular salience in the context of paramedics. EMTs respond to 911 calls just like the officer in *Montanez*, but the purpose of their response is to triage medical emergencies, not initiate criminal investigations. A paramedic who responds to a call and subsequently assaults a victim (sexually or otherwise) almost certainly does so free from Fourth Amendment scrutiny. This nonpolice actor is doubly insulated: not only are they assaulting people who are not criminal suspects or arrestees, but unlike the officer in *Montanez*, they were never responding to a criminal emergency at all.

Though there exist "very few cases dealing with the Fourth Amendment's application in the context of paramedics rendering emergency medical assistance," limited case law on this point seems to confirm as much.[19] For example, in *Peete v. Metropolitan Government of Nashville and Davidson County*, a case involving EMT response to a seizure of an epileptic man, the Sixth Circuit Court of Appeals "f[ound] no case authority holding that paramedics answering a 911 emergency request for help engage in a Fourth Amendment 'seizure' when restraining the person to render aid."[20] This appears to be the case even though the restraint applied typically would fall within the Fourth Amendment definition of *seizure* and even when that restraint otherwise would constitute excessive force. For example, in *Peete*, paramedics restrained the man by "using their bodies to apply weight and pressure to [the man's] head, neck, shoulders, arms, torso, and legs, tied his hands and ankles behind his back and continued to apply pressure to [him] while he was in prone position" until he died.[21] But because the paramedics acted solely to provide medical aid and not to investigate for a criminal or administrative purpose, the Fourth Amendment did not apply to this clearly unreasonable seizure.[22] The Sixth Circuit, in somewhat callous language, made clear what the refusal to apply the Fourth Amendment meant for the case brought by the man's estate: absent a Fourth Amendment claim, there is no "constitutional liability for the negligence, deliberate indifference, and incompetence" of medical professionals.[23]

Relying on *Peete*, the Fifth Circuit Court of Appeals considered a Fourth Amendment excessive force claim by the estate of George Cornell, a man transported to an emergency room by police officers during a suspected paranoid mental health disturbance. Upon his admission, Mr. Cornell alerted physicians to his high blood pressure and tachycardia, a heart condition resulting in arhythmic, unusually fast heartbeats. Medical staff did not complete a full diagnostic screening before giving Mr. Cornell a tranquilizing drug cocktail to reduce his paranoia and agitation. When Mr. Cornell remained agitated, medical staff twice transported him to different rooms and injected additional drugs before eventually pinning Mr. Cornell to the ground, face down, for fifteen straight minutes. Witnesses described Mr. Cornell becoming motionless long before medical staff released him from his prone position. When Mr. Cornell did not respond, he was transported to yet another room, where he was pronounced dead. The medical examiner found three primary causes for Mr. Cornell's death: his underlying health conditions, exacerbated by the drug cocktail and exacerbated further by being compressed and pinned for a quarter hour.[24]

After an investigation, the Center for Medicaid Services found the hospital to be grossly deficient in failing to provide full medical screenings to patients like Mr. Cornell upon arrival, and further found medical staff's restraint to far exceed the maximum one-minute prone position restraint in which medical staff are trained. Yet despite the fact that a government investigation concluded government doctors killed Mr. Cornell by applying grossly excessive force, the Fifth Circuit dismissed the Fourth Amendment claim. The court concluded that there is no "controlling authority—or a robust consensus of persuasive authority, suggesting that medical personnel 'seize' patients when restraining them in the course of providing treatment." In doing so, the court quoted the Sixth Circuit's opinion in *Peete* that the medical staff "acted in order to provide medical aid" and did not act "to enforce the law, deter, or incarcerate."[25]

A similar reluctance to apply the Fourth Amendment to seizures initiated by mental health responders informs the limited case law addressing the issue. Courts have refused to apply the Fourth Amendment even when the seizure at issue—potentially lengthy involuntary commitment to a mental health facility—"raises concerns that are closely analogous to those implicated by a criminal arrest."[26] In *Scott v. Hern*, the Tenth Circuit did not inquire into whether the Fourth Amendment applied to a government psychiatrist's decision to forcibly restrain someone in a psychiatric hospital, because the decision was motivated by a desire to help an ill patient, not investigate a crime.[27] Even though the court acknowledged that mental health evaluations and criminal arrests are "equally intrusive" and involve similar bodily restraints, the uniform worn by the government actor imposing this intrusion appeared to make all the constitutional difference.[28]

These cases create concerning precedent for the new public safety. Mental health emergency responders enjoy broad support across ideological lines, with more than 2,700 mental health crisis intervention teams authorized to respond to 911 calls around the country.[29] Intervention teams are often empowered to take actions—including sending individuals in crisis to involuntary civil commitment—that are equally as intrusive as criminal arrests. Yet under current precedent, these actions appear not to trigger a Fourth Amendment excessive force analysis, even though they unquestionably constitute a "seizure," plainly understood. And while determinations about civil commitment may not appear analogous to traditional excessive force cases involving physical violence, both the significant restraint on liberty itself and the force necessary to effectuate such a restraint make these cases critically relevant to the question of whether and to what extent nonpolice actors can ever be held liable for unreasonable seizures.

The Structural Violence of Mental Health Crisis Response

Perhaps more than any other nonpolice public safety approach, the history of mental health crisis response and treatment in this country has been defined by persistent structural violence that at times looks indistinguishable from the violence of arrests, convictions, and incarceration.

Prior to the mid-1800s, most people with serious mental illness ended up in local prisons and were subjected to deplorable conditions of confinement, kept in "cages, closets, cellars, stalls, pens."[30] The creation of mental health institutions known as "asylums" was seen as a humane alternative, allowing people to receive psychiatric treatment from doctors instead of punishment from wardens. But patients remained confined to small, locked rooms against their will, often for life. And many thousands experienced regular, daily physical restraints on their bodily movement in the form of straitjackets, bed straps, and even handcuffs. As the use of asylums increased, particularly following the end of World War II, the populations in these institutions grew far beyond capacity. By 1955, when nearly half a million people were committed to state-run psychiatric facilities, "staff struggled just to keep up with patient needs . . . and the resulting conditions looked remarkably similar to those seen in jails and prisons today."[31]

With FDA approval of effective antipsychotic medications like chlorpromazine in 1954 and the rise of the civil rights movement in the 1960s, activists and lawmakers began moving away from the institutionalization model. After President Kennedy signed the Community Mental Health Centers Act into law in 1963, which promoted community-based outpatient care as an alternative to inpatient hospitalization, "the asylums were essentially emptied. The once colossal psychiatric inpatient registry would ultimately decline to 30,000 by the 1990s."[32] While long-term civil commitment remained an important part of government-run mental health treatment, a series of Supreme Court cases aimed at protecting the rights of patients mandated that civil commitment prioritize the "least restrictive setting" necessary, be justified by some threshold finding of dangerousness to self or others, and be proven necessary by a finding of "clear and convincing evidence" as determined by a neutral judge.[33] This intermediate burden of proof, which is more than a civil lawsuit "preponderance of the evidence" standard but less than a criminal case "beyond a reasonable doubt" standard, was introduced in recognition of the "quasi-criminal" nature of involuntarily committing someone to a confined setting for an indeterminate period of time that could easily extend to the end of one's life.[34]

Long-term civil commitment remains an option for the most seriously mentally ill, but populations in these facilities today are "negligible" compared to a few decades ago. Unfortunately, large-scale funding for the types of outpatient community mental health centers contemplated by the 1963 act signed by President Kennedy never materialized. Instead, rising numbers of mentally ill people were thrust into the streets during the same period that tough-on-crime policies like the War on Drugs and broken windows policing took root, fueling the mass incarceration epidemic. Not surprisingly, prison populations exploded with nonviolent, nondangerous people with mental illness.[35] People in need of mental health resources being locked behind bars and treated as criminals exacerbated rather than alleviated their underlying conditions, almost guaranteeing a cycle of recidivism and reincarceration.

Los Angeles stands as the poster child for this "human rights disaster": "Los Angeles is home to the largest jail system in the country—including Twin Towers Correctional Facility, which the Los Angeles County Sheriff's Department calls the 'nation's largest mental health facility.' Over 14,000 people are currently locked up within the county's jails. According to the sheriff's department, 43% of those people are mentally ill. And 25% of all people incarcerated in Los Angeles jails are homeless."[36] With this backdrop, alternate response agencies focused on providing triaged mental health services to people in crisis instead of locking them away in a prison sounds like a welcome and necessary change. And it is. The "help, not handcuffs" model is an admirable and sensible one. But as with long-term institutionalization and incarceration models, too often short-term psychiatric holds rely on physical force, brutality, and violence that are neither justified nor subject to traditional constitutional restrictions.

As discussed in chapter 3, the initial determination of whether to initiate a psychiatric hold, whether made by a police officer or a psychiatrist, is typically subject to a weakened probable-cause analysis of Fourth Amendment "special needs reasonableness." Thus, the decision to place someone in a temporary "quasi-criminal" treatment setting is subject to fewer constitutional checks than a typical investigation and arrest. Once placed in the involuntary hold, patients are subject to significant physical force against their will, including through the use of round-the-clock restraints, forced medication, and powerful chemical sedation. These acts of physical violence fall entirely outside the reach of Fourth Amendment excessive force law.

Regarding forced medication and chemical sedation, the Supreme Court has held that an arrested pretrial criminal suspect retains Fourth and Fourteenth Amendment rights to refuse treatment with antipsychotic drugs unless such treatment is deemed to be "medically appropriate."[37] But in doing so, the Court confirmed that traditional Fourth Amendment objective reasonableness standards for excessive force do not apply, holding that "due process allows a mentally ill inmate to be treated involuntarily with antipsychotic drugs where there is a determination that 'the inmate is dangerous to himself or others and the treatment is in the inmate's medical interest.'"[38]

But when the person subjected to forced medication is not an arrested inmate or criminal suspect but a committed psychiatric patient, it remains unclear whether even these reduced rights apply. On October 8, 2014, Frederick Brown called 911 after using drugs and alcohol and experiencing "crazy thoughts" and auditory hallucinations, claiming he did not want to "end up being hurt." The Los Angeles County Fire Department responded and placed Brown in a temporary psychiatric hold. At the treatment facility, members of the Behavioral Response Team placed Brown in four-point restraints, locking his arms and legs to the bed. When Brown awoke and became disoriented and agitated, a hospital psychiatrist injected him with a powerful sedative cocktail of Haldol, Benadryl, and Ativan. Brown was quickly sedated but later suffered an allergic reaction to the Haldol.[39] When Brown brought a Fourth Amendment excessive force claim against the psychiatrist for unreasonably injecting him with medication when he was already restrained, the court acknowledged that *arrested detainees* have a right to refuse involuntary medication. But it found "no authority holding that involuntary sedation [of] . . . a patient who is subject to a 5150 psychiatric hold . . . is a constitutional violation."[40]

Failing to subject forced chemical sedation to more exacting constitutional scrutiny is unjustifiable, given the intense invasion of bodily integrity and autonomy it entails. One patient equated the practice to "biological rape," and the United Nations Special Rapporteur on Torture observed that in many contexts the practice meets the international definition of torture.[41] The United Nations report noted that supposed "best interests" and "medical necessity" justifications for chemical sedation "generally involve highly discriminatory and coercive attempts at controlling or 'correcting' the victim's personality, behaviour or choices and almost always inflict severe pain or suffering."[42]

This observation accurately describes many of the common uses of powerful sedatives in the US forced psychiatric treatment context. The Food and Drug Administration "has not approved any of the drugs used as chemical restraints in healthcare settings. These drugs are developed and approved for patients suffering from specific psychiatric and behavioral disorders, yet they are used off-label as chemical restraints on patients largely without regard to whether they have been diagnosed with these indicated health concerns."[43] Indeed, the use of these powerful antipsychotic medications off-label is a hallmark of short-term psychiatric detention, because the drugs are not actually prescribed to patients but are used "for their calmative effect ... singularly, intermittently, or as needed to change patients' mood or behavior."[44] In raising the alarms about these off-label uses in the context of nursing homes, Associate Director Dr. David Graham of the FDA Office of Surveillance and Epidemiology warned that extensive off-label use of these powerful drugs for sedation purposes is significantly correlated with sharp rises in mortality rates.

The use of restraining sedatives gained notoriety in recent years after the death in 2019 of Elijah McClain, who was stopped by police and brutally restrained by paramedics before being injected with a lethal amount of ketamine.[45] While the paramedics who administered the dose ultimately were convicted of criminally negligent homicide, the case remains an outlier for finding liability against a nonpolice actor using chemical sedatives in a medical response capacity. And while that and other paramedic cases arise in the context of EMT emergency triage response, the reasoning used by courts in those cases to reject liability for acts of nonpolice brutality applies equally to hospital psychiatrists. Paramedics, in using chemical sedatives, are "not acting to enforce the law, deter, or incarcerate. . . . They [are] attempting to help [mentally ill patients], although they [may] badly botch the job. . . . A plaintiff's excessive force claim looks like a medical malpractice claim rather than a Fourth Amendment or Due Process violation."[46] Likewise, "using a therapeutic drug to sedate an arrestee [or mentally ill patient] to be taken safely at the [psychiatric] hospital" does not trigger Fourth Amendment scrutiny, because both the paramedic and the psychiatrist "intended to provide medical care" and did not intend to support a criminal investigation and arrest.[47]

THE NARROW MEANING OF *SEIZURE*

These experiences with brutal violence at the hands of medical and mental health personnel all involve physical force that unquestionably would be considered a "seizure" under the Fourth Amendment, if only the courts would extend the amendment's reach to these nonpolice actors. Labeling a violent action a "seizure" is critically important, because an unreasonable seizure "acts as the constitutional hook" for excessive force claims.[48] But unless the violent act in question constitutes a "seizure," the Fourth Amendment does not apply at all, and government actors—police and nonpolice alike—can behave as arbitrarily and violently as they want and not trigger scrutiny. Unfortunately, courts have narrowly defined the word *seizure* to almost entirely exclude an important and increasingly common alternate responder action: violent homeless encampment destructions and dispersals of the unhoused.

The classic Fourth Amendment seizure involves a traditional arrest, with police placing handcuffs on someone and taking her to the police station for booking. The Supreme Court has also held that circumstances short of an arrest can constitute a seizure "if, in view of all the circumstances surrounding the incident, a reasonable person would have believed he was not free to leave."[49] But the Court does not recognize a "seizure" when someone is free to *leave* an area but not free to *stay* in that area.

For example, an officer seeking to disperse a crowd of protesters often uses force to do so, but that officer's "intent often is not to make the protester succumb to the officer's grasp, but to disperse the crowd and make the protester go away."[50] This type of forceful, often brutal, restraint on liberty does not trigger the Fourth Amendment, because "a restraint on movement only constitutes a Fourth Amendment seizure if that restraint renders someone not 'free to leave' as opposed to being not 'free to stay.'"[51]

In *Dundon v. Kirchmeier*, the District of North Dakota dismissed excessive force claims against police brought by people protesting construction of the Dakota Access Pipeline through Indigenous lands.[52] One night while protesters slept, police used fire hoses, rubber bullets, concussion grenades, and bean bag projectiles to force protesters to leave, injuring two hundred people in the process. The court held that "the Fourth Amendment did not apply at all to any of the police conduct," because "police sought to disperse [the activists], not arrest them."[53] Likewise, in *Edrei v. New York*, a case involving the violent dispersal of demonstrators protesting the death of Eric Garner, the court declined to apply the Fourth Amendment to police use of long-range acoustic devices to force protesters to leave, finding that a "seizure" takes place only when police use "force to intentionally restrain a person and gain control of their movements."[54]

MASS DISPLACEMENT: HOMELESS ENCAMPMENTS

This reluctance to find a seizure "where suspects are free to leave but not free to go about their business" has important implications for alternate responders and the unhoused.[55] Cities increasingly rely on homeless outreach as alternatives to police to respond to protracted public health and safety issues. But in doing so, they rely on these outreach teams to forcibly disperse and relocate people sleeping outside unlawfully, either alone or in large encampments. Some cities have crafted "convoluted policies like a new camping ban in Portland, Oregon that prohibits homeless camping during the hours of 8am to 8pm" and have given outreach teams the right to forcibly move anyone violating this ban.[56]

Other cities, like San Diego, California—recently dubbed "the most expensive city in America" owing largely to its runaway real estate prices compared to modest median incomes[57]—have created "safe-sleeping sites" throughout the city, forcibly relocating the unhoused into these sites and breaking down unsanctioned encampments outside these sites.[58] While

San Diego police have assisted in these forced relocations and made at least one arrest, the bulk of the relocation effort has been carried out by nonpolice members of the city's HOT team.[59] HOT members enter large encampments unannounced, give residents notice that they are in violation of the city's new ordinance, break down any dwellings, and force residents to disperse, typically through a verbal show of authority (and if necessary, physical force) that traditionally would satisfy the "means intentionally applied" element for Fourth Amendment seizure purposes.[60]

But the intent of these HOT members using force to disperse the unhoused from encampments appears indistinguishable from that of police attempting to disperse protesters from a city street. In both cases, the government actor is trying to make people leave "rather than to detain and arrest them."[61] Given courts' reluctance to find a Fourth Amendment seizure in the protest policing context, it seems similarly unlikely that a court will find a seizure in the mass homeless displacement context. Thus, neither the forcible destruction of one's home nor the forcible movement of an individual's person—even, presumably, by brutal physical means— would give rise to a Fourth Amendment excessive force claim.

THE LIMITS OF DUE PROCESS CLAIMS

Much of the violent conduct discussed above that fell outside the Fourth Amendment's purview was also analyzed by courts under the Constitution's Fourteenth Amendment's Due Process Clause.[62] Even where government brutality does not constitute excessive force, the misconduct might still have violated a victim's constitutional due process rights.[63] It is reasonable to ask, then, why it matters so much whether physical brutality gets remedied under the Fourth Amendment when there exists another constitutional remedy. The answer lies in the nature of the Due Process Clause as a weak catch-all provision, a vague constitutional right of "last resort" that rarely provides victims of brutality with adequate relief.[64]

The Due Process Clause provides that no state shall "deprive any person of life, liberty, or property, without due process of law."[65] Among other things, this clause prohibits the government from depriving someone of their life, liberty, or property in a way that is so arbitrary and uncivilized that it "shocks the contemporary conscience."[66] Unlike the Fourth Amendment, this "shocks the conscience" test applies to all state actors and all state conduct, including government alternate responders. This test arose in large part as a right of last resort where a government agent engaged in egregious behavior but that behavior did not neatly fit into one of the more narrowly defined constitutional guarantees like the Fourth Amendment right to be free from unreasonable seizures.[67] Indeed, "The entire premise behind substantive due process requires that no other explicit constitutional protection exists."[68] Given courts' reluctance to apply the Fourth Amendment to claims of nonpolice brutality, what is left to fill in the gaps is the Due Process Clause's "shocks the conscience" test.

This test fails victims in three primary ways. First, the threshold for a violation of this test is much higher than the Fourth Amendment's unreasonable seizure and excessive force tests.[69] To truly "shock the conscience," a government actor's conduct must be "beyond the pale," and it must leave no doubt about the egregious wrongness of the action.[70] As the Fourth Circuit explained in Hodge v. Jones, the "residual protections of 'substantive due process' ... [require] allegations of 'state action so arbitrary and irrational, so unjustified by any circumstance of governmental interest, as to be literally incapable'" of explanation.[71] Thus, unlike the Fourth Amendment, where courts balance the governmental interest in using force against the important liberty interests of citizens, the due process "shocks the conscience" test requires a finding that no governmental interest did or could possibly exist.

Here again, police sexual misconduct cases provide a helpful, if discouraging, illustration. Despite the obvious lack of any legitimate government interest, police sexual assault cases turn on archaic notions of what kinds of sexual violence are truly "shocking." The analysis often depends on how and where the officer touched the victim, for how long, how many times, whether and to what extent brute physical force was used, whether and to what extent the victim physically resisted, and whether the encounter "sounds more like 'harassment' than an 'egregious assault.'"[72] The only unanimous agreement on this point is that forcible rape shocks the conscience.[73] All other types of sexual assault, including compelled nude photography, forcible oral sex, and other horrific behavior, only occasionally "shock the conscience" of judges and juries weighing the constitutional culpability of government predators.

This reality highlights a second way this test fails victims of government violence: it relies on the subjective beliefs of judges about what "shocks the conscience" rather than the objective "seizure" and "reasonable use of force" tests of the Fourth Amendment. In a judiciary "that lacks the diversity of the American people, a judge's conscience may not accurately represent the collective conscience of society."[74] Particularly on the federal bench, where unelected political appointees serve for life, the demographic makeup of the federal judiciary fails to mirror that of the general population.[75] An older, whiter, disproportionately male federal bench may not share the same values for what shocks the conscience as contemporary society.[76]

For example, in the Seventh Circuit Court of Appeals case *Alexander v. DeAngelo*, Judge Richard Posner (one of the most well-known and influential appellate judges of the last half century) considered whether an officer's sexual assault sufficiently shocked the conscience to amount to a due process violation.[77] The officers, under a false threat of imprisonment, forced the victim to perform oral sex as part of a prostitution sting.[78] Judge Posner, while ultimately agreeing with his colleagues that the officer's conduct "narrowly" violated the victim's due process rights, observed that it was a close case because "she may think oral sex no big deal (some young people nowadays do not consider it 'real' sex at all), . . . she did not express indignation," and the assault itself was no worse than "the usual risk of being beaten up . . . by a drug dealer."[79]

This case illustrates the third way due process inadequately protects victims of government brutality. Unlike the objective inquiry of the Fourth Amendment, courts assessing potential due process violations take into account the subjective motivations of government actors and may find no violation if otherwise shocking behavior was conducted for what the actor thought were legitimate motives.[80] In *Alexander*, the officers claimed that their sexual misconduct was part of the "act" of being undercover and trying to root out a dangerous prostitution ring.[81] While the argument ultimately failed, the fact that the officer's subjective motivations were relevant at all further highlights the weakness of this catch-all remedy.

PRIVATE ALTERNATE RESPONDERS, PUBLIC HARMS

The Fourth Amendment applies only to government actors or those functioning as government actors, what is often called "acting under color of state law." Many alternate responders are public employees who thus might be subject to the Fourth Amendment, including paramedics, public hospital doctors and psychiatrists, government social workers, publicly funded homeless outreach teams, and even independent agencies like CAHOOTS and STAR. But many health care providers, drug treatment providers, and violence interrupters work for privately owned and operated companies. Does the Fourth Amendment apply at all to them?

It depends on the function of the private alternate responder. The Supreme Court has explained that, where a private employee fills a "traditional public function" like firefighting, police activity, and prison services, that employee acts "under color of state law" and is subject to Fourth Amendment scrutiny.[82] Thus, a state prisoner can sue a private prison guard for deprivation of constitutional rights, because the private prison guard fills a traditional public function.[83] Private health care workers can also fill such a public function by contract, such as private doctors contracting to provide medical care to prisoners or psychiatrists providing state-mandated mental health services through a government-run and administered diversion program.[84]

At first blush, this public function test seems to help subject more alternate responder activity to Fourth Amendment scrutiny, but that likely is not the case. It is true that many alternate responders are being and will continue to be tasked with the traditional public function of public safety even if they remain private employees. But categorizing a private doctor or crisis worker as filling a public function and thus "acting under color of state law" only confirms that the Fourth Amendment *could* apply to their conduct, not that it will. Indeed, there is no question that police officers are public actors subject to the Fourth Amendment, and yet entire swaths of their public activity are deemed beyond the reach of the amendment, either because they cannot be characterized as a "search" or "seizure" or because the officers are engaged in noncriminal "community caretaking" activities. Likewise, whether the alternate responder is a private or public employee, their conduct is subject to Fourth Amendment scrutiny in only limited circumstances, given the Supreme Court's decision to narrowly limit its application outside its "primary purpose" of crime control.

In this sense, any analogy between private alternate responders and private prison guards tends to fall flat. Private prison guards replace public prison guards. They fill the exact same job with the exact same duties and responsibilities in the exact same role, just on private property. Alternate responders, by their very nature, do not replace police in the same way. They exist not to fill the same duties and responsibilities as traditional crime-fighting police but expressly as an *alternative* to those carceral criminal investigative motives. So while private alternate responders may fill a public function, it is not one that automatically subjects them to Fourth Amendment scrutiny.

However, finding that a private alternate responder was acting in a purely private instead of public capacity may actually benefit victims of violence seeking compensation for their injuries. Here private security guards provide a useful example. Stephen Brock was an off-duty deputy serving as a security guard for Big Time "Wings" Sports Grill in Chilton County, Alabama. When bar patron Carlos Ortega attempted to defuse a dispute between Deputy Brock and another patron, Brock choked Ortega, dragged him outside, and threw him out of the bar. Ortega sued for assault and battery and for violations of the Fourth Amendment. The court found that "the deputy's conduct in assaulting the patron and dragging him outside was consistent with that of a [private] security guard," thus making the Fourth Amendment inapplicable to this private conduct. But because the brutality was not committed by a "public" official, traditional government immunities shielding public employees from liability also did not apply. Thus, the court allowed Ortega's assault and battery claims to proceed against both Brock and Big Time Wings under a vicarious liability theory.[85] Had Brock been acting in a public law enforcement capacity, Alabama law likely would have shielded him from private tort liability and prevented vicarious liability against the bar. This example provides a limited context within which private state tort claims may offer greater relief for victims of nonpolice brutality, at least in those narrow circumstances where private alternate responders are acting in a purely private capacity.[86]

THE BENEFITS—AND LIMITS—OF STATE TORT LAWSUITS

Unlike unlawful searches yielding evidence used in a criminal prosecution, victims of government brutality typically are not concerned with trying to suppress evidence in a criminal trial. Instead, they seek compensation for their injuries, punishment for the bad actors, and potentially changes to government policy and practice. These victims normally do so by filing a lawsuit. As University of Virginia law professor and police reform expert Rachel Harmon has explained, these lawsuits "permit a remedy for kinds of Fourth Amendment violations the exclusionary rule does not address, such as constitutionally excessive force—which produces no evidence—and Fourth Amendment violations against those who are never charged with a crime."[87]

Throughout this chapter, we have focused almost exclusively on whether a victim of nonpolice violence can successfully bring such a lawsuit with a constitutional claim under either the Fourth or Fourteenth Amendment. But why are these claims so important? After all, can't a victim of violence sue for assault, battery, false imprisonment, and intentional infliction of emotional distress? These private state law tort claims offer the chance at monetary compensation, and they avoid the tricky questions about whether and to what extent certain constitutional provisions apply against certain government officials.

Indeed, this is true. All of the plaintiffs in all of the cases discussed in this chapter brought private tort claims against their abusers in addition to constitutional claims. For example, the plaintiff in *Montanez* who was raped by a police officer who responded to her 911 call filed claims for assault, battery, and intentional infliction of emotional distress in addition to her Fourth and Fourteenth Amendment claims. And it was these private tort claims that ultimately survived the government's attempts to dismiss the case until the parties settled for half a million dollars on the eve of trial.

But something else the plaintiff received at the end of the case illustrates one reason why constitutional tort claims are so important: her attorneys' fees. Unlike private tort litigation, constitutional claims filed under the federal civil rights law known unofficially as "Section 1983" allow the prevailing party in a litigation to recoup her attorneys' fees.[88]

Because the plaintiff in *Montanez* succeeded in maintaining her Fourteenth Amendment due process claim (though not her Fourth Amendment claim), the court awarded her attorneys' fees under this civil rights law. And while most civil rights plaintiffs do not actually pay hourly attorneys' fees out of pocket during the litigation, quality attorneys are attracted to and incentivized to take civil rights cases in no small part because of the promise of payment if they prevail. Virtually no private tort claims have a similar fee-shifting scheme, at least for the types of torts relevant to police and nonpolice brutality. As a result, if private tort plaintiffs recover anything at all, they must pay their attorneys a hefty percentage—as much as 45 percent—of the monetary recovery at the end of the lawsuit.

But money is not the only reason why constitutional litigation is so important. These cases also provide important vehicles to demand institutional change through injunctive relief (and wider media coverage) that often is not available in private lawsuits.[89] Many of the broader policy changes forced upon police departments in recent years, including changes to use-of-force policies, the use of body-worn cameras, elimination of racial profiling practices, and an end to dragnet surveillance of neighborhoods, happened as a result of so-called structural reform litigation.[90] And while "private suits for equitable relief have not played nearly as substantial a role in reforming police departments' civil rights practices as they have played in changing other public enterprises," there is hope that such structural reform lawsuits could change unlawful practices for alternate responders—if those practices were considered Fourth Amendment violations. Courts have shown greater willingness to allow plaintiffs to sue for broader equitable changes to government policies and practices when those policies and practices target innocent or common conduct or target distinct subpopulations of which the plaintiff is a part.[91] Perfect examples include HOT teams destroying unhoused person's property and mental health responders restraining and chemically sedating involuntarily committed patients. Both practices target innocent conduct of a distinct subpopulation.

Of course, private tort lawsuits can drive institutional change, albeit indirectly. When local government agencies have to pay millions of dollars in damages or settlements arising from private tort lawsuits, their insurers take notice. In 2017, St. Ann, Missouri, patrol officers pursued a driver with expired tags during rush-hour traffic at speeds exceeding ninety miles per hour for more than ten miles until the driver of the fleeing vehicle slammed into a green Toyota Camry and permanently disabled the driver of the Camry. When confronted about his officers' conduct and the resulting lawsuit that had been filed, St. Ann police chief Aaron Jimenez repeated his department's decades-old motto: "St. Ann will chase you until the wheels fall off."[92] A year and a half later, Jimenez had changed his tune, banning high-speed pursuits for traffic infractions and minor crimes. The change? A threat by the St. Louis Area Insurance Trust risk pool to cancel its liability coverage for the department without major changes to its use of chase policies. With lawsuit payouts of $12 million to the estate of Breonna Taylor and $27 million to the estate of George Floyd, other departments—and insurance companies—are taking notice.[93] But while these positive changes often result from private tort lawsuits, the victim-plaintiffs bringing those suits have to rely on the actions of these third-party insurers, who may seek different structural changes from those desired by the victim if they step in at all.

There are two reasons, however, that private tort lawsuits may provide more effective remedies than constitutional litigation, both involving legal hurdles to relief: qualified immunity and vicarious liability. Qualified immunity shields government officials from lawsuit for official actions unless those actions violate "clearly established" rights. The "qualified" nature of this immunity has metastasized into a near-absolute immunity in police brutality cases. As has been well documented for decades, even if a court finds that an act of police violence constitutes excessive force, that officer almost invariably remains shielded from liability on qualified-immunity grounds.[94] A growing chorus of scholars and activists have highlighted the Court's embarrassing and unjustified expansion of qualified immunity to protect police officers from liability at all costs.[95]

Limited case law suggests that nonpolice alternate responders may not enjoy the same kind of blanket immunity police have come to expect when facing challenges to their violent acts.[96] Many qualified-immunity cases involving nonpolice violence turn on the threshold question discussed throughout this chapter of whether such government actors can ever "seize" someone within the meaning of the Fourth Amendment.[97] If the law is not clearly established on that point, then courts grant qualified immunity.[98] However, many courts that have applied the amendment to nonpolice brutality claims have subsequently denied qualified immunity, in part because it is easier to "clearly establish" that paramedics and social workers should not hog-tie, beat up, or chemically sedate to death their patients than it is to "clearly establish" that police shouldn't use similar force when arresting a suspect. Moreover, as with private prison guards who act under color of state law but are not entitled to qualified immunity, private alternate responders filling traditional public functions also cannot shield themselves from liability through qualified immunity—if, that is, their conduct falls under the Fourth Amendment's reach. That more nonpolice brutality civil rights cases may survive qualified immunity when the Fourth Amendment applies to such cases further confirms the importance of understanding the contours of the amendment's applicability.

This legal hurdle of federal qualified immunity often applies to state tort claims, but not always. In some states, a Fourth Amendment excessive force claim may fail on federal qualified-immunity grounds, but a state claim for battery based on the same facts likely might survive. For example, the Alabama legislature has "granted statutory immunity from state tort liability to municipal police officers for 'conduct in performance of any discretionary function within the line and scope of his or her law enforcement duties,'"[99] thus preventing battery and other tort claims against police and other government officials. In contrast, California and Michigan deny immunity from tort liability for police officers who use excessive force, and likely would deny immunity to nonpolice actors who similarly face suit for assault and battery.

The second possible benefit of private tort lawsuits is that, unlike with federal civil rights claims filed under Section 1983, government employers can be held vicariously liable for the unlawful actions of their employees. For federal civil rights claims challenging unconstitutional conduct, a plaintiff can successfully sue a department, city, or county for an individual actor's misconduct only if she can show that the misconduct was directly attributable to an agency policy.[100] As a result, proving municipal liability is "not only difficult, but requires extensive, expensive discovery."[101]

Table 1   Relief for victims of nonpolice brutality and misconduct

	4th Amendment	14th Amendment (Due Process Clause)	State Tort Law
Applies To . . .	Unreasonable searches and seizures	Deprivations of life, liberty, and property without due process	Varies. Relevant torts address physical harm or privacy invasions (assault, battery, false imprisonment, trespass)
Applies Against . . .	Government actors conducting administrative or investigative activity	Government actors	All persons
Standard	Objective reasonableness	Arbitrary and capricious; shocks the conscience	Varies, but generally involves a level of intent by defendant
Burden of Proof	Preponderance	Preponderance	Preponderance
Remedies	Exclusion of evidence Monetary damages Injunctive relief (government reform)	Monetary damages Injunctive relief (government reform)	Monetary damages Injunctive relief (stay-away orders and other individual restraints)

In contrast, municipal governments can be broadly held vicariously liable for the private tortious conduct of their officers, police and nonpolice alike. While such liability is impossible in states that provide governmental immunity from suit to their officials and municipalities, many states across the country provide no such blanket immunity.[102]

In short, there exists a complicated, sometimes overlapping web of possible relief for victims of nonpolice brutality and other nonpolice misconduct from the Fourth Amendment, Fourteenth Amendment, and state tort law. None of these avenues provide perfect protection, but all of them may become relevant to a particular litigant in a particular circumstance, as illustrated in table 1.

WHERE DO WE GO FROM HERE?

Despite the very real risks of unchecked physical violence described in this chapter, some sense of perspective is appropriate as we summarize the hopes and perils of our new public safety. Alternate responders represent a positive, sensible solution to public life far too reliant on violent police responses to health and noncriminal safety concerns. And their presence reduces rates of violence, including lethal violence, when compared with police. That alone stands as cause for celebration.

But alternate responders also exist within a soft policing structure built on confinement, containment, control, and violence of a different sort. Though that violence is justified by real or imagined compassionate, medical, nonpunitive motives, far too often the results are the same as hard policing's: destruction of property, invasions of bodily autonomy, injury, illness, and sometimes death. That these violent acts fall largely outside the Constitution's purview reflects a legal loophole at risk of exploitation as our new public safety expands in size and scope. Thus, we must remain clear eyed about these dangers as we articulate the internal rules, external regulations, and legal statutes that will govern these expanded alternate response agencies. It is to that task we now turn.

5 A Safer Public Safety

The movement toward public safety specialization provides significant hope and promise for a society too wedded to the idea of police as all-purpose responders. Not only does nonpolice specialization more effectively triage the specific immediate issues of those in need, but it allows police to focus more energy on their primary area of violent criminal investigative expertise. It also helps remove many of the harms inflicted by a violent and aggressive police force appearing where force and criminal sanction have no natural place.

Of course, alternate responders themselves pose health and safety risks to the communities they serve. This book highlights two in particular. First, many of the structures of nonpolice response rely too frequently on nonconsensual liberty deprivations, physical violence, and coercion in ways that closely mirror traditional policing. Involuntary psychiatric holds, homeless encampment sweeps, and social worker fraud investigation home visits utilize aggressive soft policing powers focused more on control and containment than help and healing. Second, the laws protecting us from these overzealous soft policing practices are weak and ineffective compared to laws protecting us from law enforcement, if such laws apply at all.

This chapter offers a range of proposals to address both of these issues with the aim of making the new public safety safer for those who interact with and rely on it. These proposals take the form of affirmative regulation, either internal regulation of alternate responder agencies or state and local legislation restricting the powers of these responders. Some features are common to all types of alternate responders: limits on search and seizure powers, strict limits on the ability to use force or coerce any actions or statements, communication firewalls between alternate responders and police, and prohibitions on the use in criminal trials of evidence gathered by alternate responders. These features can help close the legal loopholes left by courts declining to extend the protections of the Fourth Amendment to nonpolice entities. Other proposals are tailored to specific agencies and are aimed more at reducing the harmful soft policing effects of existing noncriminal public safety structures.

Given the relative newness of complete independent alternate response agencies, there exist few comprehensive models for regulations granting or limiting powers to alternate responders. But where they do exist, these proposals highlight what works, what does not, and what should be revisited by government agencies finding a balance between public safety and individual liberties.

MEDICAL PERSONNEL

University of Utah law professor Teneille Brown recently posted a draft of an important law review article entitled "When Doctors Become Cops."[1] It begins by perfectly encapsulating the risks of nonpolice medical professionals untethered from the Fourth Amendment and unregulated in the field of criminal enforcement:

> The lines between law enforcement and health care are blurring. Police increasingly lean on doctors to provide them with genetic samples, prescription histories, and toxicology results that they could not obtain on their own. This often occurs without a warrant or the patient's consent. At the same time, legislatures are using physicians as regulatory levers to police pregnant and transgender bodies. And due to chronic underfunding of social services, many Americans now receive pseudo-mental health treatment

through the courts rather than clinics. Together, these things paint a sinister picture of law enforcement being thrust into medicine in ways that are deeply troubling and vastly under-explored.[2]

Other than police, EMTs and emergency room doctors are the most common first responders to a whole range of emergencies implicating criminal activity, from drug overdoses to gunshot wounds. But when doctors are expected or required to cooperate with law enforcement, it diminishes public safety in important ways. It diverts doctors' and EMTs' attention from their primary objective of treating a patient in need. It breaks trust between those patients and their doctors so that patients will withhold potentially incriminating information that is vital to treatment, such as the type or quantity of an ingested drug. And it pushes sick and injured people away from seeking medical assistance at all. Even though federal law prohibits doctors from disclosing a patient's drug use to police, the medical profession's otherwise close collaborative relationship with police creates a chilling effect on what should be an open and trusting relationship.

Thus, medical professionals should have the ability—the obligation—to create a clear firewall between them and police "that allows medical providers to focus on serving patients while maintaining independence from police."[3] State and local laws "should establish the autonomy of healthcare providers and healthcare institutions."[4] This firewall protects the relationship between providers and patients and recognizes the different goals of police and medical professionals. Although EMTs and police may work together in responding to emergencies, "the police are oriented to public criminal justice goals while medical professionals are oriented to individual patients' well-being."[5] To respect each responder's independent objectives, "medical providers on the scene with police should not be treated as an arm of law enforcement. The relationship must be carefully managed to maintain medical providers' independence."[6] Any trust in medical providers depends on "sovereignty and ability to exercise independent judgment within their respective spheres of expertise."[7]

Relatedly, medical professionals should be prohibited from voluntarily sharing any information with police, not just drug use history. As we saw in chapter 3, police routinely put pressure on doctors to invasively search for and provide physical and testimonial evidence to support an arrest. Doctors routinely provide it. And patients, recognizing this risk, avoid doctors as a result. Breaking this system of evidence sharing between police bound by the Fourth Amendment and doctors largely not so bound plugs one of the major legal loopholes present in alternate response public safety. And rather than frustrate police investigations, it simply prevents police from exploiting this loophole by requiring them to develop probable cause for whatever evidence they seek from the doctor, to secure a warrant, and then to execute it.

These firewall regulations should go beyond simply preventing medical professionals from sharing information with police. State and local laws "should affirm that police may not directly or indirectly pressure medical providers to take any actions during emergency encounters," and police "should not participate in healthcare providers' discussion of a person's condition or possible treatments."[8] And police should have no say in a medical provider's decision whether or not to use restraints to provide care, including the use of chemical restraints. Not only should officers resist the impulse to enlist medical providers to provide assistance seizing patient-suspects for criminal investigative purposes, but it should be illegal for them to act on that impulse.

Finally, medical professionals should receive "training on how to respond if a police officer inserts themselves into the medical decision-making process." Giving medical providers clear language to use in response to improper requests "would empower them to respond appropriately. This training could reduce the chances that medical professionals misuse or weaponize chemical restraints in pursuit of the interests of the criminal justice system."[9] Allowing medical professionals to respond independently of police, including providing legal protections from forced disclosure or assistance, and training them to resist any such entreaties, gives agency to these alternate responders and promotes delivering potentially life-saving treatment. A true commitment to public safety and health as an alternative to punitive impulses, arrests, and convictions must be premised on the legal and practical ability of nonpolice medical professionals to pursue health and safety objectives free from police and carceral influences.

MENTAL HEALTH RESPONDERS

Mental health first responders play an increasingly important role in non-criminal public safety. Unresolved mental health issues often are the root cause of many public safety disturbances for which police used to be the only option, including houselessness, addiction, and petty criminal activity. But they also stand as the gatekeepers of an invasive and often destructive involuntary civil commitment system that puts vulnerable people "somewhere else" without actually treating them or improving public health and safety outcomes.

There are those, including abolitionists and the United Nations Office of Human Rights, that want to see forced psychiatry in all its forms completely abolished. I disagree. There are limited circumstances where one's severe mental illness exhibits itself in volatile, dangerous ways that create imminent risks for that person and those around them. There also exist limited situations where a mental illness has become so significant that a person has lost all ability to care for herself. In these very narrow situations, involuntary psychiatric holds are the best, and often the only, option.

But significant change is needed to the current system. The movement toward expanding the scope of involuntary holds to include not just imminent risk of harm but foreseeable risk of some future harm invests too much discretion in police and alternate responders who might feel compelled to "clean up the streets" by placing someone experiencing crisis "somewhere else." And it ensnares too many people into a system authorizing significant restrictions on freedom without a clear need to do so. Involuntary holds should be justified in only one very narrow situation: *where there is an imminent risk of serious bodily harm to oneself or others*. This standard also allows for commitment where one's inability to care for oneself gives rise to an imminent risk of serious bodily harm.

There are important reasons for limiting involuntary psychiatric holds. First, while there certainly are more situations beyond imminent risk of harm where mental health treatment would be beneficial, there remains the ability to provide onsite mental health treatment and to offer voluntary inpatient and outpatient resources. No one is denied the ability to voluntarily access potentially helpful resources. Second, forcing someone into treatment in a psychiatric ward entails a dramatic "quasi-criminal" restriction on liberty akin to an arrest, and that power ought to be reserved for the most emergent and necessary situations. Third, psychiatric hospitals far too often fail to meaningfully improve outcomes for the mentally ill and may even exacerbate illness by further traumatizing patients.

In this respect, involuntary commitment practices require significant overhaul. It is beyond the scope and expertise of this book to discuss the intricacies of mental health treatment. But from a rights perspective, three changes are warranted. All forced medication practices should end. Forced chemical sedation intrudes upon the most basic concepts of bodily integrity and autonomy, and this type of "biological rape" shares many hallmarks of traditional torture. Moreover, Orwellian surveillance systems, with cameras in every patient room, should be dismantled to respect patient privacy as much as possible, and patients should be given the dignity to dress, undress, and use bathrooms without being monitored. And, physical restraints ought to be used as a last resort in case-specific situations instead of automatically as a matter of "safety" practices.

Finally, given the significant arrest-like liberty restrictions of involuntary holds and the prison-like liberty restrictions of psychiatric hospital treatment, mental health holds should be subject to traditional Fourth Amendment scrutiny, not a "special needs" analysis. Decisions to involuntarily commit someone for treatment should be based on probable cause and supported by the grant of a warrant from a neutral and detached magistrate, unless exigent circumstances require immediate action prior to the issuance of a warrant. And any commitment decision made without a warrant should be reviewed by a judge as soon as possible, no later than forty-eight hours after the commitment order has been issued. These are the basic probable-cause and warrant requirements for traditional law enforcement searches, seizures, and arrests, and they should govern psychiatric holds as well.[10]

Similarly, traditional safeguards should apply to the psychiatric hospital setting itself and should protect patients from unwarranted privacy intrusions and excessive force. While Fourth Amendment privacy rights from suspicionless searches do not apply to prisoners, they should attach to psychiatric patients who, despite current hospital practices, are not prisoners and have done nothing wrong.[11] And patients should have the ability to challenge excessive force used against them by hospital staff under traditional Fourth Amendment seizure standards, whether that force comes in the form of a tie-down restraint, forced sedation, or sexual assault.

Finally, as with medical professionals, a clear firewall of information must be erected between police and mental health personnel. Patients cannot be expected to freely and openly discuss their mental health and medical histories with psychologists and psychiatrists if there remains a risk that such information could be provided to police for prosecution. In the field, mental health experts should take all steps necessary to shield divulged information from police when triaging a noncriminal mental health emergency. In the clinical setting, mental health experts must remain in compliance with doctor-patient confidentiality and refuse to disclose any information to police outside limited mandated reporting requirements involving imminent risk of harm to others.

HOMELESS OUTREACH TEAMS

Homeless outreach teams represent a tremendous opportunity to rethink our collective relationship to and responsibility for public safety. Being without shelter is one of the most vulnerable positions in which any of us could find ourselves. And while mental illness and addiction do play a significant role in the unhoused population, the country's spiraling affordable housing crisis threatens a much larger and diverse percentage of the population with housing insecurity than at previous times in our history. Large homeless encampments also pose health and safety risks for their residents and for those living and working nearby. And the traditional law enforcement response of arrest, citation, seizure of property, and demands to "move it along" has utterly failed to reduce homelessness. If anything, the collateral financial and reputational consequences of homelessness-related convictions only further entrench these marginalized community members on the margins of the community.

Unfortunately, most HOT teams currently mirror these same failed policies, only without a badge and a gun. Most major-city HOT teams expressly state that their goals include giving citations for illegal camping and destroying permanent encampments, even though they know that the unhoused cannot pay the citations and that the cities for which they work lack adequate available shelter to keep the unhoused off the streets. No amount of shuffling unhoused populations from one part of town to another actually reduces the homeless population.

Thus, two major changes are needed. First, homeless outreach alternate responders must cease issuing "quality of life" citations to unhoused persons who are simply doing the basic things necessary for life that the rest of us can do in the privacy of our homes—sleeping, sitting, eating, drinking, pissing, shitting. Despite the Supreme Court's holding to the contrary, criminalizing these "acts of homelessness" is equivalent to criminalizing the status of homelessness, something that is both unconstitutional and immoral.

Second, encampment "sweeps," in which shelter tents and personal property are destroyed and unhoused persons are forced to relocate, must end. Not only are sweeps dehumanizing and cruel exercises of government authority to reduce someone's entire life belongings to rubble, but they increase insecurity for people whose only collective community ties exist within the encampments without providing alternatives to setting up a new encampment. Instead, cities would be well served to follow the lead of grassroots coalitions like San Francisco's "Solutions Not Sweeps" and Los Angeles's "Services Not Sweeps."[12] While a permanent solution to the nation's homelessness crisis involves the creation of millions more shelter beds and millions more affordable housing units, these organizations focus on practical, immediate solutions to the public health and safety issues presented by encampments. Instead of "sweeping" encampments, HOT teams can assist with "cleaning" them by providing a combination of standard trash pickup, litter removal, and assistance with "helping encampment residents trim their collections."[13] These teams can also provide and maintain portable toilets or other bathroom solutions to reduce health hazards present in camps, while also providing cleaning, hygiene, and sanitary supplies to residents.

Some cities have pushed back on these commonsense ideas, claiming that "if a city provides services, they are recognizing that people are staying there."[14] As one homeless advocate explained, "We get accused that we're just enabling people to be on the street, that we're fighting for people to sleep outside. We all say we know that housing is the solution, but that's going to take so long, we need to start treating people with dignity and respect now."[15] Indeed, to the extent that one wants to view trash pickup and Porta Potties as a dangerous acknowledgment of the existence of homeless populations, one should place the blame for this "danger" not with those forced to live on the streets but with city, state, and federal leaders unable and unwilling to provide real housing solutions. In the wealthiest nation in human history, homelessness is not an individual failure but a societal one. Pretending the issue does not exist by denying basic human dignity to those most affected by it ignores reality and decreases health and safety for all of us.

But providing basic municipal services like trash and sanitation to encampments also presents an opportunity for HOT workers and other alternate responders. So much of this book has examined how alternate responder effectiveness correlates significantly with the ability to create trusting relationships with the people these responders serve. An easy and lasting way to build that trust between HOT personnel and the unhoused community is to show up consistently in these communities, be present with basic support services like cleaning supplies, and use that engagement as an opening to discuss possible longer-term solutions like outpatient mental health treatment, drug treatment centers, or temporary shelter housing. This kind of voluntary engagement—*without the presence of police*—is far more likely to promote the ultimate goal of unhoused persons finding for themselves solutions to reintegrate fully with society.

SOCIAL WORKERS

Truly independent social work response is perhaps the most difficult objective to achieve among alternate responders. Social workers have a varied caseload with public safety concerns ranging from the wholly non-criminal to the violently criminal. Government social workers address impoverishment, homelessness, substance abuse, child neglect and abuse, and domestic and sexual violence.

This reality creates a "dilemma" for social workers: "If they continue collaborating with police, how do they prevent the well-documented harms of policing? If they reject collaboration with police, how do they meet procedural standards for the many social work activities that rely on law enforcement?"[16] More than fifty thousand social work students graduate annually in the United States, yet few legal and ethical guidelines exist to help social workers individually or collectively navigate this dilemma.[17] Debates between the National Association of Social Workers and thousands of social workers over the proper role of social work-police collaboration have spilled into the open, with charges of white supremacy leveled at both the institution of police and the institution of social work.[18] And few social workers are trained in the legal nuances of constitutional applicability to their work, much less the impact police presence may have on that applicability.

Existing police-social worker collaborations suffer from institutional mistrust stemming from different goals and perspectives on public safety. In one study involving the response to domestic violence, social workers were motivated by a culture of "advocacy, social justice values, and cooperation, with human well-being as the primary goal."[19] Police, in contrast, were influenced by a "culture characterized as having a hierarchical, patriarchal structure, with the ultimate goal of maintaining community order and safety by way of coercion and force."[20] These contrasting priorities made true collaboration difficult.

But the single largest impediment to social workers promoting public safety without police is the mandated reporting requirement under which social workers operate in every state in the country. Current statutory guidelines require social workers to report all sorts of information to law enforcement and immigration officials, including personal health information, drug use records, child welfare records, and other sensitive private information that may result in criminal prosecution or immigrant deportation.[21] In fact, a growing chorus of so-called radical social workers reject replacing police, not because they want to continue collaborating with police, but because they believe social work itself should be dismantled in its current form. The reason: requirements "by law to collect and report clients' personal health information, which, in some cases, winds up harming their clients."[22] These social workers "believe working in these settings and under these constraints contradicts their code of ethics mandate to respect clients' rights to self-determination" and obligations not to actively harm clients.[23]

These social workers have a point. Any commitment to transforming public safety with greater commitments to health and well-being and fewer punitive responses must begin by allowing those frontline workers capable of addressing health and well-being to do so without assisting the carceral state. Social workers regularly treat clients already ensnared in the criminal legal system, including those "held in prisons and jails, at inpatient psychiatric facilities, and in detention centers."[24] They also treat vulnerable clients at risk of criminal consequences, including the drug addicted, sex workers, and the homeless. If we actually believe social workers have the ability to improve the health, safety, and well-being of their clients—and perhaps more importantly, if we as a society care about the well-being of these people—we must relieve social workers of their mandated reporting requirements and consider the social worker-client relationship to be as sacrosanct as the doctor-patient or attorney-client relationship.

This firewall reform is urgently needed for two reasons. First, social workers regularly report problems developing the trust necessary to have open communication with clients to address issues, because clients fear having their personal information and behaviors passed on to police.[25] The risk of arrest and incarceration alone stunts the process before it can truly begin. Imagine if attorneys were required to report any illegal client behavior to police, or if doctors had the same obligation to report any illegal patient behavior. Those relationships would be infected with distrust and they would fail. That is what current mandated reporting laws do to the social worker-client relationship.

Second, even if social workers can develop a trusting relationship with clients, mandated reporting obligations threaten to prematurely end those relationships or frustrate the goals of the relationship. If a social worker attempting to repair a domestic relationship or put a drug addict on the path to recovery has to report criminal activity to police, the risk always exists that the client or someone close to them will be arrested and prosecuted prior to reconciliation or sobriety. The punitive impulse of police threatens to short-circuit more holistic reforms. For example, migrant children in social services settings are encouraged to open up to doctors and social workers, in part so social workers can help reunify and stabilize families. But mandated reporting requirements often result in children's medical and psychological records being used as evidence in immigration removal proceedings, destroying any hope for reunification or stabilization.[26]

In a study about "the urgency of firewalls" between social workers and immigration authorities, researchers noted the unsustainable "balancing acts that many social workers face" in delivering services:

> Social workers first have to balance their duty to obey the law versus their duty to adhere to professional values. Second, confidentiality is one of the core values of the social work profession and hence needs to be upheld. If confidentiality is undermined, clients will not engage with social work services and treatment. Providing information to comply with immigration laws may then actually lead social workers to undermine the value of confidentiality. Third, . . . social workers may be forced to decide between the welfare of one client versus the well-being of the whole institution.[27]

These "balancing acts" all exist for one reason: mandated reporting requirements. If social workers were not bound to "obey [reporting] law," they would not have to balance that against professional values. If they had no duty to report, confidentiality would not be threatened. And if social workers were not forced to participate in the evidence-gathering process for the immigration or criminal legal systems, they could focus on what should be the first priority, the individual client, rather than the integrity of entire systems. If we truly care about public health and safety beyond criminal enforcement, and not simply making officers' criminal evidence-gathering responsibilities easier, we must radically rethink social worker mandated reporting requirements.

Finally, if we value the nature of social work as centered on holistic healing of clients instead of bureaucratic soft policing, we must dismantle suspicionless snooping programs like Project 100% and stop utilizing social workers as fraud investigators. Clients who know that their social workers can arrive unannounced and search the most intimate details of their lives looking for evidence of "gaming the system" naturally will remain distrustful of and antagonistic to these workers. Social workers who are required to serve these dual functions—healer and investigator— will carry that distraction and conflict of interest with them into case settings, disrupting the healing process. While governments may have a legitimate interest in ensuring that taxpayer-funded services are not funneled to people committing fraud, tightly regulated independent investigators ought to carry out that function, not the people directly providing those services.

Of course, governments would do well to recognize the inefficiency of these sweeping fraud investigation programs. Historically, the cost of the investigations far exceeds the money recovered, or even alleged to have been lost, from fraudulent activity. These broad investigative programs have most succeeded in traumatizing and demonizing poor, often minority, members of our community struggling to survive on the financial margins while feeding tropes about "welfare queens." In contrast, the nation's largest-ever welfare fraud scandal was perpetrated by government actors against the poor and needy. In Mississippi, the nation's poorest state, where more than 90 percent of welfare applications are denied, journalist Anna Wolfe exposed how $77 million in federal welfare funds were redirected by white state officials away from qualified Black women and children to professional athletes, pet projects, and government associates. Among the recipients were Hall of Fame quarterback Brett Favre, who received $1.1 million for "promotional activities," and his alma mater, the University of Southern Mississippi, which received $5 million to build a volleyball facility for a team that included Favre's daughter.[28] For her reporting, which ultimately implicated Governor Phil Bryant, Anna Wolfe received a Pulitzer Prize, a defamation lawsuit from Bryant, and a threat of jail time if she does not reveal her confidential sources.[29] When we begin to acknowledge that the fraud and wasteful spending threats come not from the marginalized but from the powerful, perhaps true transformation can begin.

VIOLENCE INTERRUPTERS

The existence of violence interrupters, more than perhaps any other alternate responder, rests on an acknowledgment that some police presence is necessary to prevent and respond to violent crime, particularly gun crime. This nation is awash in firearms. At the end of 2022, American civilians owned approximately 393 million firearms.[30] That is 46 percent of the total worldwide civilian firearm total and amounts to 1.2 guns for every man, woman, and child in the country.[31] The year 2023 was on track to become a "record book year" for firearms purchases in the United States, "with 2024 looming large too."[32] And with relaxed purchase, carry, and use regulations taking effect in statehouses across the country, buttressed by recent Supreme Court rulings expanding constitutional protections for who can carry what type of firearm where and when, there is no end in sight to America's addiction to guns and gun violence.[33]

Eliminating police will eliminate neither violent crime nor the guns at the heart of this crime. But violence interruption as an alternative approach to traditional policing may help, especially when one considers the primary sources of gun violence. Outside of domestic violence, one of the greatest violent threats to public safety as measured by violent crime rates comes from organized and quasi-organized criminal enterprises. Most such criminals are not part of highly organized mafia-style crime families or entrenched hierarchical gangs like MS-13, but instead loosely knit groups of young men involved in black market commerce for guns and drugs while engaging in deadly skirmishes with rival groups. The statistical surge in gun violence in this country is not driven by highly publicized mass shootings but by individual killings carried out by domestic partners and members of these loosely organized gangs.[34]

Violence interrupters can play an important role in disrupting the cycle of violence for this second group. Most interrupters are former gang members or violent criminals themselves, and they can use that experience to both better understand the driving forces behind organized street crime and build the trust necessary to reach its perpetrators.[35] As with other alternate responders, however, the potential for ineffectiveness and rights abuse exists without carefully crafted programmatic regulations. One of the only reasons violence interrupters have trust and legitimacy with gang members, many of whom are actively involved in criminal activity, is that they can play a role as a trusted confidant and provide alternatives to arrest and imprisonment. That trust cannot be maintained if violence interrupters merely act as conduits for police investigation and arrest. Herein lies one of the trickiest aspects of violence interruption. The "clients" interrupters serve are themselves potential or actual violent criminals, many of whom create the types of public safety risks that even police reformers admit may require police intervention. But violence interrupters can only truly work as an alternative to police approaches that have largely failed to reduce organized crime violence if they can work independently of police and promise some protection from arrest if gang members work with them to break the cycle of violence.

Whether violence interrupters can persuade would-be criminals depends in part on the extent to which they can provide the carrots of supportive social services to aid with the transition away from crime and the sticks of criminal consequences for failure to heed the advice. This in turn depends at least partly on cooperation with police, which threatens the whole process. A good example of this conundrum comes from Columbus, Ohio, where in 2021 the Columbus Violence Prevention Office met with seventeen at-risk youth who were involved in street crime ranging from small-scale property theft and drug use to major drug distribution and aggravated assault.[36] Violence prevention officers met with them privately, but they were joined by federal law enforcement officials who were able to gather identifying information and evidence about the individuals.[37] During the session, each of the seventeen individuals was asked to pledge to sign an agreement to step away from their criminal enterprises and take advantage of "resources to aid them stay out of trouble, including help with job placement and financial assistance," with the goal of helping them stay "safe, alive, and out of prison."[38]

Of the seventeen men present, sixteen signed on. The one "who didn't is now facing prison time."[39] According to Columbus police Sgt. Shawn Gruber, who leads the division's gang unit, "The second he walked out of these doors, we found out he jumped right back into the game. . . . One-week investigation . . . We got all his guns, all his money, all his dope."[40] Based on the "success" of the first program, the Columbus violence prevention office held a second session with nine more at-risk youth, joined this time by the Columbus Division of Police, Columbus mayor Andrew Ginther, the U.S. Attorney's Office for the Southern District of Ohio, the Franklin County Prosecutor's Office, Mothers of Murdered Columbus Children, and the Franklin County Coroner's Office.[41]

There are two ways to view this approach. One could call the sessions a success, based on the fact that sixteen of seventeen alleged gang members pledged to take a different path, thus improving public safety for all involved. Nine more men chose to attend a second session. And the one gang member who refused help is now behind bars, thus protecting citizens who could have been harmed by his actions.

But why were these sessions so small? Present during these sessions were police officers and state and federal prosecutors, all of whom gathered valuable evidence that could be used in a future prosecution just by virtue of these men showing up. Their presence calls into question whether enough of the target audience—organized gang members—feel that it is worth the risk of incarceration to openly admit to criminal activity by attending these sessions. Perhaps far more individuals would have attended and taken advantage of the programs had police and prosecutors not been present.

This example illustrates the need for a firewall between violence interrupters and police. Unlike any other alternate responders, violence interrupters specifically work for and with people actively engaged in criminal activity, often violent criminal activity. If the threat of arrest *increases* for these individuals when working with violence interrupters, one cannot expect these programs to have anything other than a minimal impact.

CIVILIAN TRAFFIC ENFORCEMENT

By far the most radically transformative change to policing, in terms of both size and contact with the public, would be the removal of police from traffic enforcement. For most of us, our primary (if not only) contact with police takes place in the context of driving or riding in an automobile. This status quo of police enforcing traffic laws may seem impossible to change if for no other reason than it is all we are used to. Given the ubiquity and routine nature of police pulling over motorists, its presence in our collective consciousness, many of our personal experiences with it, and the lack of any existing alternative approach, it almost seems that police enforcement of traffic laws is the only possible approach.

But we know this is not the case. Other countries, including the United Kingdom and New Zealand, enforced traffic laws for decades without police involvement. And while these much smaller countries cannot provide a perfect template for the United States because they do not have many of the challenges making roadway safety in America so difficult— particularly with respect to the prevalence of guns in this country—useful lessons can be gleaned from their experiences. Indeed, the fact that the United States is awash in guns animates a seemingly counterintuitive proposal for civilian traffic enforcers: they should be unarmed.

A primary reason to remove police from traffic enforcement involves the unnecessary violence an armed and jaundiced officer primed to fight violent crime injects into routine traffic stops. To address this issue, traffic monitors must remain unarmed during the course of their on-duty work. Prohibiting traffic monitors from being armed puts otherwise nervous drivers at ease and prevents a worried and trigger-happy traffic monitor from turning a speeding ticket into a tragedy. Studies show that a significant reason why many motorists flee or confront police during traffic stops is fear of lethal violence from police. Removing that threat of arrest and death from the traffic enforcement equation reduces the risk of firearms-related death on the side of the road.

But what about the safety of the traffic monitor? After all, it has long been common knowledge that traffic stops are among the most deadly parts of a job for an armed police officer. An oft-cited truism is that more officer fatalities occur at traffic stops than anywhere else, because an officer does not know who, or what, is in a vehicle she has just forcibly stopped on the side of a potentially busy and dangerous highway.[42] If an armed officer is in so much danger, how can an unarmed traffic monitor hope to remain safe?

Several reasons exist to think that removing the gun—and the cop— from the equation will actually make traffic stops safer for all involved. First, as with so much common knowledge, this wisdom appears to be more myth than reality. According to the National Fraternal Order of Police, only approximately 7 percent of all officer fatalities occur at traffic stops.[43] While any loss of life is tragic, the commonly held belief that traffic stops are the most dangerous part of the job simply is not true. Indeed, given that over two-thirds of all police contacts with individuals come at traffic stops or accidents but account for only 7 percent of all officer fatalities, the data shows that traffic stops are among the safest aspects of what remains a dangerous job, at least from an officer death standpoint.

But the "overstatement" of the danger to officers at traffic stops actually creates greater danger at traffic stops for drivers and their passengers. As

District Attorney Sam Gill observed, "We get into what I would call anticipatory killings," where officers are primed with false narratives about the
dangers of traffic stops and respond with overaggression.[44] Under a conservative estimate, "The rate for a felonious killing of an officer during a
routine traffic stop was only 1 in every 6.5 million stops, [and] the rate for
an assault resulting in serious injury to an officer was only 1 in every
361,111 stops."[45] Yet there is "an overstatement, ingrained in court precedents and police culture, of the danger that vehicles stops pose to officers.
Claiming a sense of mortal peril—whether genuine in the moment or only
asserted later—has often shielded officers from accountability for using
deadly force."[46] Of over four hundred unarmed passengers who were
killed by officers in a five-year period where neither drivers nor passengers
posed a threat, only five officers were ever charged and convicted.[47]

In fact, "In case after case, officers said they had feared for their lives.
And in case after case, prosecutors declared the killings of unarmed motorists legally justifiable."[48] In a Pulitzer Prize–winning multiyear investigation, the *New York Times* documented thousands of cases of police violence
at traffic stops. A review of the evidence in dozens of these cases found
"questionable police conduct" and evidence that "often contradicted the
accounts of law enforcement officers."[49] Dozens of encounters appeared to
turn on what criminologists describe as officer-created jeopardy: officers
regularly—and unnecessarily—placed themselves in danger by standing
in front of fleeing vehicles or reaching inside car windows, then firing
their weapons in what they later said was self-defense.[50] In many cases,
local police officers, state troopers, or sheriff's deputies responded aggressively to disrespect or disobedience—a driver talking back, revving an
engine, or refusing to get out of a car, what officers sometimes call 'con-
tempt of cop.'"[51]

One study showed that if the police officer began the encounter by issuing a command or not giving a reason for the stop, it was three times more
likely that the interaction would escalate into a violent encounter.[52]
According to the abovementioned *New York Times* report, "Officers,
trained to presume danger, have reacted with outsize aggression. For hundreds of unarmed drivers, the consequences have been fatal."[53] The report
pointed to three particularly egregious examples illustrating this overaggressive stance:

1. In response to a driver swerving over double yellow lines, an officer approached the vehicle and yelled, "Open the door now, you are going to get shot!"
2. In response to a driver speeding recklessly, an officer approached the vehicle and yelled, "Hands out the window now or you will be shot!"
3. In response to a driver carrying an open beer bottle, an officer yelled, "I am going to shoot you—what part of that don't you understand?"[54]

So what does all of this tell us? The risk of violence facing government officials during traffic stops, whether police or civilian monitors, is not nearly as significant as commonly believed. That misconception actually increases the risk of violence by unnecessarily heightening tensions. And those tensions are exacerbated far too frequently by the police officers sworn to protect but primed to fight. Removing both the officer and the firearm from traffic stops has the potential to change this reality and significantly reduce unnecessary motorist fatalities without increasing risks to monitors who enforce vehicle codes.

Beyond remaining unarmed, other traffic enforcement limitations sound similar in nature to those discussed with other alternate responders, but they apply slightly differently during traffic stops.

Limited Seizure Authority

A traffic monitor needs authority to stop and temporarily detain drivers in moving vehicles. This initial part of the traffic monitor's job would look much like a police officer's job today; the monitor would indicate an intention to stop a vehicle through the use of flashing lights, and that show of authority would legally require a driver to comply and pull over the vehicle. But after the initial stop, a traffic monitor's seizure authority would be limited in several important ways. First, seizures would have to be limited to investigating for and citing only the infraction justifying the stop and any other immediately apparent driving-related infraction. Traffic monitors, unlike police, should not have the ability to engage in pretextual stops, nor be allowed to investigate motorists or passengers to attempt to uncover evidence of non–motor vehicle infractions or criminal activity. Nor should they be authorized to prolong traffic stops beyond the time necessary to issue citations or conduct such investigations. A monitor who pulls over a motorist for speeding may discover, during a routine stop, evidence of other vehicle-related infractions. A driver may have a suspended license. A driver may be clearly impaired. These immediately apparent traffic infractions can be addressed and cited appropriately. But no further prolonged investigations, interrogations, or searches may take place. Second, seizures must be limited to the temporary roadside detention to allow for a citation to be issued. Unlike police, traffic monitors must have no ability to effectuate an arrest. Local governments empowering traffic monitors should affirmatively prohibit monitors for conducting custodial arrests. Their objective should be limited to promoting public safety on roadways through the use of citations.

One potential complication with these limitations is that not all traffic violations are equally dangerous. Driving five miles over the speed limit or with a broken taillight creates far less concern than driving fifty miles over the speed limit or with a .25 blood alcohol content. Current criminal codes recognize this by criminalizing as serious misdemeanors or felonies some of these most dangerous moving vehicle violations. In lieu of the power of arrest, traffic monitors should be empowered with two very narrowly limited avenues through which to contact police for assistance. Traffic monitors should be authorized to extend a roadside detention in only the most serious, exigent, felonious public safety emergencies to call for police backup to respond and make an arrest where absolutely necessary. These scenarios should be specifically limited and articulated in appropriate legislation and should include both cases of obvious and dangerous driver intoxication and cases where it is immediately apparent through no further investigation that a violent crime is occurring or has just recently occurred. Also, in the event that a traffic monitor identifies such serious criminal activity but the driver flees, monitors should be empowered to contact police with the relevant identifying information about the car and driver to trigger a police all-points bulletin (APB) to apprehend the suspect.

This last scenario—driver flight from a traffic monitor—highlights another concern for critics of removing police from traffic enforcement. While motorists occasionally flee from police officers attempting to pull them over, the vast majority of motorists dutifully pull over when they see the blue lights flashing in their rearview mirrors. Other than an intrinsic desire to comply with the law, motorists comply with police because of their enormous power to apprehend suspects, the certainty of enhanced penalties for evading police, and the risk of being subjected to (potentially deadly) force by police. Traffic monitors, critics contend, wield no such influence and deterrent power. Why, then, would anyone stop for these "meter maids"?

Fair point. But aside from the fact that most citizens willingly cooperate with government directives and are likely to continue complying with the signal of blue flashing lights from a traffic monitor in the way they would for a police officer, carefully crafted regulations can also address this issue. Police officers have, and traffic monitors can have, great technological power to scan and run license plates and other identifying markers of vehicles involved in infractions. If a motorist evades a traffic monitor and does not willingly submit to a monitor's show of authority, the motorist should be automatically cited for the original offense and for evading the monitor. And by evading a monitor, the motorist should automatically waive any right to contest either citation. This type of contactless automation both decreases the possibility of a violent confrontation and creates a deterrent for motorists who might think they can ignore the commands of a nonpolice traffic monitor.

No Use of Force

Traffic monitors should be strictly prohibited from using force to effectuate or prolong a roadside detention. Nothing prohibits traffic monitors from defending themselves in the same way any of us are lawfully allowed to when aggressed, but other than traditional common law self-defense authorizations, traffic monitors may not use weapons, handcuffs, or brute physical force to restrain motorists. This restriction differs significantly from the powers of police, who are allowed to use any force that is "objectively reasonable" to detain and arrest suspects, even if that force turns deadly. In addition to leveraging nonpolice expertise in public safety, one primary goal of alternate responders is to improve public safety by limiting the amount of unnecessary force perpetrated by the government against hapless citizens. Traffic monitors would take over the enforcement role for minor vehicle infractions; physical force to carry out these duties should never be a part of the equation.

No Search Authority

Given the limited authority traffic monitors have to seize and ticket drivers solely for traffic offenses, it should come as no surprise that traffic monitors would have no search capabilities beyond what is necessary to investigate and issue citations. But this prohibition on general investigative searches is critical. Police officers have enormous power to prolong traffic stops based on reasonable suspicion to attempt to find evidence of a crime, including the ability to conduct warrantless roadside searches of drivers, passengers, and every nook and cranny of a car if probable cause of any criminal offense can be developed.[55] Often, that "probable cause" determination is as threadbare as the faint smell of marijuana justifying an invasive, top-to-bottom thrashing of a car and the seizure of all valuables from the car, even if those valuables are not connected to the crime being investigated.[56] This "automobile exception" to the warrant requirement has been abused for decades. Courts have chastised entire police departments for manufacturing probable cause and "testilying" with the exact same magic words—"I detected an odor of marijuana"—to justify broad vehicle searches.[57] And unjust civil asset forfeiture laws allow police to seize and keep for their departments the valuables found during such a search, including cash and jewelry, even if these items are never connected to a crime and even if the suspect is never convicted or even charged with a crime.[58]

Limiting search authority for traffic monitors thus serves two distinct purposes. First, it imposes natural limits on what a monitor's lawful role is in public safety—to issue tickets based on publicly observable traffic violations that do not require any investigative search activity during the stop. Second, it closes off one of the most problematic and often-abused aspects of police investigation: the unwarranted search and seizure of motorists and their possessions during a state of heightened vulnerability on the side of a road.

Clear Firewall

Removing a traffic monitor's ability to invasively search for criminal evidence, not to mention removing the firearm from the traffic monitor's waistband, will help alleviate some of the danger to drivers and passengers that exist currently with police-initiated traffic stops. There is good reason to believe that removing the gun, the investigative authority, and the police officer from the equation will reduce tensions all around. As law professor and former police officer Tyler Burgauer explains, many (if not most) pulled over drivers or passengers who attempt to flee officers or respond to stops with violence do so out of fear of what else will be discovered by the officer.[59] Driver-initiated violence is not the product of anger about being pulled over for speeding; it is the product of fear that the officer will discover the heroin in the glovebox, the unlicensed handgun in the trunk, or the outstanding arrest warrant in the database.

Because traffic monitors are limited to issuing tickets for traffic violations and are affirmatively prohibited from investigating other unlawful activity or from searching or arresting vehicle occupants for other unlawful activity, this risk disappears entirely. According to Professor Burgauer, removing that risk lowers the temperature, so to speak, of the vehicle occupants and brings the tension inherent in any traffic stop down considerably.[60]

But this can only be the case if drivers and passengers truly believe that traffic monitors will not act as backdoor informants for police. Thus, any regulations establishing a traffic agency must create clear firewalls between the monitors and the police. Traffic monitors must not only be able to operate independently of police; absent narrow and well-delineated exceptions, they must be required to do their jobs without police involvement. Only a clear firewall between monitors and those charged with criminal enforcement can create the level of trust and comfort necessary to allow monitors to enforce traffic laws without contributing unnecessarily to a bloated carceral state or a violent confrontation on the side of the road.

EXPANDED REMEDIES FOR VIOLATIONS

No number of laws restricting alternate responder authority will fully protect citizens without sufficient accountability for violations of those laws. The next chapter will describe ways that courts ought to reinterpret the US Constitution to include alternate responders within its purview and provide meaningful civil rights relief as it does with police and other government officials. But state and local governments need not wait for federal judges to correct decades of jurisprudential missteps. They can, and should, combine alternate responder regulations with two important expanded remedies for violations of those regulations.

First, no evidence obtained by alternate responders during the course of their work should be allowable as evidence at a criminal trial, whether that evidence is tangible or testimonial. This restriction supports the overall purpose of alternate responders in several ways. First, it promotes open and honest communication between alternate responders and the people they serve, much like affirmative firewalls between alternate responders and police. Second, it reduces the incentive for any rogue alternate responders to serve as eyes and ears for police or prosecutors. Third, it puts teeth to the big idea animating this new public safety: that we really do care about finding other ways to address public health and safety besides arresting people and locking them in cages.

This approach goes farther than the Fourth Amendment's traditional exclusionary rule, which prohibits only the introduction of unlawfully obtained evidence. This rule prohibits the introduction of any evidence. But of course, if regulations prohibit alternate responders from searching, seizing, or conducting criminal investigations, most such evidence will have been obtained unlawfully. Moreover, this limitation does not mean that evidence alternate responders find is entirely off limits from the government; it simply means that other government officials will have to uncover that evidence through other lawful means. Thus, an alternate responder cannot report to police the drug use discovered in a homeless encampment, but an officer can independently develop the probable cause necessary to secure a warrant and search for that evidence. An affirmative prohibition on alternate responders supporting criminal prosecutions does not doom those prosecutions; it only redirects them to the agencies left with the task of doing the prosecuting.

Second, states ought to expand the availability of remedies for private tort lawsuits against all government actors involved in public safety, both police and nonpolice. In the absence of available constitutional claims against alternate responders, victims of unlawful searches or violence must turn to private suits for assault, battery, and trespass. Most states

provide some form of governmental immunity from individual or municipal suit for these claims, and virtually no state authorizes attorneys' fees
for plaintiffs who win their tort lawsuits against government actors. These
limitations exist in large part to allow public officials to do their jobs freely
and without the constant fear of being sued by the public and second-
guessed by courts. Proponents of qualified immunity argue that the risk of
being second-guessed is particularly acute with police officers and other
public safety agents who must make split-second decisions about whether
and how to use their immense powers, though studies have shown that the
narrative of police work as tense, emergent, and requiring split-second
decisions is overstated.

But this defense of qualified immunity highlights its principal flaw: it
shields from liability the very government actors who hold the greatest
ability to inflict harm. Those engaged in the work of public safety, including police and alternate responders, have the authority and obligation to
use force against citizens, involuntarily detain them, search their bodies
and homes, confine them in hospitals and prisons, inject them with powerful drugs, and subject them to the criminal and "quasi-criminal" legal
systems. It is for that precise reason that qualified immunity ought to be
more narrowly restricted in the area of public safety, not expanded to the
current formless, limitless shape it has taken at the federal level. States
need not follow the Supreme Court's unilateral police-protective expansion of qualified immunity for federal civil rights claims and can restrict or
eliminate that shield for private state tort lawsuits.

With that shield limited or removed, plaintiffs asserting private tort
claims against public safety actors should have greater access to equitable
remedies like injunctive relief and attorneys' fees for prevailing in the suit.
Federal civil rights lawsuits provide imperfect but useful vehicles for structural reforms through injunctions mandating policy changes, and those
suits often succeed because of the work of highly skilled attorneys finan-
cially incentivized to take on the uphill, complex fight. But where these civil
rights lawsuits fail, either because of qualified immunity or because of constitutional legal loopholes exempting alternate responders from Fourth and
Fourteenth Amendment scrutiny, private tort lawsuits ought to fill that role
and provide an adequate vehicle to drive structural change. That can only
happen if states authorize fee-shifting and equitable relief in these actions.

Some might argue that such significant legal risks will deter people from joining the ranks of alternate responders. I disagree. In my work with and research on the professionals who work as EMTs, crisis interventionists, social workers, and homeless outreach personnel, it is clear that their overriding desire to provide compassionate, meaningful care to the most vulnerable among us is as sincere as their desire to find alternatives to mass incarceration. Rather than being deterred by these changes, they will see them for what they are: sensible and needed protections for the most marginalized among us against individual and structural government overreach. These enhanced legal protections will serve not to punish the work of most alternate responders but to help refine through policy and litigation the contours of a new experiment in nonpunitive public safety.

6　A Constitution That Serves "We the People"

In *Escobedo v. Illinois*, Justice Arthur Goldberg remarked that, "if the exercise of constitutional rights will thwart the effectiveness of a system of law enforcement, then there is something very wrong with that system."[1] And yet, in the sixty years since this statement, the Supreme Court has worked tirelessly to change, weaken, and add exceptions to those constitutional rights to benefit law enforcement. This near-uniform movement to adapt the protections of the Fourth and Fifth Amendments to the work of law enforcement and not the other way around has led some scholars to declare that the Supreme Court has "abdicated" its role in police oversight.[2] And in the process, the Court has all but eliminated protections for vulnerable citizens when caught in the snare of an overzealous alternate responder in the soft policing system. Indeed, an increasing chorus of scholars have highlighted the impotence of federal constitutional rights in preventing and redressing police abuse and have advocated for bypassing traditional constitutional redress altogether.[3]

This final chapter pushes back on that notion and posits that any just and effective public safety system must include at its core a robust role for the protection and vindication of federal constitutional rights. As we have seen, even the most rights-protective regulations are irrelevant to the determination of whether an alternate responder's unlawful actions are "unreasonable" under the Constitution.[4] In other words, where an alternate responder violates local law by exceeding her authority and seizing contraband for criminal prosecution, whether she does so with excessive force or not, that illegal conduct alone does not automatically trigger Fourth Amendment scrutiny and require exclusion of the ill-gotten evidence.

Given this reality, changes to constitutional jurisprudence are sorely needed. This chapter proposes a series of changes to the way courts should interpret and apply the "criminal procedure amendments" that place the focus of these amendments back on the people they were designed to protect: us. As explored throughout this book, the Court currently determines whether and to what extent these rights apply based on the subjective intent, purpose, and profession of the government actor. This approach has it exactly backwards. Constitutional provisions designed expressly to protect the people from unwarranted government conduct ought to be viewed from the perspective of those whose protections have been violated.

There exists significant support for this change. The text, history, and original design of the Bill of Rights and the Reconstruction Amendments support robust application in all government actions, including with alternate responders. The Fourth Amendment was crafted to protect us from all unreasonable government intrusions on our privacy and dignity, and neither the text nor early precedents limit its applicability to police. Indeed, the Framers themselves were most directly inspired to adopt the amendment in response to oppressive general warrants executed by British customs officials—not constables—that violated the common law prohibition against "promiscuous search and seizure."

Moreover, the linchpin of our Fourth Amendment privacy and dignity protections—"reasonableness"—inherently contemplates a line-drawing, values-laden balancing between liberty and security in government-citizen interactions. That balance of determining what constitutes "reasonable" conduct is not static, nor was it designed to be. Instead, as society evolves and citizens articulate different desired preferences for their relationship with government public safety actors, so, too, should that realignment inform what constitutes a "reasonable" government intrusion. As alternate responders form a larger part of that apparatus, their conduct ought to be included in that analysis.[5]

Of course, it is one thing to say there should be more robust federal constitutional protections and another thing entirely to make it so. Altering the current constitutional framework would require abandoning existing doctrines and occasionally overruling cases. While the current Supreme Court has shown an increased willingness to overrule decades-old precedent, it is unlikely to do so in a way that would expand individual rights and limit the government's police power, broadly defined.

But even if these proposals do not find resonance at the highest court, they may find more favorable reception at the state level. Most states have versions of the Fourth and Fourteenth Amendments in their respective constitutions, and state courts are free to interpret these provisions in ways that enhance rights protections for their citizens. The US Constitution provides a "floor" for fundamental rights below which states may not go, but states may provide more expansive rights above this federal floor. And they often do in the area of the criminal procedure amendments.

What follows are a series of proposals, modest and sensible in isolation, that together could radically transform the nature of constitutional rights for our new public safety.

THE CONSTITUTION PROTECTS PEOPLE, NOT UNIFORMS

Expanding the rights of citizens under the Fourth Amendment can only work if those amendments apply to government conduct in the first place. Much of this book has highlighted courts' refusal to apply the protections of these provisions at all with regard to nonpolice conduct. In doing so, they have focused almost exclusively on the subjective motivations of the government actor, informed by the profession of the actor.

Deciding whether to restrain government conduct based on the uniform worn by that government employee makes little sense. Focusing on the government actor ignores the purpose of these rights: to protect people from all government excess, not to grant limitless power to certain government agencies. This approach also selectively applies restrictions against only some government actors when no such "police only" restriction exists in the text or history of the amendment.

To correct these issues, I propose flipping the lens through which we view the Fourth Amendment so that we can reframe the focus not on the subjective motivations of the government but instead on the objective invasions of liberty and privacy suffered by the citizen. This "objective intrusion theory" redirects the analysis away from the subjective motivations of the government actor and toward the target who deserves the constitutional privacy and autonomy protections afforded by the Constitution. For example, instead of assessing whether the Fourth Amendment's protections apply by divining the subjective intent of a government doctor in nonconsensually drawing blood from a suspect, objective intrusion theory would assess whether nonconsensual blood draws amount to an unreasonable search of a citizen.

This approach has intuitive appeal in resolving some of the Fourth Amendment's thorniest applications. Courts have refused to apply the Fourth Amendment at all to some deeply invasive nonconsensual government searches and seizures—including blood draws, surgical intrusions, involuntary commitment, and lethal restraints—simply because the action was not subjectively motivated by a desire to investigate a crime.[6] These decisions rest on arbitrary line drawing justified by questionable factors like primary versus secondary subjective intent and the formal role or uniform worn by the actor. By removing the guesswork of intent, courts can more easily and consistently apply the protections of the Constitution.

Early "special needs" cases involving nonpolice actors reflect this initial understanding of the amendment's reach. The Supreme Court once recognized that "the focus of the [Fourth] Amendment is on the security of the person, not the identity of the searcher or the purpose of the search."[7] Indeed, while the Framers may have envisioned constables executing writs of assistance for the Crown, their overriding concern in adopting the Bill of Rights was one of preventing unwarranted intrusion from all government actors, not just police. That the Framers likely could not have envisioned today's sprawling, vast administrative state and complicated public safety apparatus that subjects Americans to regular, suspicionless searches should not work against application of the Fourth Amendment to these entities when their activities plainly implicate the amendment's reasonableness clause.[8]

OBJECTIVE RESTRAINTS ON LIBERTY

Objective intrusion theory also helps resolve issues arising from the Supreme Court's artificially narrow definition of *seizure*. The Court's refusal to recognize broad categories of dispersal-motivated excessive force as seizures creates a dangerous zone of impunity for homeless outreach teams and other alternate responders forcibly relocating vulnerable citizens. But courts should not focus on what type of physical force the government actor used; instead, the inquiry should center on whether that force restrained citizens' liberty by making them stay or making them go away. A "restraint on liberty" theory of seizure would trigger the Fourth Amendment anytime a government actor intentionally used force or a show of authority to restrain someone's freedom of movement, whether that restraint resulted in submission (in the case of an arrest) or dispersal (in the case of a homeless encampment sweep).

This expansive view of "seizures" not only promotes "the goal of deterring [non]police misconduct" but accords with the fundamental liberty rationale underlying the Fourth Amendment.[9] The historical purpose of the amendment was not only to protect the privacy of individuals from the oppressive intrusion of general warrants but also to protect citizens from unwarranted government coercion and force.[10] Where protection from unreasonable searches is premised on the fundamental precept of privacy from a snooping government, protection from unreasonable seizures is premised on the equally fundamental precept of liberty from a violent government in all its forms.

Admittedly, this approach opens the door to constitutional scrutiny of potentially large swaths of routine government conduct. But that is a good thing. Calling more government conduct a seizure does not declare it unlawful; it just requires a decision on whether that seizure was reasonable. Subjecting more invasive government conduct to judicial scrutiny benefits everyone when that conduct involves often tense and delicate public safety emergencies with vulnerable citizens.

IF IT'S ILLEGAL, ISN'T IT ALSO UNREASONABLE?

Alternate responders' power to search, seize, interrogate, and use force ought to be tightly circumscribed by internal regulation or state and local law. But current Supreme Court precedent deems violations of such sub-constitutional laws irrelevant to the Fourth Amendment: if a search or seizure is permitted as reasonable under the Fourth Amendment, it does not matter whether the action violated a separate statutory or administrative regulation.[11] As we saw in chapter 3 in *Virginia v. Moore*, the Court found it entirely irrelevant for Fourth Amendment purposes that a Virginia state trooper arrested someone for expired tags even though Virginia state law prohibited arrests for such offenses.[12] Because an arrest for minor infractions like expired tags is a "reasonable seizure" according to the Court, the trooper's arrest in *Moore* was also a constitutionally *reasonable* seizure, regardless of whether the arrest was a statutorily *lawful* seizure.[13]

Reflecting on *Moore*, Harvard Law School professor Daphna Renan rightly observed that the Court views "the content of the Fourth Amendment right [as] independent of statutory and administrative mooring."[14] Likewise, Stanford law professor Orin Kerr noted that the Court has "largely detached statutory law from the Fourth Amendment" and that "grants or limits on statutory authority are thought to no longer have constitutional relevance."[15] Thus, if an alternate responder engages in an administratively impermissible but constitutionally permissible search and finds evidence of criminal wrongdoing, that evidence can be used at trial.

Imagine not a Virginia state trooper but a Virginia civilian traffic monitor, vested by state or local law only with the power to stop motorists for traffic violations and to issue citations for those violations but not the power to search for, seize, or notify police about the presence of evidence of criminal activity. Say the traffic monitor nevertheless ignores those prohibitions, like the trooper in *Moore*, searches the car, finds a small amount of marijuana, and turns it over to police. The traffic monitor's clear violation of multiple laws would have no bearing whatsoever on whether his actions were constitutionally reasonable under the Fourth Amendment, creating the possibility that the marijuana could be used at trial and thus frustrating the purpose of nonpolice public safety response.

This view of Fourth Amendment reasonableness merits reconsideration. Determinations of Fourth Amendment reasonableness, at their core, involve value judgments about what society is expected to endure at the hands of the government.[16] At the very minimum, shouldn't we be able to assume that if the actions of a government official are *actually illegal*, they are, by definition, unreasonable? Why else prohibit activity by law if not to communicate that such activity is unreasonable? The very least we can expect from what has become a watered-down Fourth Amendment is protection from actually, affirmatively illegal searches and seizures.

This approach also promotes local democratic governance. Professor Renan notes that the Supreme Court's current view of Fourth Amendment reasonableness "lacks a structural dimension; it is an exercise of judicial interest balancing devoid of interbranch considerations."[17] In other words, the Court views itself as supreme in deciding by itself what is reasonable for all, despite clear and often contradictory input from the legislative and executive branches passing laws to prohibit certain conduct. Our political system has long recognized the supremacy of the Court when it comes to interpreting the Constitution. But a willfully blind judiciary that refuses to be informed by what we the people view as a "reasonable" search or seizure risks acting arbitrarily in the unique context of public safety and the Fourth Amendment.

The two most important words of the Fourth Amendment—*[un]reasonable* and *probable*—are inherently flexible, require value and interest balancing, and thus are and should be more adaptable to changing societal standards. This deliberate "construction of the Fourth Amendment's 'reasonableness' clause should properly change over time to accommodate constitutional purposes more general than the Framers' specific intentions," in large part because the Framers themselves constructed it that way.[18] But by retaining absolute jurisdiction over this reasonableness balancing inquiry without any input from the more democratic branches, the Court ignores the need for participatory expression in defining the contours of what an evolving society deems reasonable. Few governance issues require full citizen voice and participation more than the determination of the appropriate balance between individual liberty and collective security. And few societal evolutions strike at the heart of what constitutes a "reasonable" exercise of government conduct more than a public safety reimagining that replaces armed police with unarmed alternate responders *precisely to limit searches, seizures, arrests, and uses of force.* This kind of reimagining, as it comes to pass, upends not only what we mean by public safety but also what we mean by a reasonable search or seizure.

These types of "subconstitutional" restraints—regulations restricting the search, seizure, and interrogation tactics of nonpolice responders—should inform the meaning of the Fourth Amendment. They serve a much-needed democratizing function where tensions between liberty and security lie at the heart of both the criminal procedure amendments themselves and society's age-old struggle with granting sufficient but not overwhelming power to the government to secure the public safety. They allow this balance to be drawn and informed, not just by nine unelected justices, but also by the representatives of the millions of Americans directly affected by where that line is drawn.

We have begun to see an example of subconstitutional restraints informing courts' Fourth Amendment reasonableness analysis from an unlikely place: police internal protocols governing use of force. Organizations like the Police Executive Research Forum (PERF) have adopted a range of tactical decision-making practices for officers in use of force situations, including de-escalation, the use of warnings, the use of nonlethal force where possible, and "train[ing] on how to avoid getting into a predicament in the first place."[19] These de-escalation protocols "take police departments to 'a higher standard than the legal requirements'" set forth by the Supreme Court, which does not require courts to consider whether officers de-escalated or exacerbated a situation.[20]

This subconstitutional approach appears to be having a constitutional impact.[21] Courts have long been more sensitive to the importance of police tactics in assessing excessive force claims, so the fact that verbal "warnings before using force have become far more systematic" across departments has inclined courts to find unreasonable uses of force where verbal warnings could have been but were not given.[22] For example, in *Mattos v.*

Agarano, the Ninth Circuit Court of Appeals found that an officer's failure to warn before deploying a Taser "pushed this use of force far beyond the pale."[23] Similarly, in *Casey v. City of Federal Heights*, the Tenth Circuit Court of Appeals found "the absence of any warning" before using a Taser "especially troubling" in an excessive force lawsuit.[24] In both cases, the courts noted how commonplace and standard practice it had become for officers to offer pre-force warnings.

This approach may seem sensible, but it also has risks. Consider: What if a new generation of "tough on crime" politicians sweep statehouses across the country and pass laws granting police broad surveillance powers that would normally run counter to Fourth Amendment protections? Should these new laws, which presumably reflect the will of the constituencies electing these politicians, inform what constitutes a reasonable police practice? Should "the people" of the Fourth Amendment be able to redefine reasonableness this way, giving carte blanche to invasive, suspicionless searches and egregious uses of force in the name of public safety? Put another way, if "the people" can strengthen Fourth Amendment protections, can they also weaken or erase them?

In a word: no. To do so would contradict the history, intent, textual design, and very essence of constitutional liberty in the Bill of Rights generally and the Fourth Amendment in particular.[25] The Bill of Rights was designed as a constitutional floor that can be raised by citizens through positive law and through state courts through interpretation of state constitutional provisions. Nonconstitutional data points like local regulations may allow "Fourth Amendment doctrine [to] be resuscitated, making the constitutional floor 'higher' and more informative."[26] As Professor Kerr has observed in his writings on the original function of the Fourth Amendment, this type of legislatively informed Fourth Amendment reasonableness accords with early understandings of the amendment itself: "The Fourth Amendment generally required affirmative authorization, either granted by statute or common law, to make a search or seizure constitutional. This concept has been forgotten."[27]

This type of constitutional one-way ratchet, whereby the democratic process can broaden but not shrink constitutional protections, accords with the design and purpose of the Bill of Rights itself. These ten amendments, added during the Constitutional Convention to gain the support of antifederalists who feared a tyrannical centralized federal government that infringed upon the rights of individual citizens, set the floor of liberties below which the government cannot sink.[28] These amendments also are designed to protect the liberties and rights of unpopular minorities against the "tyranny of the majority" who might want to inequitably restrict certain rights. Just as state and local governments cannot pass laws denying disfavored religious minorities from assembling peacefully or exercising their faith freely, so too should state and local governments be denied the opportunity to redefine Fourth Amendment reasonableness in a way that narrows the rights protected there, including through evidence exclusion.

A TARGET THEORY OF FOURTH AMENDMENT SEIZURES

In Fourth Amendment search law, only someone whose personal Fourth Amendment privacy rights have been violated can challenge an unlawful search.[29] For example, if police unlawfully search my purse while it is on my person and find illegal drugs that are then used in a criminal prosecution against you, you cannot challenge introduction of the evidence in your trial, since police violated only my Fourth Amendment privacy rights, not yours.[30] The Supreme Court has rejected the so-called target theory of standing, which would have granted you standing to challenge introduction of the drugs since you were the "target" of the search.[31]

These issues almost never arise in the seizure context. "Although lower court case law is thin, apparently there is no doubt that a person may challenge a seizure of her own person."[32] This makes sense, because anyone who is personally seized and subjected to unlawful violence as a result has simultaneously suffered both the constitutional violation and the harm from that violation. But while standing to challenge a seizure rarely presents problems, the Court's narrow application of the "unreasonable seizures" clause outside police-dominated criminal investigations implicitly ignores the target of the constitutional violation: the victim of government-sponsored violence. Conditioning application of the amendment in clear cases of excessive force on the subjective motivations or job title of the government agent committing the violence ignores the rights and injuries of the "target" of the violence. Courts have refused to apply the Fourth Amendment at all to some deeply invasive acts of government violence, such as lethal restraints used by EMTs, simply because the action was not committed by a police officer or subjectively motivated by a desire to investigate a crime or arrest a suspect. These outcomes are unjustifiable; unlike with searches, in the seizure context the rights holder and the target of the injury are always inseparable, and refusal to apply the right to the injured party implicitly denies the victim "standing" without historical, textual, or precedential justification.[33]

Thus, I propose a target theory of Fourth Amendment seizures, which redirects the inquiry away from the government actor committing the rights violation and instead considers the objective intrusion into a citizen's liberty and bodily dignity interests. This approach removes justiciability issues inherent in divining the intent of government actors and allows courts to more easily and consistently apply the Fourth Amendment to clear cases of excessive force.[34] This approach also accords with the original purpose of the Fourth Amendment.[35] While most nonpolice Fourth Amendment cases involve administrative searches instead of seizures, the reasoning of these cases reflecting the original design of the amendment applies with equal force here: "If the government intrudes on a person's property, the privacy interest suffers whether the government's motivation is to investigate violations of criminal laws or breaches of other statutory or regulatory standards."[36]

This approach views the Fourth Amendment fundamentally as granting liberty and privacy rights to individuals who can seek redress when the government unlawfully infringes on those personal rights, rather than as granting and restraining power of only certain types of government actors. While the text of the amendment limits what types of conduct trigger scrutiny (searches and seizures), it does not limit what type of government actor is subject to it. A target theory of seizures focuses on the conduct and gives rights of redress to those injured by the conduct, regardless of the uniform, job title, or intent of the government actor.

NONPOLICE ENTANGLEMENT WITH POLICE

Even if these proposals subject more nonpolice conduct to Fourth Amendment scrutiny, there remains the reality that courts have long subjected such nonpolice conduct to far weaker "special needs" and "community caretaking" reasonableness standards. These standards have proven ineffective in protecting vulnerable citizens from the abusive side of soft policing. However, a small body of Fourth Amendment case law may allow for more rigorous probable cause and warrant requirements to apply to nonpolice conduct when alternate responders co-respond with or otherwise collaborate closely with police. In such cases, courts consider whether this "extensive entanglement with law enforcement" renders the nonpolice conduct functionally indistinguishable from "general crime control" conduct.[37]

In these cases, "the purpose for [the conduct] has been the most important factor in deciding whether [it] deserves a legitimate special need unrelated to law enforcement, or instead 'is ultimately indistinguishable from the general interest in crime control.'"[38] For example, in *Ferguson v. City of Charleston*, a state hospital implemented a policy to identify pregnant patients suspected of drug abuse that allowed staff members to test patients without their consent and report positive drug tests to the police.[39] The Supreme Court recognized that "the ultimate goal of the program may well have been to get the women in question into substance abuse treatment" but held that the immediate objective of the searches "was to generate evidence for law enforcement purposes in order to reach that goal."[40] Given that the institutional "purpose of the Charleston program [ ] was to use the threat of arrest and prosecution in order to force women into treatment," this "extensive involvement of law enforcement officials" made the policy "indistinguishable from general crime control."[41] As a result, traditional probable-cause and warrant requirements applied.[42]

At first blush, this case seems inapplicable to nonpolice alternate responders, whose purpose is to find noncriminal, noncarceral pathways toward public safety. But an alternative institutional purpose approach would allow courts to assess whether the purpose of a nonpolice agency is tied to investigating activity that remains formally criminal but unlikely to be prosecuted as a practical matter. Substance abuse counselors, social workers, and homelessness outreach teams (at least in jurisdictions with anticamping ordinances)[43] are tasked with addressing public safety issues arising from criminal activity even if the goal may be to find a resolution short of investigation and referral for arrest. While divining the subjective intent of these alternate responders would remain difficult, the institutional purpose prong of *Ferguson* and related extensive entanglement cases may provide the proper Fourth Amendment hook in cases of nonpolice brutality. Moreover, while *Ferguson* focuses on probable-cause requirements for *searches*, an analogous argument can be made based on extensive entanglement that nonpolice agents should in similar circumstances be subject to the full force of Fourth Amendment *seizure* law.

Nonpolice brutality claims based on impermissibly extensive entanglement with law enforcement are likely have the most resonance in co-responder programs where alternate responders ride along and respond to calls with police officers.[44] Here extensive entanglement claims should extend to whether the programmatic practice of the agency invites a criminal investigation, regardless of the stated or actual purpose.[45] When crisis interventionists respond to 911 calls with law enforcement, a criminal investigation and arrest are more likely than when an interventionist responds on her own without police. In some cases, the presence of a non-police agent on the scene may actually invite a more successful criminal investigation to the extent that the citizen-suspect trusts and confides in the alternate responder in ways they would not with law enforcement.[46] An officer on the scene with goals often in conflict with the alternate responder may attempt to pressure the nonpolice actor to seek relevant information or exert physical force to further a criminal investigation.[47] In such cases, where a program's practice is likely to lead to a penal response regardless of its stated purpose, the Court has found extensive entanglement with law enforcement and has applied the Fourth Amendment accordingly.[48] Thus, a citizen in crisis subjected to nonpolice violence at the hands of an overly aggressive mental health first responder may find success sustaining an excessive force claim if a police officer is also present on the scene. This reconceptualization of extensive entanglement doctrine provides at least one practical, achievable measure of protection for citizens subject to nonpolice brutality.

"Extensive entanglement with law enforcement" aptly describes most major cities' current homeless response policies, which rely on HOT teams co-responding with police to break down and destroy encampments while citing and arresting unhoused people for violating anticamping ordinances. Most courts have refused to apply the Fourth Amendment's probable-cause and warrant requirements to such conduct, even though both the purpose and the outcome of the government action were a seizure of property and a law enforcement response.

Courts may be prepared to take a different approach if one recent case is any indication. A class of seven disabled, mentally ill, unhoused Berkeley, California, residents filed suit against the city for sending homeless "outreach and abatement" teams into their encampment, alleging that

> at 6:20 a.m. on October 4, 2022, [the City] moved in with heavy machinery, a phalanx of Berkeley Police officers, and city officials, to destroy 29 tents, three structures, and impound and then crush four vehicles that unhoused residents were relying on for shelter. During the eviction, Peter Radu [the assistant to the city manager] admitted that there were more residents than available shelter beds, which is why the City was not asking people to leave. However, despite the lack of beds, the City proceeded to destroy many residents' only source of shelter, offering no alternative or replacement.
>
> [The City] threw away Plaintiff Rufus Lee White Jr.'s tent and all his belongings, including all his pants, despite his protests. He was offered a two-person tent but cannot access a two-person tent because his mobility disability prevents him from being able to get into the tent. Plaintiff White was left in his wheelchair without pants, completely without shelter. He ended up sleeping outside—wherever he got tired—for several days before LifeLong Medical donated a new tent to him.[49]

The complaint also alleged that city officials enticed an unhoused resident to leave her RV behind and accept shelter in a hotel. After she checked into the hotel, the city took the keys to her RV, then impounded it and destroyed it, along with all her belongings inside.[50]

In its motion to dismiss the plaintiffs' Fourth Amendment claim, the City of Berkeley claimed that all of its actions fell within the community caretaking exception, which granted it broad power to seize and destroy property for the protection of public health and safety. Judge Edward Chen rejected the argument, explaining that there existed no imminent risk to public safety justifying the permanent destruction of unabandoned property, including the tents and cars in which these vulnerable citizens lived. Instead, Judge Chen subjected the city's co-responding police and homeless outreach personnel to a traditional Fourth Amendment analysis, finding that, as alleged, the warrantless seizure and destruction of property were per se unreasonable.[51]

This sensible approach to overaggressive soft police enforcement action provides a template for other courts considering how to balance this new public safety with age-old constitutional protections. Hopefully, the proposals in this chapter can assist in that balancing act.

Conclusion

AN URGENT PLEA FOR COMMON GROUND

As I write this conclusion from my kitchen table, I sit in the middle of a neighborhood in transition. My suburban street has long been part of a solidly middle-class community that in recent years has seen a significant amount of upheaval. Many elderly residents on my street have lived here for over fifty years and are experiencing mobility and cognitive decline. Older, dilapidated apartment complexes housing the working class sit next to luxury apartments filled mostly with college students from the local university. Restaurants and shopping malls cater to those traveling in to watch a concert or sporting event at the outdoor stadium a few miles away. At the bottom of the hill, along the banks of the river bisecting the city, sits a growing encampment of the unhoused, along with their possessions that line an ever-growing number of sidewalks.

Perhaps not surprisingly, drug use and public mental health episodes in the neighborhood appear to be on the rise, both from the younger college-aged demographic and from those in crisis experiencing housing insecurity. As a parent of two young children, I admit to feeling the urge at times to want police to "just come in and clean it all up." And I do not fault or demonize those who share similar sentiments about their neighborhoods, suburbs, and cities. But these feelings fade and give way to compassion for my fellow neighbors. I know that "clean it all up" far too often means "get it out of my sight" without any regard to helping people in need or fixing these public health and safety issues for all of us. Locking someone up over and over with no wraparound resources, sweeping them from one part of town to the next, or simply ignoring their problems does nothing to help and often makes matters worse.

Some might call this approach naive, even dangerous. After all, shouldn't my first priority be protecting my family from these threats? Yes, absolutely. And I will gladly protect my family from danger when needed, including calling the police to respond to any violent threats to my home, partner, or kids. But that obligation to protect does not give me the right to call upon the most powerful arm of our government, the most powerful police force on earth, to proactively sweep away and lock up nonviolent people in crisis simply because they make me in my privilege feel uncomfortable. Nor should that right extend to the police, or more broadly the government itself. "Help, not handcuffs," is not merely effective policy; it is a moral command.

I firmly believe in the words of congressional chaplain Richard Doerr that, "once grace has been extended to you, you do not have the right to decide who is among the deserving poor to receive that grace. We are all deserving of grace." Had someone decided to call the cops to sweep me away when I was in the throes of my own struggles with mental illness and substance abuse I likely would not be sitting here, writing these words. But I was lucky. Lucky, of course, because my race made me appear less of a threat to those around me. Lucky, because my biological sex afforded me unearned privileges and made me oblivious to dangers uniquely faced by women and girls in crisis. Lucky, because I had the love and support of a patient family, the institutional support of an Ivy League institution, and enough disposable income to seek help. But those things made me lucky, not more deserving.

I feel privileged to live where I do because I have gotten to know many of the people whom outsiders might view as a risk. And there have been times where my concern for their well-being has caused me to want to pick up the phone and seek help. But for many of the reasons articulated in this book, I hesitate to do so. Indeed, that hesitation is why I wrote this book.

By virtue of my research on public safety, I know that the town in which I live staffs many alternate response public safety agencies that deploy to homes and encampments, including adult protective service and elder abuse agencies, psychiatric emergency response teams, and homeless outreach teams. I know that the individuals who staff these agencies, including members of my own family, have valuable expertise and training and possess overwhelmingly a sincere desire to provide compassionate care. I also know that they have the lawful authority to involuntarily restrain, commit, disperse, and destroy the property of those in need, even when those heavy-handed approaches only make matters worse. And I know that these agencies, when dispatched for emergency (and many nonemergency) calls, are accompanied by police as a matter of practice, ready to use force and criminal sanction as a remedy for a public health crisis.

I wrote this book because we need a better way. Throughout these pages, we have confronted the absurdity of relying so singularly on police to respond to and solve all of our complex health and safety problems. We have highlighted many of the promises and perils of a new public safety shifting the focus away from general-purpose armed police and toward specialized nonpolice alternate responders. And we have explored various constitutional, legislative, and regulatory solutions to the continued risks of harm posed by this new public safety. In these final pages, I want to summarize what I believe to be the best, most achievable set of proposals on which we should focus our efforts. In doing so, I urge all of us to put aside the polarizing politics that far too often dominates such policy discussions and frustrates opportunities for popular, meaningful reform.

Whether you consider yourself a conservative supporter of law enforcement or a progressive critic of police abuse, I hope the proposals in this book can resonate with you. When people talk about "police reform," we tend to divide into two camps and harden our opinions. It is beyond the scope of this book to discuss the many reasons why our discourse has become so polarized, including our siloed media consumption, extreme gerrymandered congressional districts, and obsession with cheering for the "red" or "blue" team as if our collective welfare were a sporting event. But I urge us to move beyond these labels and impulses. Instead, I want to suggest that all of us can find a more sensible, more popular approach to public safety that transcends our tiresome polarized climate if we are willing to try.

"WE ARE MORE POLARIZED THAN EVER!"

The popular wisdom is that Americans are more divided today than ever before. That assertion almost certainly is not true as a matter of historical accuracy—after all, we did fight a civil war that literally tore the country in two. But it is true that the rhetoric around a whole host of hot-button political issues has become more divisive, fraught, aggressive, and extreme. Whether talking about immigration, guns, or LGBTQ+ rights, partisan shouting that stakes out a position on one far end of the ideological spectrum and demonizes as dangerous anyone who disagrees increasingly dominates political discourse—if it can even be called that. There appears little strategic value in listening to people with whom one might disagree and even less value in finding compromise. The result, at least with most difficult social issues facing the country today, is that politicians talk past each other instead of to each other, and the party managing a razor-thin electoral victory passes as much partisan legislation as possible until the next party takes control and does the exact opposite. This so-called democratic process plays out both in Washington, D.C., and in state houses across the country. The irony is that many—if not most—of the extreme positions finding their way into law have neither the support of a majority of constituents nor the benefit of actually solving problems.

Policing and police reform is one of these partisan issues. Broadly speaking, those on the political and ideological right support a robust, well-funded, and well-armed police force, view police as valiant bulwarks forced to use violence to protect innocent civilians from a large and dangerous criminal underclass, and paint even mild police critics and reformers as naive "soft on crime" radicals. Those on the political and ideological left highlight the discriminatory and disproportionate bias in policing, decry the epidemic of unlawful police violence, demand accountability for police abuses, and at times belittle supporters of police as racist authoritarians.

Within that tiresome binary political vortex, many of the reforms discussed in this book, most notably reducing the role of traditional law enforcement and replacing at least some police with alternate nonpolice responders, might be labeled as "leftist" or "liberal." But nothing could be further from the truth. Increasing the role of trained nonpolice experts improves community health and safety by leveraging professional expertise, including police expertise. By handing over nonviolent public safety issues to alternate responders, police can focus on their expertise— investigating, responding to, and preventing serious violent crime. While proposed reforms that reallocate public safety resources away from armed police also have the benefit of redressing many of the problems endemic in the institution, that does not make them "antipolice" reforms. Far from being antipolice, these reforms have the support of an increasing number of police themselves.[1] Moreover, the proposals in this book recognize the value of and continued need for a police role in public safety, something at odds with the more liberal stance of total abolitionists.

These reforms, far from being "liberal," have the benefit of broad popular support if framed correctly. When surveyed about many of the alternate responder reforms proposed in this book, large majorities of people across the political spectrum support them.[2] That support grows when people learn about or have direct experience with the success of pilot programs designed to leverage nonpolice expertise.[3] But support for these programs depends in large part on how one describes alternate response public safety.

A NOTE ON FRAMING

Following George Floyd's murder on Memorial Day 2020, the police reform conversation became dominated by the movement to "defund the police."[4] What quickly became apparent, however, was that the sensible, popular, and achievable reform ideas behind this movement were obscured by the controversial and divisive slogan itself. Rather than focusing on positive change or practical solutions, the phrase "defund the police" identified a problem ("police") and claimed a mechanism to remove the problem ("defund") without offering any replacement to this central American institution. President Obama famously declared in late 2020 that the "snappy slogan" loses "a big audience the minute you say it. . . .

[The slogan] makes it a lot less likely that you're actually going to get the changes you want done."[5] Indeed, the word *defund* itself, long associated with politically divisive movements to abolish something undesirable (think "Defund NPR" or "Defund Planned Parenthood"), carried only negative connotations almost certain to create backlash.[6]

And backlash it created. The "Blue Lives Matter" movement, a countermovement showing solidarity with police that began in 2014 in response to the Black Lives Matter movement, exploded in popularity.[7] Politicians who had vocally supported police reform in 2020 backed away within months of the backlash, and municipalities that had promised to drastically reduce police budgets quietly approved double-digit departmental increases.[8]

How, then, can we move beyond hashtag slogans destined to divide and engender conflict and toward a collectively popular yet still transformative set of reforms necessary to radically reimagine public safety? One way is to look at the actual messages animating the "Defund the Police" movement and recognize their broad popularity. Johanna Wald and Nat Kendall-Taylor of the Frameworks Institute, a Stanford University-affiliated nonprofit dedicated to changing narratives to drive popular social change, identified the two main themes underlying the activism of "Defund the Police":

> Theme One: Police are expected to play a wide range of human-service roles for which they're ill-equipped. They are called upon to serve as first responders to a host of non-criminal matters. Communities of color suffer disproportionately from officers' use of excessive force and coercion in situations that warrant a much lighter touch and/or a public health orientation. We need to transform the culture and mission of policing to make it more responsive to the communities police serve, while simultaneously diminishing law enforcement's overall footprint in those communities.

> Theme Two: America historically has under-invested in communities of color, denying them the resources required to address needs such as housing, education, recreation, transportation, jobs and access to health and mental health services. A "reimagined public safety" system is more fundamental and far-reaching than reallocating resources from policing to other services; it is about investing in communities of color in ways that reflect their priorities and promote wellbeing.[9]

"The good news is that polling data tell us that support for these ideas is significant, and has the potential to grow."[10] Whether support for these ideas does in fact grow and, more importantly, turns into tangible policy change depends in large part on how we talk about police reform moving forward. With the balance of this chapter, I hope to frame the conversation around police reform in a way that demonstrates the sensibleness and popularity of reimagined public safety without shying away from the transformative nature of these proposals.

POPULAR REFORMS FOR A CHANGING SOCIETY

Recognizing that some type of reallocation in public safety is both popular and achievable, what do we do with that information? This book has articulated a series of suggestions for how we should go about rethinking and remaking public health and safety in America. These proposals can be grouped broadly into three categories: specializing independent public safety, regulating alternate responders, and protecting citizen rights. Keeping in mind the relative popularity of these proposals when they are framed correctly, I summarize each of these categories of proposals below.

Specializing Independent Public Safety

More than anything else, the "new public safety" is defined by the decision of state and local governments to turn away from police having a monopoly on public safety as twenty-four-hour general all-purpose responders. Nearly every major city in the country has separate, specialized agencies handling discrete aspects of crisis, including adult/elder protective services, child protective services, homeless outreach, mental health psychiatric response, and social work. While many of these agencies funnel money and services through nonemergency, long-term contract relationships, an increasing number of nonpolice entities do respond to and triage emergency situations once addressed solely through 911 calls and armed police response. *That trend should continue, it should expand, and it should prioritize wholly independent nonpolice response separate from law enforcement absent a clear, well-defined need for police intervention.* In particular, three types of alternate responders who alone can address a large majority of the nonviolent health and safety issues affecting our communities should be allocated additional funding and empowered to operate outside law enforcement hierarchy: mental health first response, homeless outreach, and substance abuse medical response.

Mental illness, homelessness, and drug addiction are issues that are ripe for specialization and disaggregation from the policing function. Each is complicated and complex and requires advanced training and understanding of their root causes beyond enforcing criminal laws. Each tends to embody some of the most stubborn, intractable issues in society, with untreated mental illness, chronic homelessness, and serious drug addiction proving both hard to overcome on an individual level and vexing for communities to eliminate on a societal level. None of these conditions are inherently morally blameworthy and thus all three are uneasy fits for criminal sanction. Likewise, none of these conditions respond neatly or entirely rationally to criminal punishment. Convicting a mentally ill or drug-addicted person of a crime driven by mental illness or addiction will not cure them of their underlying condition. Neither will a criminal conviction for acts related to homelessness deter someone from being homeless when they cannot afford to live anywhere else. And given the stickiness and intractability of these conditions, "recidivism rates" (to the extent that such a term is appropriate for these decidedly noncriminal conditions) are extremely high, promising to suck up a disproportionate amount of scarce law enforcement resources.

Removing mental illness, homelessness, and drug addiction from police jurisdiction is a win-win. It frees up law enforcement resources bogged down by nonviolent repeat players and lets police redirect their attention to preventing and solving violent crime. It ends ineffective arrest-and-convict responses to these nonviolent, noncriminal, nondeterrable conditions, responses that often exacerbate rather than ameliorate the problem. And it puts the experts specially trained in these issues on the front lines to help develop the trusting relationships necessary to deliver effective, holistic services that are designed to create lasting change.

But these agencies can work effectively only if they are allowed to work independently. And this is the most significant change in current practice. Many, if not most, of our neighbors suffering from untreated mental illness, addiction, and chronic homelessness have endured multiple scary, unhelpful, and sometimes violent encounters with police officers who cannot or are not interested in solving underlying problems. If alternate responders capable of solving these problems are forced to respond together with police or report back to police, these most vulnerable neighbors in our communities will naturally resist any sort of cooperation or trusting dialogue to help them get the treatment they need. Treating schizophrenia and other serious mental illness requires a long-term relationship with psychotherapists and psychiatrists that begins with trusting the first responder to connect to the right resources without fear of punishment. The same goes for serious drug addiction, especially given the reality that most drug addiction involves the regular use of illegal drugs that can lead to serious criminal consequences. Likewise, a chronically homeless individual who, in addition to potentially suffering from untreated mental illness or drug addiction, has suffered the indignity of being swept away by police and their belongings discarded will not voluntarily work with a homeless outreach team member co-responding with or reporting to law enforcement. We have to stop not only treating these noncriminal matters as crimes but also responding to these noncriminal matters with crime fighters.

That means separate, firewalled emergency hotlines for these agencies, similar to the 988 national suicide hotlines implemented in 2022. That means authorizing these agencies to respond without police backup and prohibiting police from responding unless specifically requested to do so by the alternate responder on the ground. That means strictly limiting when alternate responders can call police or share details with police, especially when illegal drug use, camping, or other nonviolent acts associated with these underlying conditions are present.

And perhaps most importantly, it means increased funding—in many cases, lots of it. If we are actually serious about addressing the underlying causes of most health and safety issues in our communities, we must first get serious about devoting the resources necessary to do so. What the recent Supreme Court litigation fight over criminalizing homeless encampments showed us was that everyone agrees there is a woeful lack of adequate affordable housing and temporary and permanent shelter beds across the country, in large cities and rural communities alike.

Similar underfunding plagues government-run mental health and drug addiction services, both of which require long-term treatment and not short-term Band-Aids.

But increased funding is easier to call for than to make a reality. Significant tax increases to pay for these services are unlikely to pass, but they may not be necessary. If we rightly reconceptualize "public safety" spending by governments as spending not just for "police, firefighters, and (maybe) EMTs" but for all public safety entities broadly, we may find that we have enough funding already. In nearly every major city, police department budgets make up the largest single segment of financial expenditure, with far smaller amounts devoted to noncriminal public safety like drug treatment and homelessness outreach. By reimagining public safety broadly as one large pot of money and allocating those resources more effectively and efficiently in a way that recognizes the need for police funding for violent crime, mental health funding for intractable mental illness, drug addiction funding for drug treatment centers, and homeless funding for triage and shelter, we may find that we already allocate enough resources and funding to public safety. All we need to do is reallocate that money more efficiently in a way that recognizes the benefits of public safety specialization. And that is a proposal with broad support.

Regulating Alternate Responders

A major component of ensuring that alternate responders retain independence from police involves strictly regulating alternate response agencies and limiting their authorized powers. Many of these proposed regulations were summarized in chapter 5, and they involve restricting responders' ability to conduct searches and seizures for evidence, preventing responders from sharing any criminal evidence (including testimonial evidence) with police, prohibiting the use of force except where absolutely necessary, and otherwise insulating alternate responders from law enforcement and criminal investigations. These sorts of regulations are best crafted and passed by the municipal government empowering and funding the agency.

Of course, regulating how these alternate responders work with police only solves the unintended consequence of nonpolice agents acting as eyes and ears for the police. An equally important issue involves the role of alternate responders as their own injurious soft police. Some soft policing reforms could be implemented through negative prohibitions like preventing homeless outreach teams from destroying property or forcibly removing the unhoused from public property. But the most sinister aspects of soft policing, particularly in the medical and mental health arena, will require a top-to-bottom reimagining of these systems.

This country is undergoing a reckoning with its health and health care systems. From a renewed focus on ultraprocessed foods and vaccine safety under the guise of "Making America Healthy Again" to a simmering outrage over health insurance barriers to quality medical care, we stand at the cusp of a potential major reordering of how we think about, promote, and treat health. This conversation hasn't yet, but should, include a penetrating look at how we have failed those with long-term and untreated mental illness.

The decline of permanent institutionalization and the rise of medication-supported outpatient programs in the latter half of the twentieth century marked a promising evolution in mental health treatment. Unfortunately, state and federal funding to treat in outpatient settings the millions of Americans suffering from mental illness did not follow, and the natural public health and safety crisis that emerged was addressed by the public safety actors never short on funding: police. That history led the Los Angeles County Jail to become the largest mental institution in the country. Positive movement has been made to change this reality, with many major cities employing mental health first responders to attempt to triage and address what might appear to be dangerous criminal behavior deserving of arrest but is instead a mental health episode requiring medical intervention. But with the expansion of these first responders has come the expansion of the uglier sides of mental health treatment: involuntary psychiatric commitment when not warranted or necessary, forced medication akin to torture, inhumane institutionalized treatment focused on provider safety over patient treatment, and summary discharge back into the community with little reentry assistance.

Solutions here will not be easy, but three immediate legislative fixes may curb some of the more egregious excesses. First, state standards for who qualifies for a short-term involuntary psychiatric hold have consistently broadened in recent years to include not just those who are at imminent risk of harm to self or others but those who appear to not be able to care for themselves at some point in the future. Such standards are far too amorphous and prospective and sweep in thousands of marginalized individuals who might benefit from some financial or housing assistance but who are not so incapable of care that they require immediate restrictive psychiatric intervention. Far too often, "5150 holds" and other short-term commitment solutions are used as a quick-fix way to put people "somewhere else" without regard to patient holistic treatment. States should reintroduce stringent, narrow standards for who qualifies for this kind of restrictive, involuntary commitment.

Second, given how similar involuntary commitment is to traditional arrest, states ought to require a warrant from a judge supported by probable cause prior to commitment. While there exist good reasons to allow nonpolice actors to secure a warrant and make the decision about commitment, given mental health care providers' expertise in the area compared with police officers', the significant intrusion upon one's liberty and bodily integrity ought to require a heightened level of proof and judicial scrutiny before authorization.

Third, forced medication, including with sedatives and powerful psychotropic drugs, ought to be strictly monitored and limited to settings where absolutely necessary to address either a psychiatric condition for which the drug in question has been prescribed to that patient by a medical doctor (an "on label" use), or where necessary to prevent an imminent physical threat of harm to the patient or others. The extreme overuse of powerful sedatives for the convenience of psychiatric hospital staff has been recognized as problematic by high-ranking federal FDA officials and labeled as torture by the United Nations. While there may exist rare circumstances where forced medication is necessary, it should be the exception and not the norm.

Protecting Citizen Rights

Finally, we must protect the rights of citizens who interact with alternate responders when their rights are infringed upon by these nonpolice actors. Much of this book has considered the ways in which the abusive conduct of nonpolice actors falls outside the protections of the US Constitution and has explained why the Supreme Court's jurisprudence on these issues should change to protect people from all government misconduct, not just police misconduct. The legal advocacy work necessary to create that judicial change is important, but given current realities that project is a long-term, generational movement. In addition to this movement, there are two readily achievable, popular, and effective reforms state and local governments should adopt to protect citizens from nonpolice abuse: strengthened civil tort lawsuit protections, and exclusion of evidence from criminal trials.

As discussed in chapters 3 and 4, the types of police and nonpolice misconduct that could theoretically give rise to a constitutional claim—invasion of privacy in conducting a search and physical brutality—often also correspond with private tort claims for assault, battery, trespass, and false imprisonment. But many of these tort claims fail because states protect police and other government officials from lawsuit by providing a form of qualified immunity from suit. These immunities are designed to allow public officials to carry out their public service duties without constant fear of having to defend themselves in court. But these limited immunities can be expanded beyond their reasonable limit, as with the Supreme Court's expansion of qualified immunity for police from constitutional liability to a doctrine of near "absolute immunity" from all but the most horrific and shocking acts of police abuse.

But unlike constitutional qualified immunity, which the Supreme Court created and controls through its precedents, state governments have the power to limit or eliminate public qualified immunity for tort claims. And there is good reason to do just that for nonpolice alternate responders. While we want these responders to confidently carry out their duties in delivering much-needed, often lifesaving services, their role in public safety is naturally limited to prevent the types of physical violence or privacy invasions that might create legal liability. In other words, unlike police, who must at times use lawful force and invade private spaces to carry out their duties, alternate responders need not inherently rely on force and intrusion to carry out their duties. Because these actions are less justified, they ought to receive less immunity from suit. By narrowing or eliminating immunity from private tort lawsuits, state and local

governments can provide both powerful protections for victims of nonpolice abuse and powerful incentives for agencies to carefully train, super-
vise, and monitor their nonpolice employees.

A similar powerful protective and deterrent incentive would include a
rule preventing the use at criminal trial of any evidence collected by an
alternate responder, at least any evidence collected through an illegal
search or seizure. One of the greatest unintended risks of removing police
from public safety enforcement is that the primary remedy for police
overreach—the exclusion of evidence illegally obtained by police—also
would cease to apply. As discussed in chapter 3, that reality very likely
remains true for federal constitutional claims under the Fourth
Amendment. But states are free to craft their own evidentiary exclusionary rules, including ones that prevent the introduction of evidence collected by certain agencies or collected in violation of affirmative state or
local laws. Since proposed alternate responder regulations themselves
would prevent nonpolice agencies from collecting or passing to police
such evidence, doing so anyway would violate an affirmative local law.
Excluding such illegally obtained evidence would protect citizens from
alternate responder overreach, deter such misconduct, and promote a primary goal of the new public safety: disentangling nonviolent, noncriminal
conduct from the tentacles of the carceral state.

ACTING LOCALLY, AND WITH GRACE

I like to run early in the morning before the bustle of kid lunches, school
drop-offs, and work email begins. I typically wake up at 5:00 a.m. and run
a familiar route along the river in a remote area between high-rise condos
and the local sports stadium. Beginning a few months ago, I started notic-
ing a recurring pattern. Most days, the banks of the river would have hallmarks of homelessness: full shopping carts, tarps, cardboard boxes, piles
of clothes and shopping bags. But every other Monday, I would find an
ambulance and two police cruisers parked along the river with two large
trash bins. For the next day or two afterwards, I noticed a sizable increase
in unhoused people walking through the neighborhood, pushing
shopping carts and pulling behind them a small mountain of personal

belongings. By the end of the week, I would again spot on my morning run the familiar hallmarks of homelessness along the riverbank, while those same unhoused people seemed to disappear from view.

It is obvious what's happening. Twice a month the local police clear out a known encampment, dispersing the people in it and throwing away what gets left behind. And the unhoused people in turn gather up what belongings they can carry with them, wander the streets until the coast is clear, and then head right back to the same spot. Public safety resources have been wasted, vulnerable lives have been disrupted, property has been destroyed, and nothing has changed. It is so frustrating to watch marginalized people get shuffled around for no benefit by my government with my tax dollars, while those same government resources and tax dollars could be put to better use actually solving the problem and actually investigating serious crime.

I wonder if you can find similar kinds of public safety inefficiency in your community. As I hope the discussion and proposals in this book have encouraged you to think about how we address public safety in this country, I also hope they spur you to think about how it works on the ground in your town. Whether you live in a rural mountain community like my hometown in the Blue Ridge Mountains or in a major metropolitan area where I currently find myself, I suspect you won't have to look too hard to find waste in how your local government allocates its public safety resources. Maybe your community doesn't have the same visible homeless crisis as mine, but maybe it is one of the thousands ravaged by the opioid epidemic. Or there is a lack of mental health resources for communities disproportionately affected by mental illness, like veteran populations, resettled refugees, or the working poor. Maybe your community has prioritized municipal funding through traffic tickets, "broken windows" fines, court costs, and "pay to stay" jail fees over the provision of resources and opportunities to those in a revolving door of impoverishment and petty crime exacerbated by entrenched poverty, underlying mental health or drug conditions, and the financial and collateral costs of criminal conviction. Whatever it is that defines the public safety problem in your community, I hope this book helps you notice it and encourages you to take action to fix it.

Nationwide programs backed by federal funding can be great. But at its core, all public safety is local. Each city, town, and rural community is distinct and carries with it its own beauty, strengths, and health and safety challenges. And each local government overwhelmingly funds, trains, and writes the rules governing its public safety personnel, police and nonpolice alike. The local governments responsible for writing these rules and passing these budgets are not primarily responsive to national politics or politicians, or to famous celebrities or athletes, and certainly not to book-writing academics like me. They are primarily responsive to you, the citizen voter with the actual power to change the direction of how your community funds and addresses public health and safety. If the last few years of intense political polarization have shown us anything, it is that regular everyday people engaging in the political process—whether parents speaking up at local schoolboard meetings or concerned citizens speaking out about COVID or other public health protocols at city council meetings—can and do drive real change in their communities. All you have to do is make your voice heard.

You don't have to run for local office to do so, though you could! Because public safety is by definition public, there are many regular opportunities to attend and participate in community meetings and hearings about public safety. Most regular city or county council meetings are open to the public and either devote substantial time to public safety issues or allow residents to add items to the agenda. Many police departments have community liaisons who hold public meetings and listening sessions to get feedback from the communities they serve. A growing number of communities have police citizen oversight boards tasked with investigating on behalf of the public instances of police abuse, and most of these boards hold regular public meetings. Local papers are starving for constituent content about local issues, either as letters to the editor or as opinion editorials. And communicating directly with elected representatives— through phone calls, letters, and organized petitions—leads to far greater response and direct action than you might think.

Perhaps it seems strange to end with a call for democratic participation to solve a problem in a time where more and more of us claim that democracy in this country is broken. Fewer of us trust the democratic process or democratic institutions. And yes, there is good reason for concern about election processes and the responsiveness of our elected officials, regardless of political party. But most of these concerns really focus on the national political landscape and on the election of and governance by federal officials in Washington, D.C. Local politicians and governing authorities remain responsive to those few of us who actively and regularly engage them on policy matters, and given the outsized amount of our money spent on public safety, we owe it to ourselves to take a more active role in how that money is spent.

We also owe it to each other as members of a shared community to work toward helping those most vulnerable and most in need of help. And it is this sentiment that poses the most vexing problem for public safety reform. Before we can work together to solve these issues, we must first agree that the poor and vulnerable among us are deserving of help. Unfortunately, that is a belief not uniformly shared. Perhaps the most difficult problem to confront in this public safety debate is one of perspective. Is the homeless person along the riverbank I pass by on my run a dangerous vagrant who puts other people at risk of disease and theft, who made his poor choices and now must face the consequences, and who shouldn't get our money and resources when there are more deserving people in need? Or is the homeless person along the riverbank a vulnerable and sick person who is himself at risk of theft and violence, who suffered from poor life circumstances thrust upon him by childhood or exorbitant housing and health care costs, and who will never recover his full humanity without critical services and support of his community?

Of course, every person's situation is different. But for most vulnerable people there is some truth in both perspectives, just as there is about you and me, about all of us. Each one of us has benefited from the help, assistance, and unearned grace of others, whether we like to admit it or not. Hard work and good choices go a long way toward success. So do good fortune, kindness, and community support. None of us is an island, and none of us succeeds alone. For those of us privileged enough to live in relative safety and security, it is our moral imperative to support those less privileged with the specialized help and treatment they need to reintegrate into society instead of the handcuffs we may think they deserve. And as a matter of public safety, this moral imperative also happens to be smart policy. Let us work together to see it through.

Notes

INTRODUCTION

1. Meko and Kriegstein, "He Was Mentally Ill."
2. Viscusi and Jeffrey, "Damages to Deter Police Shootings," 250.
3. The facts of this case are recited in *McKenna v. Edgell*, 617 F.3d 432 (6th Cir. 2010).
4. Lopez, "He Helped His Overdosing Friend."
5. Meko and Kriegstein, "He Was Mentally Ill"; Hause and Melber, "Half of People Killed"; Ruderman Family Foundation, "Media Missing the Story."
6. Selsky and Willingham, "'Tragic Outcomes.'"
7. Guarino, "Few Americans Want."
8. Guarino, "Few Americans Want."
9. Woods, "Traffic Enforcement Would Be Safer"; Harrison, "Stop, Start, or Continue?" (survey finding that 42 percent of officers never received training about traffic stops, 46 percent disagree or strongly disagree that they have received adequate training, and 13 percent support a reduced role for police in traffic enforcement).
10. Throughout the book, I refer alternately to "nonpolice public safety agents" and "alternate responders" when discussing the nonpolice actors and entities that have replaced and might replace police in certain public safety situations. The first term comes from my *University of Chicago Law Review* article "The

Fourth Amendment without Police." I borrow the phrase "alternate responders" from Simmons, "Constitutional Double Standards."

11. Kaba and Ritchie, *No More Police*, 118.

12. Kaba and Ritchie, *No More Police*, 97.

CHAPTER 1. WHY ARE POLICE EVERYTHING EVERYWHERE ALL AT ONCE?

1. Scott, *"Everything Everywhere."*

2. Michaela Lee and Du, *"Everything Everywhere."*

3. Lamin and Teboh, "Police Social Work," 9.

4. Treger, "Police Social Work," 22.

5. Alexander, *New Jim Crow;* 24. Fields, *Neighborhood Watch*, 18.

6. Fields, "Procedural Justice Industrial Complex," 585.

7. Friedman, "Disaggregating the Policing Function," 955.

8. Statista Research Department, "Number of Arrests"; Shourd, "They Called for Help" ("A conservative estimate says 900,000 people with mental illness end up in our jails every year"); Friedman, "Disaggregating the Policing Function," 945 (As many as 20 percent of all police contacts [over fifty million per year] involve persons with mental illness or alcoholism, about one-quarter of which [or 2.5 million] are arrested for low-level offenses).

9. Jun, DeVylder, and Fedina, "Police Violence among Adults," 82–85; Lowery et al., "Distraught People."

10. Chalfin and McCrary, "Are U.S. Cities Underpoliced?," 172–77.

11. D. Thompson, "Unbundle the Police."

12. Fletcher, "Erasing the Thin Blue Line," 1465 " (The police are authorized to employ the government's monopoly on violence"); Leider, "State's Monopoly of Force," 48 ("Even if a state has a monopoly on the legitimate use of violence, nothing inherently requires state officers to exercise the state's monopoly of force").

13. Leider, "State's Monopoly of Force," 48.

14. Friedman, "Disaggregating the Policing Function," 940.

15. Dennis, Berman, and Izadi, "Dallas Police Chief Says."

16. Friedman, "Disaggregating the Policing Function," 931 (quoting Liederbach and Frank, "Policing Mayberry," 59–60).

17. Friedman, "Disaggregating the Policing Function," 931.

18. Friedman, "Disaggregating the Policing Function," 931 (quoting Liederbach and Frank, "Policing Mayberry," 59–60).

19. Treger, "Police Social Work," 24.

20. Friedman, "Disaggregating the Policing Function," 950–51.

21. Liederbach and Frank, "Policing Mayberry," 60.

22. Selsky, "How Some Encounters"; Graham, "Stumbling Block."

23. D. Thompson, "Unbundle the Police"; Watson et al., "Improving Police Response," 362–64.

24. Dean et al., *Social Work and Police Partnership*, 40.

25. Friedman, "Disaggregating the Policing Function," 982.

26. D. Thompson, "Unbundle the Police"; Dillon, "Parents of Schizophrenic Man."

27. Mundell, "Most Homeless Americans."

28. Yglesias, *"End of Policing."*

29. D. Thompson, "Unbundle the Police"; Citrus Heights Sentinel, "CHPD."

30. Johnson v. City of Grants Pass, 50 F.4th 787, 800 (9th Cir. 2022).

31. Kendall, "Exclusive."

32. City of Grants Pass v. Johnson, 144 S.Ct. 2202, 2230 (2024).

33. Newsom, "Governor Newsom Orders."

34. Western, *Homeward*, 47.

35. D. Thompson, "Unbundle the Police."

36. D. Thompson, "Unbundle the Police."

37. Balko, *Rise of the Warrior Cop*, 20.

38. Kirkpatrick, "Pulled Over." The *New York Times* won a Pulitzer Prize for this in-depth investigative reporting.

39. Kirkpatrick, "Pulled Over."

40. R. Goldstein, Sances, and You, "Exploitative Revenues."

41. Subramanian et al., *Revenue over Public Safety.*

42. Subramanian et al., *Revenue over Public Safety.*

43. Pierotti, "I Was a Cash Cow."

44. Pierotti, "I Was a Cash Cow."

45. Pierotti, "I Was a Cash Cow."

46. Pierotti, "I Was a Cash Cow."

47. Subramanian et al., *Revenue over Public Safety.*

48. Subramanian, *Revenue over Public Safety*; R. Goldstein, Sances, and You, "Exploitative Revenues," 8.

49. Subramanian et al., *Revenue over Public Safety*; Plant-Chirlin, "Saddled with Debt."

50. Cook, "Burden of Criminal Justice Debt."

51. *Harvard Law Review*, "Policing and Profit," 1726–27.

52. Wilson and Kelling, "Broken Windows."

53. Cummings, "Cost of Crazy," 287.

54. Fields, *Neighborhood Watch*, 87. The book collects and summarizes multiple studies. See also Bishop et al., "Racial Disparities."

55. Bishop et al., "Racial Disparities."

56. Bishop et al., "Racial Disparities."

57. Ortiz, "Inside 100 Million"; Pierson et al., "Large-Scale Analysis."

58. Maiarechi, "What the Data Really Says"; KPIX, "Study Shows California Cops."

59. Police Accountability Task Force, "Recommendations for Reform."

60. LaFraniere and Lehren, "Disproportionate Risks."

61. LaFraniere and Lehren, "Disproportionate Risks."

62. Rudovsky and Rosenthal, "Debate," 120.

63. Tyler Burgauer, law professor and former law enforcement officer, interview by author, September 22, 2023.

64. Rhoden, "Jayland Walker Shooting."

65. *Washington Post*, "Fatal Force"; Neusteter, "Every Three Seconds."

66. US Census Bureau, "U.S. and World Population Clock."

67. Zimring, *When Police Kill*, 74–85; Lartey, "By the Numbers"; Statista, "Rate of Civilians Killed."

68. Yee, "Yes, U.S. Locks People Up."

69. Cheatham and Maizland, "How Police Compare."

70. Friedman, "Disaggregating the Policing Function," 7–11; C. Lee, "Reforming the Law," 636.

71. J. Kelly, and Nichols, "We Found 85,000 Cops."

72. J. Kelly and Nichols, "We Found 85,000 Cops."

73. Carbado and Rock, "What Exposes African Americans?," 1505; Akbar, "Abolitionist Horizon," 1797.

74. Edwards, Lee, and Esposito, "Risk of Being Killed."

75. See Tran, "FBI Chief"; C. Ross, "Multi-level Bayesian Analysis."

76. National Safety Council, "Preventable Deaths: Odds of Dying."

77. See Lowery, "Aren't More White People."

78. Fryer, "Empirical Analysis"; see also Bui and Cox, "Surprising New Evidence."

79. Goff et al., "Science of Justice"; Williams, "Study Supports Suspicion."

80. Hetey et al., "Data for Change"; Jackman, "Oakland Police."

81. Ritchie, *Invisible No More*, 2–3.

82. Ritchie, *Invisible No More*, 112–13. The book cites a 2003 study of young women in New York City, where "almost two in five young women described sexual harassment by police officers. Thirty-eight percent were Black, 39 percent were Latinx, and 13 percent Asian or Pacific Islander."

83. Ritchie, *Invisible No More*, 91–92. The book traces how historically pseudoscientific connections have been made between race and mental illness, with Black women escaping enslavement described as "lunatic slaves," Indigenous women resisting reservation agents described as "Indian defectives," and the "resistance to slavery pathologized as mental illness inherent in African-descended people." See also Jones, "Aggressive Encounters," 2058.

84. Ritchie, *Invisible No More*, 128; Fields, "Elusiveness of Self-Defense," 980.

85. Ritchie, *Invisible No More*, 128.

86. Akbar, "Abolitionist Horizon," 1789 ("Police are a regressive and violent force in a historical power struggle over the distribution of land, labor, and resources, and their power has historical, material, and ideological bases"); Fields, "Weaponized Racial Fear," 941.

87. Fields, "Weaponized Racial Fear," 941.

88. Akbar, "Abolitionist Horizon," 1789; National Law Enforcement Officers Memorial Fund, "Slave Patrols: An Early Form of American Policing"; Hadden, *Slave Patrols*, 4; N. Brown, "Black Liberty in Emergency," 715–17.

89. Akbar, "Abolitionist Horizon," 1789.

90. A. Davis, *Are Prisons Obsolete?*, 12.

91. Vitale, *End of Policing*, 24.

92. Vitale, *End of Policing*, 24.

93. Guarino, "Few Americans Want."

94. *The Economist*/YouGov Poll, "June 14–16, 2020."

95. *The Economist*/YouGov Poll, "June 14–16, 2020."

96. Klick and Tabarrok, "Using Terror Alert Levels," 15.

97. MacDonald, Klick, and Grunwald, "Effect of Privately Provided Police," 838–39.

98. Chalfin and McCrary, "Are U.S. Cities Underpoliced?," 172–77.

99. Sharkey, "Why Do We Need the Police?" ("One of the most robust, most uncomfortable findings in criminology is that putting more officers on the street leads to less violent crime").

100. Yglesias, *"End of Policing."*

101. Yglesias, *"End of Policing."*

102. D. Thompson, "Unbundle the Police."

103. Kaba, "Yes, We Mean Literally."

104. Kaba, "Yes, We Mean Literally."

105. Kaba, "Yes, We Mean Literally."

106. Kaba, "Yes, We Mean Literally."

107. Kaba, "Yes, We Mean Literally."

108. Uetricht, "Policing Is Fundamentally a Tool."

109. Kaba, "Yes, We Mean Literally."

110. Kaba, "Yes, We Mean Literally"; see also Song, "Policing the Emergency Room," 2648–50.

111. Reiss, *Police and the Public*, 63.

112. Chaplain, "Inefficacy."

113. Friedman, "Disaggregating the Policing Function," 943 ("Much harm occurs because we send armed people—who are trained and see their mission as force and law—to deal with myriad problems not particularly susceptible to this solution").

114. Bell, "Police Reform," 2065.

115. Bell, "Police Reform," 2065. One reason may be the composition of police forces. "Women make up just 12.6% of all police officers. The[se] gender disparities distort American policing. Controlling for differences in assignments, studies show female officers are significantly less likely to use force than male officers, more likely to display empathy and more likely to de-escalate fraught encounters." See R. Brooks, "One Reason for Police Violence?"

116. D. Thompson, "Unbundle the Police."

117. Beekman, "Seattle City Council"; R. Ellis, "Portland City Council Approves"; Associated Press, "LAPD Funding Slashed."

CHAPTER 2. THE NEW PUBLIC SAFETY

1. CBS News, "Police Use Crisis Intervention Team."

2. CBS News, "Anne Arundel County."

3. CBS News, "Police Use Crisis Intervention Team."

4. N. Anderson and Faheid, "Bodycam Video."

5. Levenson, "Step-by-Step Look."

6. Aaron, "'Why Did They Shoot Me?'"; Gold and Closson, "What We Know"; Krumrey, "Siblings of Juneau Man."

7. Parafiniuk-Talesnick, "In Cahoots."

8. Parafiniuk-Talesnick, "In Cahoots."

9. CAHOOTS home page, accessed January 24, 2022, https://whitebirdclinic .org/cahoots/. CAHOOTS also offers crisis counseling, suicide prevention, conflict resolution, substance abuse counseling, housing crisis services, and transportation to services.

10. CAHOOTS home page.

11. Peha, "Lewis Proposes."

12. Eugene Police Department, "CAHOOTS Program Analysis"; McCord, "Fourteen Lost Clinics."

13. Gerety, "Alternative to Police."

14. Gulley et al., "Mobile Crisis Teams."

15. National Alliance on Mental Illness, "Crisis Intervention Team Programs."

16. Morgan, "Policing under Disability Law," 1412, discusses "police violence as it affects disabled people," including the mentally ill. See also Pearson, "Actors, Mentally Ill," who notes that police "received more than 130,000 so-called 'emotionally disturbed person' calls [in 2014], about 23,000 more than in 2011."

17. Rogers, McNeil, and Binder, "Effectiveness of Police Crisis Intervention."

18. Georgia Public Safety Training Center, "Georgia Crisis Intervention Team (CIT) Program."

19. Atlanta Police Department, "APD Officer."

20. City of Durham, "Crisis Intervention Team (CIT)."

21. Rogers, McNeil, and Binder, "Effectiveness of Police Crisis Intervention."

22. Smith, "What Happens."

23. Nir, "On City Streets."

24. Smith, "What Happens."

25. Smith, "What Happens."

26. Miller, "Reformers Want Police to Step Back."

27. Friedman, "Disaggregating the Policing Function," 987; Bratton, *Broken Windows*.

28. Friedman, "Disaggregating the Policing Function," 987. Bratton, *Broken Windows*.

29. Friedman, "Disaggregating the Policing Function," 983.

30. Dean et al., *Social Work and Police Partnership*, 24.

31. Friedman, "Disaggregating the Policing Function," 984.

32. Friedman, "Disaggregating the Policing Function," 988.

33. Martinsburg Initiative, "Martinsburg Police"; Friedman, "Disaggregating the Policing Function," 988.

34. Friedman, "Disaggregating the Policing Function," 988.

35. Fields, "Fourth Amendment without Police," 1040–45.

36. Gillespie, McGilton, and Rogin, "Understanding Denver's STAR Program."

37. Lanfear, "Formal Social Control."

38. Gillespie, McGilton, and Rogin, "Understanding Denver's STAR Program."

39. Kotalik, "Denver's STAR Program."

40. Denver the Mile High City, "Support Team Assisted Response (STAR) Program."

41. Kaufman, "Ongoing Struggles."

42. A. Newman and Fitzsimmons, "New York City."

43. A. Newman and Fitzsimmons, "New York City."

44. PBS News, "U.S. Homelessness."

45. Adkins, "Homelessness in America."

46. Adkins, "Homelessness in America."

47. Houston Police Department, Mental Health Division, "Crisis Call Diversion Program"; Friedman, "Disaggregating the Policing Function," 988.

48. Friedman, "Disaggregating the Policing Function," 988.

49. Nakaso, "Social Service Workers."

50. Abraham, "Why Are So Many Cities' Homeless Policies Punitive?"

51. Abraham, "Why Are So Many Cities' Homeless Policies Punitive?"

52. City of San Diego Police Department, "Neighborhood Policing Division."

53. City of San Diego Police Department, "Neighborhood Policing Division."

54. Ireland, "City Council."

55. San Diego Mun. Code § 63.0401 et seq., "Encampments on Public Property"; Kendall, "Backers of California Homeless Camp Ban."

56. Kendall, "Backers of California Homeless Camp Ban."

57. McWhinney, "La Mesa Taps Outreach Workers."

58. McWhinney, "La Mesa Taps Outreach Workers."

59. Fields, "Weaponized Racial Fear," 935.

60. Fields, "Weaponized Racial Fear," 935.

61. *Washington Post* Editorial Board, "Opinion," challenges the "obvious illogic and cruelty of using force against a frightened, unarmed individual who poses no risk" and asks, "Couldn't people in crisis be assisted by someone other than an armed policeman?" Eldridge, "Cops Could Use First Aid," notes that officers are regularly the first responders on the scene of a medical emergency but often do not attempt to provide medical aid, focusing instead on detaining individuals.

62. CAHOOTS home page.

63. Lopez, "Evidence for Violence Interrupters."

64. Lopez, "Evidence for Violence Interrupters."

65. Gimbel and Muhammad, "Are Police Obsolete?," 1510.

66. Lopez, "Evidence for Violence Interrupters." See also Crann and Burks, "Now Better Trained"; Yang, "'Send Freedom House!,'" 1070.

67. Crann and Burks, "Now Better Trained"; Yang, "'Send Freedom House!,'" 1070; Gimbel and Muhammad, "Are Police Obsolete?," 1510. Gimbel and Muhammad, in "Are Police Obsolete?," state that "leveraging the trust and credibility of the violence interrupters" allows organizations like Cure Violence to 'mobilize the community to change norms,'" named by Cure Violence as one of the essential elements of its model (Cure Violence, "The Model").

68. Schuppe, "Biden Wants."

69. Lopez, "Evidence for Violence Interrupters," collects studies highlighting "decidedly mixed results" of programs. Gimbel and Muhammad, "Are Police Obsolete?,' 1512–13, describes the "substantial positive results" of early violence interrupter programs before funding was cut and contracts were terminated.

70. Bureau of Justice Statistics, "Contacts between Police and the Public." See also Woods, "Traffic without the Police," 1480–81 (People are "likely to violate at least one traffic law when driving from place to place").

71. Woods, "Traffic without the Police," 1481.

72. Police have used the entry point of enforcing minor moving vehicle violations to engage in broad criminal investigations unconnected to vehicle codes. The US Supreme Court has repeatedly authorized these pretextual encounters as consistent with the Fourth Amendment, in essence laundering discriminatory intent as good policing. Whren v. United States, 517 U.S. 806, 813 (1996).

73. Woods, "Traffic without the Police," 1482.

74. See City of Berkeley, "General Information," for a proposal to cut police funding by $9.2 million and use unarmed Department of Transportation employees to make traffic stops.

75. Woods, "Traffic without the Police," 1479.

76. Woods, "Traffic without the Police," 1479.

77. Woods, "Traffic without the Police," 1481.

78. Woods, "Traffic without the Police," 1492.

79. Social Service Workers United–Chicago, "NASW Is Failing Us." This open letter from a social workers' union criticizes calls for greater collaboration with police because replacing "police with social workers without eliminating these carceral aspects of social work" will perpetuate historic distrust of social workers in marginalized communities.

80. Kaba and Ritchie, *No More Police*, 115.

81. Kaba and Ritchie, *No More Police*, 114–18.

82. Kaba and Ritchie, *No More Police*, 117.

83. Kaba and Ritchie, *No More Police*, 117.

84. Méndez, *Report of the Special Rapporteur*, calls for "an absolute ban on all forced and nonconsensual medical interventions against people with disabilities, including the nonconsensual administration of psychosurgery, electroshock and mind-altering drugs such as neuroleptics, [and] the use of restraint and solitary confinement, for both long- and short-term application."

85. Kaba and Ritchie, *No More Police*, 118.

CHAPTER 3. SEARCH AND SEIZURE WITHOUT POLICE

1. Sutterfield v. City of Milwaukee, 751 F.3d 542, 545 (7th Cir. 2014).

2. *Sutterfield*, 751 F.3d at 545.

3. *Sutterfield*, 751 F.3d at 550.

4. See JL v. N.M. Dep't of Health, 165 F. Supp. 3d 996,1042 (D.N.M. 2015) (collecting cases); Ingraham v. Wright, 430 U.S. 651, 673 n.42 (1977); New Jersey v. T.L.O., 469 U.S. 325, 335 (1985).

5. United States v. Janis, 428 U.S. 433, 446 (1975) (Deterrence is the "prime purpose" of the rule, "if not the sole one").

6. Sabalow, "Bill Would Let Therapists."

7. Sabalow, "Bill Would Let Therapists."

8. City of Eugene and White Bird Clinic, "Personal Services Contract."

9. City of Eugene and White Bird Clinic, "Personal Services Contract."

10. Gardner v. Buerger, 82 F.3d 248, 252 (8th Cir. 1996); Davies, "Recovering the Original Fourth Amendment," 552.

11. United States v. Attson, 900 F.2d 1427, 1442 (9th Cir. 1990); Blasko v. Doerpholz, 2016 U.S. Dist. LEXIS 185495, *4 (D. Mass. 2016).

12. *JL*, 165 F. Supp. 3d at 1042; *T.L.O.*, 469 U.S. at 335.

13. *Attson*, 900 F.2d at 1430 (collecting cases).

14. Dressler, *Understanding Criminal Procedure*, 293.

15. Dressler, *Understanding Criminal Procedure*, 293.

16. City of Indianapolis v. Edmond, 531 U.S. 32, 37 (2000).

17. Dressler, *Understanding Criminal Procedure*, 293; Griffin v. Wisconsin, 483 U.S. 868, 880 (1987); cf. Reamey, "When 'Special Needs,'" 299–300.

18. Dressler, *Understanding Criminal Procedure*, 294.

19. York v. Wahkiakum, 163 Wn. 297, 312 (2008); Stuntz, "Implicit Bargains," 554.

20. Camara v. Municipal Court of the City and County of San Francisco, 387 U.S. 523, 530 (1967); Michigan v. Tyler, 436 U.S. 499, 510 (1978); Skinner v. Railway Labor Executives' Ass'n, 489 U.S. 602, 615 (1989); *T.L.O.*, 469 U.S. at 335.

21. Doe v. Luzerne Cnty., 660 F.3d 169, 179 (3d Cir. 2011).

22. *Attson*, 900 F.2d at 1431; see also *Blasko*, 2016 U.S. Dist. LEXIS at *52.

23. *Attson*, 900 F.2d at 1433.

24. *Blasko*, 2016 U.S. Dist. LEXIS at *50.

25. Perez v. Moore, 2019 U.S. Dist. LEXIS 148692, at *4 (N.D. Cal. Aug. 30, 2019).

26. *Perez*, 2019 U.S. Dist. LEXIS 148692, at *4.

27. Peete v. Metropolitan Government of Nashville & Davidson County, 486 F.3d 217, 219 (6th Cir. 2007).

28. Kaba and Ritchie, *No More Police*, 122.

29. Nowell, "Adora Perez Is Free."

30. Nowell, "Adora Perez Is Free."

31. E. Coleman, "Many States Prosecute."

32. American College of Obstetricians and Gynecologists, "Opposition to Criminalization."

33. Amnesty International, "Criminalizing Pregnancy."

34. E. Coleman, "Many States Prosecute."

35. Ferguson v. City of Charlotte, 532 U.S. 67, 70 (2000).

36. Shapiro and Jarenwattananon, "New Report."

37. Dellinger and Pell, "Bodies of Evidence."

38. Centers for Disease Control and Prevention, "Crisis + Emergency Risk Communication."

39. *Camara*, 387 U.S. at 393.

40. Wyman v. James, 400 U.S. 309, 320 (1971).

41. See, e.g., Sanchez v. San Diego, 483 F.3d 965, 966 (9th Cir. 2007); Wildauer v. Frederick County, 993 F.2d 369, 380 (4th Cir. 1993).

42. See *Griffin*, 483 U.S. at 880 (administrative needs of probation system justify suspicionless searches of probationers' homes); *T.L.O.*, 469 U.S. at 340 (reasonableness standard governs searches of students' persons and effects by public school authorities); *Skinner*, 489 U.S. at 612 (neither probable cause nor individualized suspicion is necessary for mandatory drug testing of railway employees).

43. Florida v. Jardines, 569 U.S. 1, 10 (2013).

44. Ocen, "New Racially Restrictive Covenant," 1565.

45. *Sanchez*, 483 F.3d at 972.

46. Doe v. Woodard, 912 F.3d 1278, 1285 (10th Cir. 2019); Andrews v. Hickman Cty., 700 F.3d 845, 855 (6th Cir. 2012); Michael C. v. Gresbach, 526 F.3d 1008, 1020 (7th Cir. 2008).

47. Kaba and Ritchie, *No More Police*, 118.

48. Sifuentes and Ross, "21-Year Fight."

49. Treatment Advocacy Center, "Grading the States."

50. Treatment Advocacy Center, "Grading the States."

51. Treatment Advocacy Center, "Grading the States."

52. McCabe v. Life-Line Ambulance Services, 77 F.3d 540, 542–43 (1st. Cir. 1996).

53. *McCabe*, 77 F.3d at 546.

54. Morgan, "Psychiatric Holds," 1427–30.

55. Primus, "Disentangling Administrative Searches," 256–57.

56. May v. City of Nahunta, 846 F.3d 1320, 1329 (11th Cir. 2017).

57. *May*, 846 F.3d at 1329.

58. United States v. Robinson, 414 U.S. 218 (1973).

59. Jina-Pettersen, "Fear, Neglect, Coercion."

60. Jina-Pettersen, "Fear, Neglect, Coercion."

61. Jina-Pettersen, "Fear, Neglect, Coercion."

62. Jina-Pettersen, "Fear, Neglect, Coercion."

63. Mind Freedom International, "Fighting Back."

64. Morgan, "Psychiatric Holds," 1398.

65. Kaba and Ritchie, *No More Police*, 122.

66. Kaba and Ritchie, *No More Police*, 122.

67. Christopherson, "Community Caretaking Function."

68. Tinius v. Carrol Cnty. Sheriff Dept., 321 F. Supp. 2d 1065, 1069–70 (N.D. Iowa 2004).

69. Gallegos v. City of Colorado Springs, 114 F.3d 1024, 1030 (10th Cir. 1997).

70. United States v. Harris, 795 F.3d 820, 826 (8th Cir. 2015).

71. Mitchell v. City of Los Angeles, 2017 U.S. Dist. LEXIS 224463, at *4 (C.D. Cal. Sep. 25, 2017).

72. Paulas, "Encampment Sweeps."

73. Paulas, "Encampment Sweeps."
74. Paulas, "Encampment Sweeps."
75. McKenna v. Edgell, 617 F.3d 432, 438 (6th Cir. 2010).
76. New York v. Burger, 482 U.S. 691 (1987).
77. Virginia v. Moore, 553 U.S. 164, 169.
78. *Moore*, 553 U.S. at 169.
79. Dressler, *Understanding Criminal Procedure*, 296.
80. Dressler, *Understanding Criminal Procedure*, 296.
81. *Moore*, 553 U.S. at 174.
82. *Moore*, 553 U.S. at 180; see also Kerr, "Cross-Enforcement," 501.
83. Litigants who fail to assert a Fourth Amendment claim may still proceed with Due Process claims under the Fifth or Fourteenth Amendment. However, those claims will be assessed under an incredibly deferential "conscience shocking" standard. See Johnson v. Newburgh Enlarged Sch. Dist., 239 F.3d 246, 252 (2d Cir. 2001).
84. See Sato, "Social Workers."
85. Agrawal, "Majority of Police"; Department of Justice, "Importance of Police-Community Relationships."
86. Fields, "Weaponized Racial Fear," 970.
87. See United States v. Matlock, 415 U.S. 164, 180 (1974) ("In their understandable zeal to ferret out crime, officers are less likely to possess the detachment and neutrality with which the constitutional rights of the suspect must be viewed").
88. Social Service Workers United–Chicago, "NASW Is Failing Us."

CHAPTER 4. BRUTALITY WITHOUT POLICE

1. Hart, "Tossed Medicine, Delayed Housing."
2. Jina-Pettersen, "Fear, Neglect, Coercion."
3. Swenson, "Teens Tied Down."
4. Vera Institute, "Redefining Public Safety Initiative." See also C. Thompson, "Sending Unarmed Responders" ("There are than 100 response teams nationwide, but experts say more research on their impact is needed").
5. Tennessee v. Garner, 471 U.S. 1 (1985).
6. Graham v. Connor, 490 U.S. 386, 390 (1989).
7. Fletcher, "Erasing the Thin Blue Line," 1465; cf. Leider, "State's Monopoly of Force," 48 ("Even if a state has a monopoly on the legitimate use of violence, nothing inherently requires state officers to exercise the state's monopoly of force").
8. See JL v. N.M. Dep't of Health, 165 F. Supp. 3d 996, 1042 (D.N.M. 2015), citing Ingraham v. Wright, 430 U.S. 651, 673 n.42 (1977), and New Jersey v. T.L.O., 469 U.S. 325, 335 (1985).

9. *JL*, 165 F. Supp. 3d at 1942.

10. United States v. Attson, 900 F.2d 1427, 1442 (9th Cir. 1990).

11. Transcript of Oral Argument at 5–7, United States v. Lanier, 520 U.S. 259 (1997) (No. 95–1717), 1997 WL 7587 (quoting Justice Kennedy's questions).

12. Ostrowsky, "#MeToo's Unseen Frontier," 267; Fontana v. Haskin, 262 F.3d 871, 882 (9th Cir. 2001).

13. Ostrowsky, "#MeToo's Unseen Frontier," 259.

14. United States v. Langer, 958 F.2d 522, 522–23 (2d Cir. 1992).

15. Poe v. Leonard, 282 F.3d 123, 130 (2d Cir. 2002).

16. Montanez v. City of Syracuse, 2019 WL 315058, at *6–8 (Jan. 23, 2019).

17. *Montanez*, 2019 WL 315058, at *15.

18. *Montanez*, 2019 WL 315058, at *15 ((citing Jones v. Wellham, 104 F.3d 620, 628 (4th Cir. 1997) (holding that officer rape of plaintiff, who was neither a suspect nor an arrestee, implicated substantive due process and not the Fourth Amendment)); see also United States v. Morris, 494 F. App'x 574, 581 (6th Cir. 2012) (casting doubt on Fourth Amendment's applicability when the officer "did not detain [the rape victim] for any legitimate law enforcement purposes" when he raped her several hours after a traffic stop); D.G. v. City of Las Cruces, No. 14-CV-368, 2015 WL 13665421, at *7 (D.N.M. Mar. 25, 2015) ("Cases in our Circuit have yet to consider the application of the Fourth Amendment to a sexual assault by an officer on a person not in custody in the typical, criminal context").

19. Martinez v. City of Los Angeles, 2021 U.S. Dist. LEXIS 146030, *23 (C.D. Cal. 2021).

20. Peete v. Metropolitan Government of Nashville and Davidson County, 486 F.3d 217, 219 (6th Cir. 2007); see also Pena v. Givens, 637 Fed.Appx. 775, 790 (5th Cir. 2015).

21. *Peete*, 486 F.3d at 222.

22. *Peete*, 486 F.3d at 222 (No seizure occurred because "the paramedics acted in order to provide medical aid" and did not act "to enforce the law, deter, or incarcerate").

23. *Peete*, 486 F.3d at 240.

24. *Pena*, 637 Fed.Appx. at 790.

25. *Pena*, 637 Fed.Appx. at 790.

26. Pino v. E.P. Higgs, 75 F.3d 1461, 1467 (10th Cir. 1996).

27. Scott v. Hern, 216 F.3d 897, 910 (10th Cir. 2000).

28. Compare *Pino*, 75 F.3d at 1468 (applying the Fourth Amendment to police officers seizing a mentally ill person for their own benefit), with *Hern*, 216 F.3d at 910 (applying Due Process Clause to psychiatrist diagnosis that led to involuntary commitment); see also Cantrell v. City of Murphy, 666 F.3d 911, 923 (5th Cir. 2012) (applying Fourth Amendment's probable-cause standard to police officers who detained mentally ill man who posed a substantial risk of harm to

himself"); *Pena*, 637 F. App'x. at 780 (granting qualified immunity to psychiatric technicians in lethal force restraint case because no controlling authority established that their conduct amounted to a seizure under the Fourth Amendment).

29. National Alliance on Mental Illness, "Crisis Intervention Team (CIT) Programs."

30. D. Dix, "'I Tell What I Have Seen.'"

31. Roth, "Truth about Deinstitutionalization."

32. Fariba and Gupta, "Involuntary Commitment."

33. Lake v. Cameron, 267 F. Supp. 155 (D.D.C. 1966); O'Connor v. Donaldson, 422 U.S. 563 (1975); Addington v. Texas, 441 U.S. 418 (1978).

34. Fields, "Debunking the Stranger-in-the-Bushes Myth," 471–72.

35. It is too simplistic to simply adopt the "Penrose hypothesis" that there is an inverse relationship between psychiatric inpatient numbers and the prison population. This hypothesis suggests that if more mentally ill people were in psychiatric hospitals, fewer people would be in prison. Exploding prison populations in the United States owe more to aggressive drug enforcement, draconian mandatory minimum sentences, and overzealous policing of minor "broken windows" social disorder. The mentally ill just happen to be swept up into this system of overcriminalization and mass incarceration. See Roth, "Truth about Deinstitutionalization."

36. O'Connor, "Los Angeles Is Locking Up More People."

37. Riggins v. Nevada, 504 U.S. 127, 135 (1992).

38. *Riggins*, 504 U.S. 127 at 135.

39. Brown v. Dias, 2019 U.S. Dist. LEXIS 73811, at *53 (C.D. Cal. Mar. 21, 2019).

40. *Brown*, 2019 U.S. Dist. LEXIS 73811, at *53.

41. Méndez, *Report of the Special Rapporteur.*

42. Méndez, *Report of the Special Rapporteur.*

43. Obasogie and Zaret, "Medical Professionals," 39.

44. Obasogie and Zaret, "Medical Professionals," 39.

45. Obasogie, "Excited Delirium," 1572; Sow, "Protect and Serve," 752.

46. *Peete*, 486 F.3d at 230.

47. *Peete*, 486 F.3d at 230.

48. *Graham*, 490 U.S. at 394.

49. United States v. Mendenhall, 446 U.S. 544 (1980).

50. Fields, "Protest Policing," 360.

51. Fields, "Protest Policing," 361.

52. Dundon v. Kirchmeier, 2017 U.S. Dist. LEXIS 222696, at 58 (D.N.D. Feb. 7, 2017).

53. See *Dundon*, 2017 U.S. Dist. LEXIS 222696, at *59 ("The Plaintiffs have neither alleged they were arrested or detained by law enforcement officials nor

alleged they were informed by law enforcement officers they were not free to leave and walk away").

54. Edrei v. New York, 254 F. Supp. 3d 565, 574 (S.D.N.Y. 2017).

55. Paradis, "Carpe Demonstratores," 338.

56. Cohen, "Cities Are Asking."

57. U.S. News & World Report, "Most Expensive Places."

58. See City of San Diego, "Safe Sleeping Program"; Encinas, "Inside Look"; Halverstadt, "San Diego's Homeless Response."

59. Dulaney, "Mayor Gloria's Push."

60. Halverstadt, "San Diego's Homeless Response."

61. Paradis, "Carpe Demonstratores," 334.

62. See *Poe*, 282 F.3d at 136; *Scott*, 216 F.3d at 910.

63. See Cottrell v. Caldwell, 85 F.3d (11th Cir. 1996) 1480, 1490; Sanchez v. Figueroa, 996 F. Supp. 143, 150 (D. Puerto Rico Feb. 23, 1998) ("Claims of excessive force outside of the context of a seizure are analyzed under substantive due process principles").

64. See Hall v. Tawney, 621 F.2d 607, 613 (4th Cir. 1980).

65. U.S. Const. Amend. XIV.

66. DePoutot v. Raffaelly, 424 F.3d 112, 125 (1st Cir. 2005).

67. Chapman, "Due Process," 1718.

68. Ostrowsky, "#MeToo's Unseen Frontier," 279n125; Chapman, "Due Process," 1721n280 ("The Due Process Clause is tucked into a compound sentence without a proper subject").

69. See United States v. Guidry, 456 F.3d 493, 506 n.8 (5th Cir. 2006); Urbonya, "Public School Officials' Use," 4.

70. Fraser v. Pa. State Univ., 654 F. Supp. 3d 443, 457 (M.D. Pa. Feb. 7, 2023); Kadakia v. Rutgers, 633 F. App'x 83, 87 (3d Cir. 2015); Hodge v. Jones, 31 F.3d 157, 167 (4th Cir. 1994).

71. *Hodge*, 31 F.3d at 167.

72. Hawkins v. Holloway, 316 F.3d 777, 785-86 (8th Cir. 2003) (describing allegations of sexual molestation as "offensive behavior in the context of junior high locker room style male horseplay," but *not* "behavior that the Constitution prohibits under the rubric of contemporary conscience shocking substantive due process").

73. State v. Brown, 550 So.2d 922, 924 (1989); Balmer, "Some Thoughts on Proportionality," 800; Kamisar, "'Comparative Reprehensibility,'" 15.

74. Ostrowsky, "#MeToo's Unseen Frontier," 277; Decker v. Tinnel, 2005 WL 3501705, at *7 (N.D. Ind. Dec. 20, 2005); County of Sacramento v. Lewis, 523 U.S. 833, 862 (1998).

75. American Constitution Society, "Diversity of the Federal Bench"; Iuliano, "New Diversity Crisis," 248.

76. American Constitution Society, "Diversity of the Federal Bench."

77. Alexander v. Deangelo, 329 F.3d 912, 915–17 (7th Cir. 2003).

78. *Alexander*, 329 F.3d at 917.

79. *Alexander*, 329 F.3d at 918.

80. *Graham*, 490 U.S. at 397.

81. *Alexander*, 329 F.3d at 917.

82. Frankel, "Regulating Privatized Government," 1453.

83. Flagg Bros. v. Brooks, 436 U.S. 149, 163–64 (1978); Lugar v. Edmonson Oil Co., 457 U.S. 922, 936–37 (1982).

84. J.K. ex rel. R.K. v. Dillenberg, 836 F. Supp. 694, 699 (D. Ariz. 1993).

85. Ortega v. Brock, 501 F. Supp. 2d 1337, 1347 (M.D. Ala. Aug. 7, 2007).

86. *Ortega*, 501 F. Supp. 2d at 1347.

87. Harmon, "Legal Remedies," 33.

88. Harmon, "Legal Remedies"; 42 U.S.C. § 1988.

89. Herman, "Beyond Parity," 1083; cf. Reinart, "New Federalism," 766.

90. Herman, "Beyond Parity," 1083.

91. City of Los Angeles v. Lyons, 461 U.S. 95, 105 (1983).

92. Kindy, "Insurers Force Change."

93. Kindy, "Insurers Force Change."

94. Schwartz, *Shielded*, 112–35; Baude, "Is Qualified Immunity Unlawful?," 82; Hassel, "Excessive Reasonableness," 118 ("The qualified immunity doctrine . . . has metastasized into an almost absolute defense to all but the most outrageous conduct").

95. Baude, "Is Qualified Immunity Unlawful?," 82.

96. Hassel, "Excessive Reasonableness," 118.

97. Thompson v. Cope, 900 F.3d 414, 422 (7th Cir. 2018).

98. *Thompson*, 900 F.3d at 422; Estate of Barnwell v. Roane Cnty., 2016 U.S. Dist. LEXIS 144359, at *7 (E.D. Tenn. Jun. 16, 2016).

99. Ala. Code 197, § 6-5-338(a).

100. Harmon, "Legal Remedies," 35; Monell v. Dep't. of Soc. Servs., 436 U.S. 658, 690–92 (1978).

101. Harmon, "Legal Remedies," 35.

102. Matthiesen, Wickert, & Lehrer, SC, "Municipal/County/Local Governmental Immunity."

CHAPTER 5. A SAFER PUBLIC SAFETY

1. T. Brown, "When Doctors Become Cops."

2. T. Brown, "When Doctors Become Cops."

3. Obasogie and Zaret, "Medical Professionals," 51.

4. Obasogie and Zaret, "Medical Professionals," 51.

5. Obasogie and Zaret, "Medical Professionals," 65.

6. Obasogie and Zaret, "Medical Professionals," 65.

7. Obasogie and Zaret, "Medical Professionals," 55.

8. Obasogie and Zaret, "Medical Professionals," 62.

9. Obasogie and Zaret, "Medical Professionals," 65.

10. County of Riverside v. Laughlin, 500 U.S. 44, 58 (1991); Gerstein v. Pugh, 420 U.S. 103, 120 (1975).

11. Hudson v. Palmer, 468 U.S. 517, 526 (1984).

12. Paulas, "Encampment Sweeps"; Human Rights Watch, "You Have to Move!"

13. Paulas, "Encampment Sweeps."

14. Paulas, "Encampment Sweeps."

15. Paulas, "Encampment Sweeps."

16. Fixler, "Police-Social Work Collaboration."

17. Fixler, "Police-Social Work Collaboration."

18. See Chamlou, "Growing Movement."

19. Chamlou, "Growing Movement."

20. Chamlou, "Growing Movement."

21. Sato, "Social Workers."

22. Sato, "Social Workers."

23. Sato, "Social Workers."

24. Sato, "Social Workers."

25. Chamlou, "Growing Movement."

26. Sato, "Social Workers."

27. Hermannson, "Firewalls."

28. Pittman and Pittman, "How Brett Favre Got $6 Million."

29. Dilanian and Strickler, "She Won a Pulitzer."

30. Kaur, "What Studies Reveal."

31. McCarthy, "U.S. Civilians Own."

32. Keane, "Americans Charted Record Book Year."

33. District of Columbia v. Heller, 554 U.S. 570 (2008); McDonald v. City of Chicago, 561 U.S. 742, 784–85 (2010); cf. Charles, "Securing Gun Rights" ("But focusing too narrowly on [the Second Amendment] neglects the vast and expansive nonconstitutional protections for gun rights in contemporary America").

34. Abt, "Violent Crime" ("Gun violence isn't spread evenly. Instead, it clusters around relatively few city blocks, among small networks of high-risk people"); Ferguson, "Big Data" ("Researchers can predict their likelihood of being a victim or perpetrator of gun violence using big data metrics, including . . . past experience with victims of gun violence and gang connections").

35. See Crann and Burks, "Now Better Trained"; Fields, "Fourth Amendment without Police," 1042.

36. Gallion, "'Call-In' Offers Aid."

37. Gallion, "'Call-In' Offers Aid."

38. Gallion, "'Call-In' Offers Aid."

39. Gallion, "'Call-In' Offers Aid."

40. Gallion, "'Call-In' Offers Aid."

41. Gallion, "'Call-In' Offers Aid."

42. See Jaqua, "Policing the Police," 367; cf. Woods, "Policing, Danger Narratives," 662.

43. Debusmann, "Why Do So Many."

44. Kirkpatrick, "Pulled Over."

45. Kirkpatrick, "Pulled Over"; see also Woods, "Policing, Danger Narratives," 665.

46. Kirkpatrick, "Pulled Over."

47. Kirkpatrick, "Pulled Over."

48. Kirkpatrick, "Pulled Over."

49. Kirkpatrick, "Pulled Over."

50. Kirkpatrick, "Pulled Over"; see also Stein, "Before the Final Frame"; C. Lee, "Officer-Created Jeopardy" 1407–8 (describing instances where officers put themselves in danger unnecessarily during traffic stops and later used force to protect themselves).

51. Kirkpatrick, "Pulled Over"; Cooper, "Cop Fragility," 640.

52. Nawaz, "Study Shows First Words."

53. Kirkpatrick, "Pulled Over."

54. Kirkpatrick, "Pulled Over"; YouTube, "Police Chase Shootout"; KGET, "KCSO Releases Summary"; YouTube, "Audio, Video."

55. United States v. Cruz-Rivera, 14 F.4th 32, 40 (1st Cir. 2021) (finding that officers can prolong a traffic stop beyond the mission of the stop if there is reasonable suspicion of criminal activity); Rodriguez v. United States, 575 U.S. 348, 369 (2015) (same); State v. Barrow, 989 N.W.2d 682, 690 (Minn. 2023) ("Under the automobile exception, police may search a car without a warrant, including closed containers in that car, if there is probable cause to believe the search will result in a discovery of evidence or contraband").

56. United States v. Jackson, 682 Fed. Appx. 86, 100 (3d Cir. 2017) ("It is well settled that the smell of marijuana alone can be enough to establish probable cause for an arrest").

57. Slobogin, "Testilying," 1040; Capers, "Crime, Legitimacy, and Testilying," 840; J. Goldstein, "Officers Said They Smelled Pot" ("'The time has come to reject the canard of marijuana emanating from nearly every vehicle subject to a traffic stop,' Judge April Newbauer wrote").

58. DuBoff, "Asset Forfeiture Scheme."

59. Tyler Burgauer, interview by author, September 22, 2023.

60. Burgauer, interview.

CHAPTER 6. A CONSTITUTION THAT SERVES
"WE THE PEOPLE"

1. Escobedo v. Illinois, 378 U.S. 478, 490 (1964).
2. T. Jacobi and Berlin, "Supreme Irrelevance," 2033.
3. T. Jacobi and Berlin, "Supreme Irrelevance"; Stoughton, "How the Fourth Amendment Frustrates," 521.
4. See Virginia v. Moore, 553 U.S. 164 (2008).
5. Fields, "Fourth Amendment without Police," 1086–90.
6. See United States v. Attson, 900 F.2d 427 (9th Cir. 1990); Scott v. Hern, 216 F.3d 897 (10th Cir. 2000); McKenna v. Edgell, 617 F.3d 432 (6th Cir. 2010).
7. Dubbs v. Head Start, Inc., 336 F.3d 1194, 1206 (10th Cir. 2003).
8. See Baughman, "Subconstitutional Checks," 1108 ("Administrative policies decide, in practice, the scope and bounds of the power to search. This may not have been the Framers' vision, but it is increasingly what search and seizure looks like on the ground"); cf. Solove, "Digital Dossiers," 1107 ("Robust Fourth Amendment protection need not be inconsistent with the administrative state, as a significant portion of modern administrative regulation concerns business and commercial activities which lack Fourth Amendment rights equivalent to those guaranteed to individuals").
9. Loor, "Tear Gas + Water Hoses," 831–32.
10. Olmstead v. United States, 277 U.S. 438, 463 (1928) (stating that the "well-known historical purpose" of the Fourth Amendment "was to prevent the use of governmental force to search a man's house, his person, his papers, and his effects, and to prevent their seizure against his will"); United States v. Martinez-Fuerte, 428 U.S. 543, 554 (1976) ("The Fourth Amendment imposes limits to prevent arbitrary and oppressive interference by enforcement officials with the privacy and personal security of individuals").
11. Fields, "Fourth Amendment without Police," 1069–70.
12. Fields, "Fourth Amendment without Police," 1066–67.
13. Moore, 553 U.S. at 178.
14. Renan, "Fourth Amendment," 1080.
15. Kerr, "Cross-Enforcement" 495.
16. Fields, "Fourth Amendment without Police," 1085 ("For an amendment driven by value-laden reasonableness balancing inquiries, the lawfulness of an actor's search or seizure is relevant to the determination that the conduct was or was not reasonable").
17. Renan, "Fourth Amendment," 1071.
18. Steiker, "Second Thoughts," 824 ("The construction of the Fourth Amendment's 'reasonableness' clause should properly change over time to accommodate constitutional purposes more general than the Framers' specific intentions").

19. Zuchel v. City of Denver, 997 F.2d 730, 739 (10th Cir. 1993) (citing expert testimony on de-escalation best practice).

20. Garrett and Stoughton, "Tactical Fourth Amendment," 219–20; see also Police Executive Research Forum (PERF), "Use of Force," 2.

21. Police Executive Research Forum (PERF), "Use of Force" (one response "to the apparent disconnect between sound police practices and Fourth Amendment doctrine is to dismiss court-made law as out of date and ill advised").

22. Garrett and Stoughton, "Tactical Fourth Amendment," 298.

23. Mattos v. Agarano, 661 F.3d 433, 451 (9th Cir. 2011) (en banc).

24. Casey v. City of Federal Heights, 509 F.3d 1278, 1285 (10th Cir. 2007).

25. Steiker, "Second Thoughts," 824n20; Donohue, "Original Fourth Amendment," 1328 (charting the history of the Fourth Amendment and concluding that the Fourth Amendment entails "a general protection against [the] government," not just police).

26. Garrett and Stoughton, "Tactical Fourth Amendment," 220.

27. Kerr, "Cross-Enforcement," 495.

28. Kerr, "Cross-Enforcement," 495.

29. Rakas v. Illinois, 439 U.S., 128, 135 (1978) (denying ability of parties "to raise vicarious Fourth Amendment claims"); Alderman v. United States, 394 U.S. 165, 180 (1969) ("We adhere to the general rule that Fourth Amendment rights are personal rights which, like some other constitutional guarantees, may not be vicariously asserted").

30. Rakas, 439 U.S. at 135.

31. Rakas, 439 U.S. at 140 ("Having rejected petitioners' target theory the question is whether the challenged search and seizure violated the Fourth Amendment rights of a criminal defendant who seeks to exclude the evidence").

32. Dressler, Understanding Criminal Procedure, 295.

33. I recognize that whether someone has "standing" to assert a claim differs from whether that claim applies to particular conduct. But analytically, the Supreme Court's substantive Fourth Amendment standing doctrine, which differs from Article III standing, provides a useful lens through which to view the failures of excessive force jurisprudence. Fourth Amendment standing in search law cares about granting redress to the person harmed by the search. Yet Fourth Amendment excessive force law denies redress to persons harmed by seizures even when the conduct otherwise would give rise to a claim.

34. Hoard v. Hartman, 904 F.3d 780, 788 (9th Cir. 2018) ("Put simply, officer intent serves as the core dividing factor between constitutional and unconstitutional applications of force").

35. Donohue, "Original Fourth Amendment, "1328.

36. Marshall v. Barlow's, Inc., 436 U.S. 307, 312–13.

37. Maclin, "Is Obtaining an Arrestee's DNA," 125.

38. Maclin, "Is Obtaining an Arrestee's DNA," 126.

39. Ferguson v. City of Charleston, 532 U.S. 67, 70 (2000).

40. *Ferguson*, 532 U.S. at 73.

41. *Ferguson*, 532 U.S. at 73.

42. *Ferguson*, 532 U.S. at 73.

43. Langley v. City of San Luis Obispo, 2022 U.S. Dist. LEXIS 96169, at *8 (C.D. Cal. Feb. 7, 2022) ("Despite this shortage [of shelter beds], the City has continued to strictly enforce ordinances to prevent unhoused residents from sheltering in the City's open spaces and streets, effectively criminalizing homelessness"); Cobine v. City of Eureka, 2016 U.S. Dist. LEXIS 58228, at *6 (N.D. Cal. May 2, 2016) ("Because the City has threatened criminal prosecution in order to enforce the notice to vacate and enforce the anti-camping ordinance, Plaintiffs contend that Eureka is effectively criminalizing homelessness").

44. Houston Police Department, "Crisis Call Diversion Program"; Friedman, "Disaggregating the Policing Function," 988.

45. Fields, "Fourth Amendment without Police," 1072–73 ("Whether nonpolice agencies have impermissibly extensive entanglement with law enforcement also should depend on whether the programmatic practice of the agency invites a criminal investigation, regardless of the stated or actual purpose").

46. See Chamlou, "Growing Movement"; Obasogie and Zaret, "Medical Professionals," 65 (discussing the need for clear firewalls between medical professionals and police to protect sensitive health information from being used in a criminal prosecution); T. Brown, "When Doctors Become Cops," 1.

47. Obasogie and Zaret, "Medical Professionals," 51.

48. See Edmond v. City of Indianapolis, 531 U.S. 32, 38, 45 (2000) (striking down suspicionless vehicle checkpoint with the noncriminal stated purpose of "interdict[ing] illegal drugs" and preventing the introduction of drugs into the city, but which in practice resulted in the arrest and prosecution of all motorists found in possession of illegal drugs).

49. Prado v. City of Berkeley, 2024 U.S. Dist. LEXIS 139836, at *6 (Aug. 6, 2024).

50. *Prado*, 2024 U.S. Dist. LEXIS 139836, at *8.

51. *Prado*, 2024 U.S. Dist. LEXIS 139836, at *8.

CONCLUSION

1. Abramson, "Building Mental Health."

2. Abramson, "Building Mental Health"; Shults, "What Officers and the Public Are Thinking"; Waters, "Calling Mental Health Workers."

3. Rahman, "Overwhelming Support" (describing poll finding significant increases in number of people who believe nonpolice agents should respond to

mental health, crises, homelessness issues, and unarmed suspects following George Floyd's murder).

4. For an overview of the varieties of meanings embedded in "defund the police," see Yglesias, "Growing Calls"; Searcy, "What Would Efforts to Defund"; Brewster, "Defund the Police Movement."

5. Ramirez, "Obama Said."

6. Concha, "Time Has Come"; Spoerre, "Missouri Republicans Push Bill."

7. B. Newman, Reny, and Merolla, "Race, Prejudice."

8. Goodman, "A Year after 'Defund'" ("The abrupt reversals have come in response to rising levels of crime, the exodus of police officers and political pressures"); Reuters, "Minneapolis Restores Police Budget" ("The 'defund the police' movement did not lead to much actual action in the end because 'there wasn't the political will, really, to do so'"); Mays, "New York Adopts" (detailing $200 million NYPD budget increase, one year after pledged cuts to the NYPD budget "failed" to materialize); Rao, "Between Defund and Defend" ("As crime rose, the mayor increased the Los Angeles Police Department's budget 3% in April").

9. Wald and Kendall-Taylor, "Keep the Ideas."

10. Wald and Kendall-Taylor, "Keep the Ideas"; Saletan, "'Defund the Police.'"

Bibliography

Aaron, Rick. "'Why Did They Shoot Me?' 14-Year-Old Linden Cameron Continues His Long Road to Recovery." *ABC4*, April 29, 2021. www.abc4 .com/news/why-did-they-shoot-me-14-year-old-linden-cameron-continues -his-long-road-to-recovery/.

Abraham, Roshan. "Why Are So Many Cities' Homeless Policies Punitive?" *Next City*, June 22, 2023. https://nextcity.org/urbanist-news/why-are-so-many- cities-homeless-policies-punitive.

Abramson, Ashley. "Building Mental Health into Emergency Responses." *Monitor on Psychology* (American Psychological Association), July 1, 2021. www.apa.org/monitor/2021/07/emergency-responses.

Abt, Thomas. "Violent Crime in the U.S. Is Surging. But We Know What to Do about It." *Time*, January 12, 2022. https://time.com/6138650/violent-crime- us-surging-what-to-do/.

ACLU of South Carolina. "New Report Documents Staggering Racial Dispari- ties in Charleston Policing Arrests and Citations." October 28, 2021. www .aclusc.org/en/news/new-report-documents-staggering-racial-disparities- charleston-policing-arrests-and-citations.

Adams, Char. "Experts Stress That More Training Won't Eradicate Police Violence." *NBC News*, April 15, 2021. www.nbcnews.com/news/nbcblk /experts-stress-more-training-won-t-eradicate-police-violence- n1264092.

Adkins, Matthew. "Homelessness in America: Statistics, Analysis, and Trends." Security.org, September 26, 2024. www.security.org/resources/homeless-statistics/.

Agrawal, Nina. "Majority of Police in the U.S. Say Their Jobs Have Gotten Harder." *Los Angeles Times*, January 11, 2017. www.latimes.com/nation/la-na-pew-report-police-20170111-story.html.

Akbar, Amna. "An Abolitionist Horizon for (Police) Reform." *California Law Review* 108, no. 6 (2020): 1781–1846.

Alexander, Michelle. *The New Jim Crow: Mass Incarceration in the Age of Colorblindness*. New York: New Press, 2010.

American College of Obstetricians and Gynecologists. "Opposition to Criminalization of Individuals during Pregnancy and the Postpartum Period." www.acog.org/clinical-information/policy-and-position-statements/statements-of-policy/2020/opposition-criminalization-of-individuals-pregnancy-and-postpartum-period#:~:text=ACOG%20believes%20that%20it%20is,and%20the%20postpartum%20period11.

American Constitution Society. "Diversity of the Federal Bench." January 25, 2024. www.acslaw.org/judicial-nominations/diversity-of-the-federal-bench/.

American Psychological Association. "Revision of Ethics Code Standard 3.04." January 24, 2024. www.apa.org/ethics/code/standard-304.

Amnesty International. "Criminalizing Pregnancy: Policing Pregnant Women Who Use Drugs in the USA." www.amnesty.org/en/wp-content/uploads/2021/05/AMR5162032017ENGLISH.pdf.

Anderson, Claire. "'No Regrets!' Shocking Video Shows Firefighter Punching Handcuffed Patient." *Express*, December 15, 2022. www.express.co.uk/news/us/1709918/miami-firefighter-suspended-Robert-Webster-punch-patient-video-dxus.

Anderson, Nic F., and Dalia Faheid. "Bodycam Video Shows Police Fatally Shooting New Jersey Woman Whose Family Told 911 She Was Having a Mental Health Crisis." *CNN*, August 17, 2024. www.cnn.com/2024/08/17/us/new-jersey-victoria-lee-police-shooting/index.html.

Armacost, Barbara E. "Police Shootings: Is Accountability the Enemy of Prevention?" *Ohio State Law Journal* 80, no. 5 (2019): 907–86.

Asher, Abe. "Unnecessary Traffic Stops by Police Make Public Safety Worse." *Jacobin*, March 6, 2023. https://jacobin.com/2023/03/public-safety-police-reform-traffic-stops-violence-racism.

Asher, Jeff, and Ben Horwitz. "How Do the Police Actually Spend Their Time?" *New York Times*, June 19, 2020. www.nytimes.com/2020/06/19/upshot/unrest-police-time-violent-crime.html.

Asirvatham, Rohit. "Are Constitutional Rights Enough? An Empirical Assessment of Racial Bias in Police Stops." *Northwestern University Law Review* 116, no. 6 (2022): 1481–1545.

Associated Press. "LAPD Funding Slashed by $150M, Reducing Number of Officers." July 1, 2020. https://apnews.com/3ad962eb78e30975354f60 36c6451022.

Atlanta Police Department. "APD Officer Uses Crisis Intervention Training to Help Man Experiencing Mental Crisis." YouTube, February 26, 2021. www .youtube.com/watch?v=t2RJSn6zlLk.

Bakare, Lanre. "Angela Davis: 'We Knew That the Role of the Police Was to Protect White Supremacy.'" *The Guardian*, June 15, 2020. www.theguardian .com/us-news/2020/jun/15/angela-davis-on-george-floyd-as-long-as-the -violence-of-racism-remains-no-one-is-safe.

Balko, Radley. *Rise of the Warrior Cop: The Militarization of America's Police Forces*. New York: PublicAffairs, 2018.

Balmer, Thomas. "Some Thoughts on Proportionality." *Oregon Law Review* 87, no. 3 (2008): 783–818.

Barr, Luke. "New York City Moves to End Qualified Immunity, Making It 1st City in the US to Do So." *ABC News*, March 29, 2021. https://abcnews.go .com/Politics/york-city-moves-end-qualified-immunity-making-1st /story?id=76752098#.

Bates, Josiah. "Much Like the Victims They Try to Help, Gun Violence Prevention Workers Have Scars." *Time*, February 17, 2022. https://time .com/6148263/gun-violence-prevention-workers-trauma/.

Baude, William. "Is Qualified Immunity Unlawful?" *California Law Review* 106, no. 1 (2018): 45–90.

Baughman, Shima Baradaran. "Subconstitutional Checks." *Notre Dame Law Review* 92, no. 3 (2017): 1071–1140.

Baughman, Shima Baradaran. "Rebalancing the Fourth Amendment." *Georgetown Law Journal* 102, no. 1 (2013): 1–58.

Becton, Charles. "The Drug Courier Profile: All Seems Infected That th' Infected Spy, as All Looks Yellow to the Jaundic'd Eye." *North Carolina Law Review* 65, no. 4 (1987): 417–80.

Beekman, Daniel. "Seattle City Council Homes In on Police Department Cuts as Defunding Proponents and Skeptics Mobilize." *Seattle Times*, July 18, 2020. www.seattletimes.com/seattle-news/politics/seattle-city-council-homes- in-on-police-department-cuts-as-defunding-proponents-and-opponents -mobilize/.

Bell, Monica. "Police Reform and the Dismantling of Legal Estrangement." *Yale Law Journal* 126, no. 7 (2017): 2054–2150.

Bishop, Elizabeth Tsai, Brook Hopkins, Chijindu Obiofuma, and Felix Owusu. "Racial Disparities in the Massachusetts Criminal System." Harvard Law School Criminal Justice Policy Program, September 9, 2020. https://hls .harvard.edu/wp-content/uploads/2022/08/Massachusetts-Racial -Disparity-Report-FINAL.pdf.

Bisram, Jennifer. "Bronx Community Calls for Accountability after Raul de la Cruz Was Shot by NYPD." *CBS News*, April 7, 2023. www.cbsnews.com /newyork/news/raul-de-la-cruz-nypd-shooting-the-bronx/.

Bratton, William J. *Broken Windows and Quality-of-Life Policing in New York City*. New York City Police Department, 2015. www.nyc.gov/html/nypd /downloads/pdf/analysis_and_planning/qol.pdf.

Breen, Thomas. "95.6% of Cops' Calls Don't Involve Violence." *New Haven Independent*, June 19, 2020. www.newhavenindependent.org/article /police_dispatch_stats.

Brewster, Jack. "The Defund the Police Movement Is Sweeping the Country— Here's What It Really Means." *Forbes*, June 10, 2020. www.forbes.com/sites /jackbrewster/2020/06/09/the-defund-the-police-movement-is-sweeping-the- country-heres-what-it-really-means/.

Brooks, Peter. *Troubling Confessions: Speaking Guilt in Law and Literature*. Chicago: University of Chicago Press, 2000.

Brooks, Rosa. "One Reason for Police Violence? Too Many Men with Badges." *Washington Post*, June 18, 2020. www.washingtonpost.com/outlook/2020 /06/18/women-police-officers-violence/.

Brown, Norrinda. "Black Liberty in Emergency." *Northwestern University Law Review* 118, no. 3 (2023): 689–754.

Brown, Tenielle. "When Doctors Become Cops." University of Utah College of Law Research Paper No. 566, January 2023. https://papers.ssrn.com/sol3 /papers.cfm?abstract_id=4346154.

Bruner, Bethany. "Ohio Social Worker Accused of Having Sexual Relationship with 13-Year-Old Client." *USA Today*, October 9, 2023. www.usatoday.com /story/news/nation/2023/10/09/ohio-social-worker-payton-shires-sex- crime-arrest/71117791007/.

Bui, Quoctrung, and Amanda Cox. "Surprising New Evidence Shows Bias in Police Use of Force but Not in Shootings." *New York Times*, July 11, 2016. www.nytimes.com/2016/07/12/upshot/surprising-new-evidence-shows-bias- in-police-use-of-force-but-not-in-shootings.html.

Bureau of Justice Statistics. "Contacts between Police and the Public, 2018— Statistical Tables." December 2020. https://bjs.ojp.gov/library/publications /contacts-between-police-and-public-2018-statistical-tables.

Butler, Paul. "The System Is Working the Way It Is Supposed To: The Limits of Criminal Justice Reform." *Georgetown Law Journal* 104, no. 6 (2016): 1419–78.

Capers, I. Bennett. "Crime, Legitimacy, and Testilying." *Indiana Law Journal* 83, no. 2 (2008): 835–80.

Caplan, Gerald M. "Questioning Miranda." *Vanderbilt Law Review* 38, no. 6 (1985): 1417–76.

Carbado, Devon. "Blue-on-Black Violence: A Provisional Model of Some of the Causes." *Georgetown Law Journal* 104, no. 1 (2016): 1479–1529.

Carbado, Devon, and Patrick Rock. "What Exposes African Americans to Police Violence?" *Harvard Civil Rights–Civil Liberties Law Review* 51 (2016): 159–87.

CBS News. "Anne Arundel County Police Department's Crisis Intervention Team Wins International Recognition." July 13, 2020. www.cbsnews.com /baltimore/news/anne-arundel-county-police-departments-crisis-intervention-team-wins-international-recognition/.

CBS News. "Los Angeles City Council Votes to Slash LAPD Budget by $150 Million." July 1, 2020. www.cbsnews.com/news/los-angeles-city-council -votes-to-slash-lapd-budget-by-150-million/.

CBS News. "Police Use Crisis Intervention Team to Respond to the Mentally Ill." YouTube, May 13, 2021. www.youtube.com/watch?v=ZQ8cSLFlB24.

Centers for Disease Control and Prevention. "Crisis + Emergency Risk Communication (CERC) in Response to an Opioid Overdose Event." www.cdc.gov /overdose-resources/pdf/Overdose-Event-Response_508.pdf.

Chalfin, Aaron, and Justin McCrary. "Are U.S. Cities Underpoliced? Theory and Evidence." *Review of Economics and Statistics* 100, no. 1 (2018): 172–77.

Chamlou, Nina. "The Growing Movement to Use Social Workers Instead of Police." Affordable Colleges, October 28, 2021. www.affordablecollegesonline .org/college-resource-center/news/social-workers-instead-of-police/.

Chaplain, Madeline. "Inefficacy of the Crisis Intervention Team Model." *Seattle University Undergraduate Research Journal* 7, no. 8 (2023): 22–30.

Chapman, Nathan. "Due Process as Separation of Powers." *Yale Law Journal* 121, no. 7 (2012): 1672–1807.

Charles, Jacob D. "Securing Gun Rights by Statute: The Right to Keep and Bear Arms outside the Constitution." *Michigan Law Review* 120, no. 4 (2022): 581–642.

Chatterjee, Rhitu. "New Law Creates 988 Hotline for Mental Health Emergencies." *NPR*, October 19, 2020. www.npr.org/sections/health-shots/2020 /10/19/925447354/new-law-creates-988-hotline-for-mental-health-emergencies.

Cheatham, Amelia, and Lindsay Maizland. "How Police Compare in Different Democracies." Council on Foreign Relations, March 22, 2022. www.cfr.org /backgrounder/how-police-compare-different-democracies.

Chohlas-Wood, Alex. "Identifying and Measuring Excessive and Discriminatory Policing." *University of Chicago Law Review* 89, no. 2 (2022): 441–75.

Christopherson, Nick. "Community Caretaking Function: A Doctrinal Overview." *Wake Forest Law Review*, September 21, 2021. www.wakeforestlawreview .com/2021/09/community-caretaking-function-a-doctrinal-overview/.

Citrus Heights Sentinel. "CHPD: Over 30% of Calls to Police Dept. Are Home-less-Related." July 21, 2016. https://citrusheightssentinel.com/2016/07/20/police-30-calls-chpd-homeless-related.

City of Berkeley. "General Information: Regular Meeting Agenda." July 14, 2020. www.cityofberkeley.info/Clerk/City_Council/2020/07_Jul/City_Council__07-14-2020_-_Regular_Meeting_Agenda.aspx.

City of Durham. "Crisis Intervention Team (CIT)." January 27, 2022. https://durhamnc.gov/3698/Crisis-Intervention-Team-CIT.

City of Eugene and White Bird Clinic. "Personal Services Contract." June 27, 2019. www.eugene-or.gov/DocumentCenter/View/56579/2019-03240-White-Bird-CAHOOTS-Services———SIGNED.

City of San Diego. "Safe Sleeping Program." January 22, 2024. www.sandiego.gov/homelessness-strategies-and-solutions/services/safe-sleeping-program.

City of San Diego Police Department. "Neighborhood Policing Division." Accessed November 27, 2024. www.sandiego.gov/police/services/neighborhood-policing-division.

Clancy, Thomas. "The Framers' Intent: John Adams, His Era, and the Fourth Amendment." *Indiana Law Journal* 86, no. 3 (2011): 979–1061.

Cohen, Rachel. "Cities Are Asking the Supreme Court for More Power to Clear Homeless Encampments." *Vox*, October 10, 2023. www.vox.com/2023/10/10/23905951/homeless-tent-encampments-grants-pass-martin-boise-unsheltered-housing.

Cohen, Rachel. "The Supreme Court Will Decide What Cities Can Do about Tent Encampments." *Vox*, January 12, 2024. www.vox.com/scotus/2024/1/12/24036307/supreme-court-scotus-tent-encampments-homeless.

Coleman, Emma. "Many States Prosecute Pregnant Women for Drug Use. New Research Says That's a Bad Idea." *Route Fifty*, December 5, 2019. www.route-fifty.com/management/2019/12/pregnant-women-drug-use/161701/.

Coleman, Justine. "Most Say Police Shouldn't Be Primary Responders for Mental Health Crises: NAMI Poll." *The Hill*, November 15, 2021. https://thehill.com/policy/healthcare/581556-majority-say-professionals-should-respond-to-mental-health-crises-instead.

Concha, Joe. "The Time Has Come: Defund the Hopelessly Biased NPR." *The Hill*, July 11, 2022. https://thehill.com/opinion/campaign/3551625-the-time-has-come-defund-the-hopelessly-biased-npr/.

Connecticut Post. "Police: Patient Assaulted by EMT in Ambulance." April 20, 2016. www.ems1.com/assault/articles/police-patient-assaulted-by-emt-in-ambulance-FjKFFw7ZU81Xqi1f/.

Cook, Foster. "The Burden of Criminal Justice Debt in Alabama." *TASC*, January 1, 2014. https://media.al.com/opinion/other/The%20Burden%20of%20Criminal%20Justice%20Debt%20in%20Alabama-%20Full%20Report.pdf.

Cooper, Frank Rudy. "Cop Fragility and Blue Lives Matter." *University of Illinois Law Review* 2020, no. 1 (2020): 621–62.

Correll, Joshua. "Across the Thin Blue Line: Police Officers and Racial Bias in the Decision to Shoot." *Journal of Personality and Social Psychology* 92, no. 6 (2007): 1006–23.

Costello, Darcy. "Emergency Calls with No Police Response? Louisville Gets Ready to Make It Happen." *Courier Journal*, October 13, 2021. www .courier-journal.com/story/news/politics/metro-government/2021/10/13 /louisville-pilot-could-mean-non-police-response-emergency-calls /8434314002/.

Crann, Tom, and Megan Burks. "Now Better Trained and Resourced, Minne-apolis Violence Interrupters to Hit Streets Next Month." *MPR News*, May 27, 2021. www.mprnews.org/story/2021/05/27/now-better-trained-and -resourced-minneapolis-violence-interrupters-to-hit-streets-next-month.

Critical Resistance. "Critical Resistance: Beyond the Prison Industrial Complex 1998 Conference." January 28, 2022. http://criticalresistance.org /critical-resistance-beyond-the-prison-industrial-complex-1998-conference.

Crocker, Thomas. "The Fourth Amendment and the Problem of Social Cost." *Northwestern University Law Review* 117, no. 2 (2022): 473–548.

Cummings, John E. "The Cost of Crazy: How Therapeutic Jurisprudence and Mental Health Courts Lower Incarceration Costs, Reduce Recidivism, and Improve Public Safety." *Loyola Law Review* 56, no. 1 (2010): 279–310.

Cure Violence. "The Model." Accessed January 28, 2022. https://perma.cc /9TVF-HPGQ.

Davidson, Adam. "Managing the Police Emergency." *North Carolina Law Review* 100, no. 4 (2022): 1209–91.

Davidson, Adam. "Procedural Losses and the Pyrrhic Victory of Abolishing Qualified Immunity." *Washington University Law Review* 99, no. 62 (2022): 1459–1530.

Davies, Thomas. "Recovering the Original Fourth Amendment." *Michigan Law Review* 98, no. 3 (1999): 547–750.

Davis, Angela. *Are Prisons Obsolete?* New York: Seven Stories Press, 2003.

Davis, Robert, Mary Lombardo, Daniel Woods, Christopher Koper, and Carl Hawkins. "Civilian Staff in Policing: An Assessment of the 2009 Byrne Civilian Hiring Program." National Criminal Justice Reference Service, 2014. www.ncjrs.gov/pdffiles1/nij/grants/246952.pdf.

Dean, Charles W., Richard Lumb, Kevin Proctor, James Klopovic, Amy Hyatt, and Rob Hamby. *Social Work and Police Partnership: A Summons to the Village. Strategies and Effective Practices.* Governor's Crime Commission, North Carolina Department of Crime Control and Public Safety, October 2000. https://soar.suny.edu/bitstream/handle/20.500.12648/2161/crj_ facpub/1/fulltext%20%281%29.pdf?sequence=1.

Debusmann, Bernd. "Why Do So Many Police Traffic Stops Turn Deadly?" *BBC*, January 31, 2023. www.bbc.com/news/world-us-canada-64458041.

Dellinger, Jolynn, and Stephanie Pell. "Bodies of Evidence: The Criminalization of Abortion and Surveillance of Women in a Post-Dobbs World." *Duke Journal of Constitutional Law and Public Policy* 19, no. 1 (2024): 1–108.

Dennis, Brady, Mark Berman, and Elahe Izadi. "Dallas Police Chief Says 'We're Asking Cops to Do Too Much in This Country.'" *Washington Post*, July 11, 2016. www.washingtonpost.com/news/post-nation/wp/2016/07/11 /grief-and-anger-continue-after-dallas-attacks-and-police-shootings -as-debate-rages-over-policing.

Denver the Mile High City. "Support Team Assisted Response (STAR) Program." Accessed November 25, 2024. https://denvergov.org/Government /Agencies-Departments-Offices/Agencies-Departments-Offices-Directory /Public-Health-Environment/Community-Behavioral-Health/Behavioral-Health-Strategies/Support-Team-Assisted-Response-STAR-Program.

Department of Justice. "Importance of Police-Community Relationships and Resources for Further Reading." January 22, 2022. www.justice.gov/file /1437336/download.

Dilanian, Ken, and Laura Strickler. "She Won a Pulitzer for Exposing How the Country's Poorest State Spent Federal Welfare Money. Now She Might Go to Jail." *NBC News*, July 2, 2024. www.nbcnews.com/investigations/anna-wolfe-pulitzer-mississippi-welfare-scandal-phil-bryant-rcna159936.

Dillon, Nancy. "Parents of Schizophrenic Man Shot Dead by Off-Duty Cop in California Costco Say They 'Begged' for Son's Life." *New York Daily News*, August 26, 2019. www.nydailynews.com/news/national/ny-parents-file-claim -lapd-officer-son-california-costco-20190826-shnyr7bssnetdowlwpnbk4vn7u -story.html.

Dix, Dorothea. "'I Tell What I Have Seen'—The Reports of Asylum Reformer Dorothea Dix." National Library of Medicine, April 9, 2006. Excerpted from Dorothea Dix, *Memorial to the Legislature of Massachusetts* (Boston: Munroe and Francis, 1843). https://pmc.ncbi.nlm.nih.gov/articles /PMC1470564/.

Dix, George E. "Federal Constitutional Confession Law." *Temple Law Review* 67, no. 1 (1988): 231–91.

Donohue, Laura. "The Original Fourth Amendment." *University of Chicago Law Review* 83, no. 3 (2016): 1181–1328.

Dove Delegates. "Utilizing Imagery of Nelson Mandela and the Symbol of a Dove of Peace, DOVE Delegates in Lousiville, Kentucky 'Lead with Healing' as a Way to 'Dismantle Systems of Oppression' through Nonviolence." January 24, 2024. www.dovedelegates.org/about.

Dressler, Joshua. *Understanding Criminal Law.* Durham, NC: Carolina Academic Press, 2017.

Dressler, Joshua. *Understanding Criminal Procedure*. 7th ed. Durham, NC: Carolina Academic Press, 2017.

Drexel University Dornsife School of Public Health. "Banged Up and Burned Out: Assaults by Patients against Paramedics and EMTs." 2022. https://drexel.edu/dornsife/research/centers-programs-projects/FIRST/In-the-media/Banged%20Up%20and%20Burned%20Out%20-%20Assaults%20by%20Patients%20Against%20Paramedics%20and%20EMTs/.

DuBoff, Gregory. "Asset Forfeiture Scheme Empowers Cops to Seize and Keep Cars, Cash and Homes Even When Owners Are Not Charged with a Crime." Rutherford Institute, March 23, 2023. www.rutherford.org/publications_resources/on_the_front_lines/government_asset_forfeiture_scheme_empowers_police_to_seize_and_keep_cars_cash_homes_even_when_owners_are_not_charged_with_a_crime#:~:text=Civil%20asset%20forfeiture%20is%20a%20practice%20where%20government,the%20local%20police%20who%20did%20the%20initial%20seizure.

Dulaney, Cody. "Mayor Gloria's Push for Homeless 'Progressive Enforcement' Leads to Eightfold Spike in Arrests." *News Source*, June 10, 2022. https://inewsource.org/2022/06/10/san-diego-homeless-arrests/.

Eaglin, Jessica. "The Drug Court Paradigm." *American Criminal Law Review* 53, no. 3 (2016): 595–640.

The Economist/YouGov Poll. "June 14–16, 2020—1500 US Adult Citizens." January 22, 2022. https://docs.cdn.yougov.com/vgqowgynze/econTabReport.pdf.

Edelman, Lauren. *Working Law: Courts, Corporations, and Symbolic Civil Rights*. Chicago: University of Chicago Press, 2016.

Edwards, Frank, Hedwig Lee, and Michael Esposito. "Risk of Being Killed by Police Use-of-Force in the U.S. by Age, Race/Ethnicity, and Sex." *Proceedings of the National Academy of Sciences*, August 5, 2019. www.pnas.org/doi/full/10.1073/pnas.1821204116.

Eldridge, Taylor. "Cops Could Use First Aid to Save Lives. Many Never Try." *Marshall Project*, December 15, 2020. www.themarshallproject.org/2020/12/15/cops-could-use-first-aid-to-save-lives-many-never-try.

Ellis, James. "Law Enforcement's Role in the Delivery of Emergency Medical Services in Maine." Homeland Security Digital Library, August 2001. www.hsdl.org/c/abstract/?docid=9016.

Ellis, Rebecca. "Portland City Council Approves Budget Cutting Additional $ 15M from Police." *Oregon Public Broadcasting*, June 17, 2020. www.opb.org/news/article/portland-police-budget-15-million-defund-cannabis-council-vote/.

Encinas, Ciara. "An Inside Look at San Diego's 2nd Safe Sleeping Site for Homeless." *ABC News 10*, October 20, 2023. www.10news.com/news/local-news/san-diego-news/an-inside-look-at-san-diegos-2nd-safe-sleeping-site-for-homeless.

Eugene Police Department. "CAHOOTS Program Analysis 2021 Update." www.eugene-·or.gov/DocumentCenter/View/66051/CAHOOTS-program-analysis-2021-update.

Fagan, Jeffrey. "Race and Reasonableness in Police Killings." *Boston University Law Review* 100, no. 14 (2020): 951–1016.

Fain, Kimberly. "Viral Black Death: Why We Must Watch Citizen Videos of Police Violence." *JSTOR Daily*, September 1, 2016. https://daily.jstor.org/why-we-must-watch-citizen-videos-of-police-violence/.

Fallon, Richard H., Jr. "Judicial Supremacy, Departmentalism, and the Rule of Law in a Populist Age." *Texas Law Review* 96, no. 3 (2018): 487–553.

Fariba, Kamron A., and Vikas Gupta. *Involuntary Commitment*. StatPearls. Treasure Island, FL: StatPearls Publishing, 2024.

Ferguson, Andrew Guthrie. "Big Data and Predictive Reasonable Suspicion." *University of Pennsylvania Law Review* 163, no. 3 (2015): 327–409.

Fields, Shawn E. "Debunking the Stranger-in-the-Bushes Myth: The Case for Sexual Assault Protection Orders." *Wisconsin Law Review* 2017, no. 3 (2017): 429–90.

Fields, Shawn E. "The Elusiveness of Self-Defense for the Black Transgender Community." *Nevada Law Journal* 21, no. 3 (2021): 975–95.

Fields, Shawn E. "The Fourth Amendment without Police." *University of Chicago Law Review* 90, no. 4 (2023): 1023–93.

Fields, Shawn E. *Neighborhood Watch: Policing White Spaces in America.* Cambridge: Cambridge University Press, 2022.

Fields, Shawn E. "The Procedural Justice Industrial Complex." *Indiana Law Journal* 99, no. 2 (2024): 563–618.

Fields, Shawn E. "Protest Policing and the Fourth Amendment." *University of California Davis Law Review* 55, no. 1 (2021): 347–400.

Fields, Shawn E. "Weaponized Racial Fear." *Tulane Law Review* 93, no. 4 (2019): 931–1015.

Fisk, Catherine, and L. Song Richardson. "Police Unions." *George Washington Law Review* 85, no. 3 (2017): 712–99.

Fixler, Alex. "Police-Social Work Collaboration and the Ethical Practice Paradox: Perspectives from Social Work's Next Generation." *Journal of Progressive Human Services*, forthcoming. https://d-scholarship.pitt.edu/44250/1/JPHS%20-%20SW_Police_Collaboration.pdf.

Fletcher, Matthew. "Erasing the Thin Blue Line: An Indigenous Proposal." *Michigan State Law Review* 2021, no. 1 (2021): 1447–87.

Fox 61. "Hartford School Social Worker Arrested for Sexual Assault." September 19, 2023. www.msn.com/en-us/news/other/hartford-school-social-worker-arrested-for-sexual-assault/ar-AA1ncmsv.

Francis, Megan Ming. "Reimagining Justice: A Primer on Defunding the Police and Prison Abolition." *Pocket*, January 28, 2022. https://getpocket.com

/collections/reimagining-justice-a-primer-on-defunding-the-police-and-prison-abolition.

Frankel, Richard. "Regulating Privatized Government through § 1983." *University of Chicago Law Review* 76, no. 4 (2009): 1449–1516.

Friedman, Barry. "Disaggregating the Policing Function." *University of Pennsylvania Law Review* 169, no. 4 (2021): 925–99.

Friedman, Barry. "Lawless Surveillance." *New York University Law Review* 97, no. 4 (2022): 1143–1214.

Friedman, Barry, and Cynthia Benin Stein. "Redefining What's 'Reasonable': The Protections for Policing." *George Washington Law Review* 84, no. 2 (2016): 281–353.

Fryer, Roland G. "An Empirical Analysis of Racial Differences in Police Use of Force." Working paper, National Bureau of Economic Research, 2018. www .nber.org/papers/w22399.pdf.

Gallion, Bailey. "'Call-In' Offers Aid to Paroled Gang Members to Stop Violence—or Face Prison Time." *Columbus Dispatch*, October 18, 2023. www .dispatch.com/story/news/crime/2023/10/18/columbus-call-in-program-offers-gang-members-choice-of-halting-violence-for-aid-or-face-consequences/71218103007/.

Garrett, Brandon. "Contaminated Confessions Revisited." *Virginia Law Review* 101, no. 2 (2015): 395–454.

Garrett, Brandon, and Seth Stoughton. "A Tactical Fourth Amendment." *Virginia Law Review* 103, no. 2 (2017): 211–307.

Georgia Public Safety Training Center. "Georgia Crisis Intervention Team (CIT) Program—GPSTC." Accessed November 25, 2024. https://access.gpstc.org /student/classes/details?gpstcCode=MC2057.

Gerety, Rowan Moore. "An Alternative to Police That Police Can Get Behind." *The Atlantic*, December 28, 2020. www.theatlantic.com/politics/archive /2020/12/cahoots-program-may-reduce-likelihood-of-police-violence /617477/.

Gillespie, Sarah, Mari McGilton, and Amy Rogin. "Understanding Denver's STAR Program." Urban Institute, August 21, 2023. www.urban.org /research/publication/understanding-denvers-star-program.

Gimbel, V. Noah, and Craig Muhammad. "Are Police Obsolete? Breaking Cycles of Violence through Abolition Democracy." *Cardozo Law Review* 40, no. 4 (2019): 1509–26.

Ginsburg, Ruth Bader. "The Role of Dissenting Opinions." *Minnesota Law Review* 95, no. 1 (2010): 1–8.

Globe, Celia. "Social Workers to the Rescue? An Urgent Call for Emergency Response Reform." *Fordham Urban Law Journal* 68, no. 4 (2021): 1024–26.

Goff, Phillip Atiba, Tracey Lloyd, Amanda Geller, Steven Raphael, and Jack Glaser. "The Science of Justice: Race, Arrests, and Police Use of Force."

Center for Policing Equity, July 2016. https://policingequity.org/images /pdfs-doc/CPE_SoJ_Race-Arrests-UoF_2016-07-08-1130.pdf.

Gold, Michael, and Troy Closson. "What We Know about Daniel Prude's Case and Death." *New York Times*, April 16, 2021. www.nytimes.com/article /what-happened-daniel-prude.html#:~:text=The%20Monroe%20 County%20medical%20examiner,according%20to%20an%20autopsy%20 report.&text=The%20report%20also%20said%20that,contributing%20 factors%20in%20his%20death.

Goldstein, Dana. "Do Police Officers Make Schools Safer or More Dangerous?" *New York Times*, June 12, 2020. www.nytimes.com/2020/06/12/us /schools-police-resource-officers.html.

Goldstein, Joseph. "Officers Said They Smelled Pot. The Judge Called Them Liars." *New York Times*, September 13, 2019. www.nytimes.com/2019/09 /12/nyregion/police-searches-smelling-marijuana.html.

Goldstein, Rebecca, Michael W. Sances, and Hye Young You. "Exploitative Revenues, Law Enforcement, and the Quality of Government Service." *Urban Affairs Review* 61, no. 1 (2020): 1–14.

Goodman, J. David. "A Year after 'Defund,' Police Departments Get Their Money Back." *New York Times*, October 10, 2021. www.nytimes.com/2021 /10/10/us/dallas-police-defund.html.

Gormley, Elena. "Social Workers Can't Help People in Crisis by Partnering with Police." *Jacobin*, April 25, 2021. https://jacobinmag.com/2021/04/social-workers-police-chicago-co-responder-model.

Graham, David. "The Stumbling Block to One of the Most Promising Police Reforms." *The Atlantic*, February 22, 2022. www.theatlantic.com/ideas /archive/2022/02/mental-health-crisis-police-intervention/622842/.

Guarino, Ben. "Few Americans Want to Abolish Police, Gallup Survey Finds." *Washington Post*, July 22, 2020. www.washingtonpost.com/nation/2020 /07/22/abolish-police-gallup-poll/.

Gulley, Jordan, Francine Arienti, Rebecca Boss, Alicia Woodsby, and Vikki Wachino. "Mobile Crisis Teams: A State Planning Guide for Medicaid Financed Crisis Response Services." California Healthcare Foundation, February 3, 2022. www.tacinc.org/wp-content/uploads/2022/01/CHCF-Mobile-Crisis-Services-State-Planning-Guide-2021-01-24_Final.pdf.

Gupta-Kagan, Josh. "Beyond Law Enforcement: Camreta v. Greene, Child Protection Investigations, and the Need to Reform the Fourth Amendment Special Needs Doctrine." *Tulane Law Review* 87, no. 2 (2012): 370–75.

Gupta-Kagan, Josh. "Reevaluating School Searches Following School-to -Prison Pipeline Reforms." *Fordham Law Review* 87, no. 5 (2019): 2013–67.

Hadden, Sally E. *Slave Patrols: Law and Violence in Virginia and the Carolinas*. Cambridge, MA: Harvard University Press, 2001.

Halverstadt, Lisa. "San Diego's Homeless Response Took a Punitive Turn in 2023." *Voice of San Diego*, December 28, 2023. https://voiceofsandiego.org /2023/12/28/san-diegos-homeless-response-took-a-punitive-turn-in-2023/.

Harmon, Rachel A. "Legal Remedies for Police Misconduct." August 9, 2017. https://papers.ssrn.com/sol3/papers.cfm?abstract_id=3015952.

Harrison, Bob. "Stop, Start, or Continue? A National Survey of the Police about Traffic Stops." Rand Corp., June 30, 2021. www.rand.org/pubs/commentary /2021/06/stop-start-or-continue-a-national-survey-of-the-police.html.

Hart, Angela. "Tossed Medicine, Delayed Housing: How Homeless Sweeps Are Thwarting Medicaid's Goals." *CNN Health*, September 11, 2024. www.cnn .com/2024/09/11/health/homeless-encampments-sweeps-san-francisco -kff-health-news-partner/index.html.

Harvard Civil Rights–Civil Liberties Law Review. "A Reform and Revolution to Fourth Amendment Jurisprudence." January 31, 2023. https://journals.law .harvard.edu/crcl/a-reform-and-revolution-to-fourth-amendment- jurisprudence/.

Harvard Law Review. "Leading Cases." 115, no. 1 (2001): 335.

Harvard Law Review. "Policing and Profit." 128 no. 6 (2015): 1726–27.

Harvard Law Review. "Prosecuting the Police-less City: Police Abolition's Impact on Local Prosecutors." 135, no. 5 (2021): 1900.

Hassel, Diana. "Excessive Reasonableness." *Indiana Law Review* 43, no. 1 (2009): 117–42.

Hauck, Grace. "Denver Successfully Sent Mental Health Professionals, Not Police, to Hundreds of Calls." *USA Today*, February 6, 2021. www.usatoday .com/story/news/nation/2021/02/06/denver-sent-mental-health-help-not- police-hundreds-calls/4421364001/.

Hause, Marti, and Ari Melber. "Half of People Killed by Police Have a Disability: Report." *NBC News*, December 1, 2015. www.nbcnews.com/news /us-news/half-people-killed-police-suffer-mental-disability-report- n538371.

Heflin, Julie. "UofL to Help Lead in Development of 911 Alternative Response Model for Louisville." University of Louisville, May 20, 2021. www.uoflnews .com/post/uofltoday/uofl-to-help-lead-in-development-of-911-alternative-response- model-for-louisville/.

Herman, Susan. "Beyond Parity: Section 1983 and the State Courts." *Brooklyn Law Review* 54, no. 4 (1989): 1057–1135.

Hermannson, Linus. "Firewalls: A Necessary Tool to Enable Social Rights for Undocumented Migrants in Social Work." *International Social Work* 65, no. 4 (2022): 1–15. https://journals.sagepub.com/doi/full/10 .1177/0020872820924454.

Herzing, Rachel. "Address to the Critical Prison Studies Caucus of the Ameri- can Studies Association: Keyword Police." American Studies Association,

November 8, 2014. www.theasa.net/communities/caucuses/critical-prison-studies-caucus.

Hetey, Rebecca C., Benoît Monin, Amrita Maitreyi, and Jennifer L. Eberhardt. "Data for Change: A Statistical Analysis of Police Stops, Searches, Handcuffings, and Arrests in Oakland, Calif., 2013–2014." Stanford SPARQ: Social Psychological Answers to Real-World Questions, 2016. https://stanford.app .box.com/v/Data-for-Change.

Houston Police Department, Mental Health Division. "Crisis Call Diversion Program." January 24, 2022. www.houstoncit.org/ccd/.

Human Rights Watch. "You Have to Move! The Cruel and Ineffective Criminalization of Unhoused People in Los Angeles." August 14, 2024. www.hrw.org /news/2024/08/14/us-los-angeles-criminalizes-unhoused-people?gad _source=1&gclid=Cj0KCQjw1Yy5BhD-ARIsAI0RbXapjOVNOR54Dft1Qt-MbwBgsLTPqC-0q4O0O_MPW3i67w4pQM5lUY4AaAh_hEALw_wcB.

Huq, Aziz. "The Consequences of Disparate Policing: Evaluating Stop and Frisk as a Modality of Urban Policing." *Minnesota Law Review* 101, no. 1 (2017): 2397–2480.

Ireland, Elizabeth. "City Council Addresses Urgent Homeless Shelter Needs, Expands Safe Sleeping Program." *Times of San Diego*, October 1, 2024. https://timesofsandiego.com/politics/2024/10/01/city-council-addresses-urgent-homeless-shelter-needs-expands-safe-sleeping-program /#:~:text=Current%20capacity%20for%20the%20Safe,the%20out-skirts%20of%20Balboa%20Park.

Iuliano, Jason. "The New Diversity Crisis in the Federal Judiciary." *Tennessee Law Review* 84, no. 1 (2016): 247.

Jackman, Tom. "Oakland Police, Stopping and Handcuffing Disproportionate Numbers of Blacks, Work to Restore Trust." *Washington Post*, June 15, 2016. www.washingtonpost.com/news/true-crime/wp/2016/06/15/oakland-police-stopping-and-handcuffing-disproportionate-numbers-of-blacks -work-to-restore-trust/.

Jackson, Jesse. "Juvenile Violence, Juvenile Justice: Reclaiming Our Youth from Violence." *Boston College Law Review* 36, no. 5 (1995): 913–26.

Jackson, Jonathan. "Centering Race in Procedural Justice Theory: Structural Racism and the Under- and Overpolicing of Black Communities." *Law and Human Behavior* 47, no. 1 (2023): 68–82.

Jacobi, John. "Prosecuting Police Misconduct." *Wisconsin Law Review* 2000, no. 1 (2000): 789–854.

Jacobi, Tonja, and Ross Berlin. "Supreme Irrelevance: The Court's Abdication in Criminal Procedure Jurisprudence." *University of California, Davis Law Review* 51, no. 5 (2018): 2033–2127.

Jaqua, Benjamin. "Policing the Police: Reexamining the Constitutional Implications of Traffic Stops." *Indiana Law Review* 50, no. 1 (2016): 345–67.

Jeanne Geiger Crisis Center. "Domestic Violence High Risk Team." January 30, 2022. http://dvhrt.org/about.

Jina-Pettersen, Nourredine. "Fear, Neglect, Coercion, and Dehumanization: Is Inpatient Psychiatric Trauma Contributing to a Public Health Crisis?" National Library of Medicine, August 9, 2022. https://pubmed.ncbi.nlm.nih .gov/35968056/.

Jonathan, Marc Blitz. "Video Surveillance and the Constitution of Public Space: Fitting the Fourth Amendment to a World That Tracks Image and Identity." *Texas Law Review* 82, no. 6 (2004): 1349–81.

Jones, Trina. "Aggressive Encounters and White Fragility: Deconstructing the Trope of the Angry Black Woman." *Iowa Law Review* 102, no. 5 (2017): 2017–69.

Jun, Hyun-Jin, Jordan E. DeVylder, and Lisa Fedina. "Police Violence among Adults Diagnosed with Mental Disorders." *Health Society and Work* 45, no. 2 (2020): 82–85.

Justice and Hope for Children. "Multi Disciplinary Team." January 30, 2022. www.capjustice.org/cap/multidisciplinary-team/.

Kaba, Mariame. *We Do This 'til We Free Us: Abolitionist Organizing and Transforming Justice.* Chicago: Haymarket Books, 2021.

Kaba, Mariame. "Yes, We Mean Literally Abolish the Police." *New York Times*, June 12, 2020. www.nytimes.com/2020/06/12/opinion/sunday/floyd-abolish-defund-police.html.

Kaba, Mariame, and Andrea J. Ritchie. *No More Police: A Case for Abolition.* New York: New Press, 2022.

Kamisar, Yale. "'Comparative Reprehensibility' and the Fourth Amendment Exclusionary Rule." *Michigan Law Review* 86, no. 1 (1987): 1–50.

Kansara, Reha. "Black Lives Matter: Can Viral Videos Stop Police Violence?" *BBC News*, July 6, 2020. www.bbc.com/news/blogs-trending-53239123.

Karteron, Alexis. "When Stop and Frisk Comes Home: Policing Public and Patrolled Housing." *Case Western Reservation Law Review* 69, no. 3 (2016): 669–729.

Kassin, Sam M. "On the Psychology of Confessions: Does Innocent Put Innocents at Risk?" *American Psychologist* 60, no. 3 (2005): 215–28.

Kaufman, Maya. "Ongoing Struggles within B-HEARD, the City's Mental Health Crisis Response Pilot." *Politico*, April 17, 2023. www.politico .com/newsletters/weekly-new-york-health-care/2023/04/17/ongoing-struggles-within-b-heard-the-citys-mental-health-crisis-response-pilot-00092093.

Kaur, Harmeet. "What Studies Reveal about Gun Ownership in the US." *CNN*, June 2, 2022. https://edition.cnn.com/2022/06/02/us/gun-ownership -numbers-us-cec/index.html.

Keane, Larry. "Americans Charted Record Book Year for Firearms in 2023, with 2024 Looming Large Too." *NSSF*, January 8, 2024. www.nssf.org /articles/2023-record-year-for-firearms-2024-looming-large/.

Kelly, John, and Mark Nichols. "We Found 85,000 Cops Who've Been Investigated for Misconduct. Now You Can Read Their Records." *USA Today*, last updated June 11, 2020. www.usatoday.com/in-depth/news/investigations /2019/04/24/usa-today-revealing-misconduct-records-police-cops /3223984002/.

Kelly, Lisa. "Abolition or Reform: Confronting the Symbiotic Relationship between 'Child Welfare' and the Carceral State." *Stanford Journal of Civil Rights and Civil Liberties* 17, no. 2 (2021): 255–70.

Kendall, Marisa. "Backers of California Homeless Camp Ban Cite 'Successful' San Diego Law. But Is It?" *Washington State Standard*, April 15, 2024. https://washingtonstatestandard.com/2024/04/15/backers-of-california-homeless-camp-ban-cite-successful-san-diego-law-but-is-it/.

Kendall, Marisa. "Exclusive: California's Homeless Population Grew Again This Year, Especially in These Counties." *CalMatters*, September 10, 2024. https://calmatters.org/housing/homelessness/2024/09/pit-count-analysis -2024/#:~:text=Sacramento%20and%20San%20Joaquin%20 counties,increased%20nearly%20a%20whopping%20160%25.

Kerr, Orin S. "Cross-Enforcement of the Fourth Amendment." *Harvard Law Review* 132, no. 2 (2018): 473–535.

Kesslen, Ben. "Calls to Reform, Defund, Dismantle, and Abolish the Police, Explained." *NBC News*, June 8, 2020. www.nbcnews.com/news/us-news /calls-reform-defund-dismantle-abolish-police-explained-n1227676.

KGET. "KCSO Releases Summary of Deadly Officer-Involved Shooting Near Fort Tejon." August 12, 2019. www.kget.com/news/crime-watch/kcso-releases-summary-of-officer-involved-shooting-near-fort-tejon/.

Kindy, Kimberly. "Insurers Force Change on Police Departments Long Resistant to It." *Washington Post*, September 14, 2022. www.washingtonpost.com /investigations/interactive/2022/police-misconduct-insurance-settlements-reform/.

Kirkpatrick, David. "Pulled Over: Why Many Police Traffic Stops Turn Deadly." *New York Times*, October 31, 2021. www.nytimes.com/2021/10/31/us /police-traffic-stops-killings.html.

Klick, Jonathan, and Alexander Tabarrok. "Using Terror Alert Levels to Estimate the Effect of Police on Crime." *Journal of Law and Economics* 48, no. 1 (2005): 267–79.

Kotalik, Liz. "Denver's STAR Program Sees Promising Results in First Six Months." *9News*, February 11, 2021. www.9news.com/article/news /denver-star-program-results-police/73-90e50e08-94c5-474d-8e94 -926d42f8f41d.

KPIX. "Study Shows California Cops More Likely to Stop Black Drivers."
    January 2, 2020. https://sanfrancisco.cbslocal.com/2020/01/02/study-
    shows-california-police-more-stop-black-drivers.
Krumrey, Yvonne. "Siblings of Juneau Man Killed by Police Demand Answers."
    KTOO, August 23, 2024. www.ktoo.org/2024/08/23/siblings-of-juneau-
    man-killed-by-police-demand-answers/.
Kushner, Rachel. "Is Prison Necessary? Ruth Wilson Gilmore Might Change
    Your Mind." *New York Times*, April 17, 2019. www.nytimes.com/2019
    /04/17/magazine/prison-abolition-ruth-wilson-gilmore.html.
Lacks, Jeremy. "The Lone American Dictatorship: How Court Doctrine and
    Police Culture Limit Judicial Oversight of the Police Use of Deadly Force."
    New York University Annals Survey of American Law 64, no. 23 (2008): 428.
LaFraniere, Sharon, and Andrew W. Lehren. "The Disproportionate Risks of
    Driving While Black." *New York Times*, October 24, 2015. www.nytimes.com
    /2015/10/25/us/racial-disparity-traffic-stops-driving-black.html.
Lahut, Jake. "Support for Defunding the Police Collapsed in 2021, with Steep
    Drops among Black Adults and Democrats, New Poll Shows." *Business
    Insider*, October 26, 2021. www.businessinsider.com/defund-the-police-
    polling-public-support-drop-democrats-pew-research-2021-10.
Lamin, Sylvester Amara, and Consoler Teboh. "Police Social Work and Com-
    munity Policing." *Cogent Society Science* 2, no. 1 (2016): 1–13.
Lanfear, Charles C. "Formal Social Control in Changing Neighborhoods: Racial
    Implications of Neighborhood Context on Reaction Policing." *City and
    Community* 17, no. 4 (2018): 1093.
Lartey, Jamiles. "By the Numbers: US Police Kill More in Days Than Other
    Countries Do in Years." *The Guardian*, June 9, 2015. www.theguardian.com
    /us-news/2015/jun/09/the-counted-police-killings-us-vs-other-countries.
Lee, Cynthia. "Officer-Created Jeopardy: Broadening the Time Frame for
    Assessing a Police Officer's Use of Deadly Force." *George Washington Law
    Review* 89, no. 6 (2021): 1362–1451.
Lee, Cynthia. "Reforming the Law on Police Use of Deadly Force: De-
    escalation, Preseizure Conduct, and Imperfect Self-Defense." *University of
    Illinois Law Review* 2018, no. 2 (2018): 629–92.
Lee, Michaela, and Josh Du. "*Everything Everywhere All at Once* Passes *Return
    of the King* as Most-Awarded Movie Ever." *IGN*, March 9, 2023. www.ign
    .com/articles/everything-everywhere-all-at-once-return-of-the-king-most-
    awarded-movie.
Lee, Michelle Ye Hee. "O'Malley's Claim about Crime Rates in Baltimore."
    Washington Post, April 28, 2015. www.washingtonpost.com/news/fact
    -checker/wp/2015/04/28/omalleys-claim-about-crimerates-in-baltimore.
Leider, Robert. "The State's Monopoly of Force and the Right to Bear Arms."
    Northwestern University Law Review 116, no. 1 (2021): 35–80.

Leo, Richard. *Police Interrogation and American Justice*. Cambridge, MA: Harvard University Press, 2008.

Levenson, Eric. "A Step-by-Step Look at How Law Enforcement's Visit to Sonya Massey's Home Went So Wrong." *CNN*, July 24, 2024. www.cnn.com/2024 /07/23/us/sonya-massey-police-shooting-what-went-wrong/index.html.

Levin, Sam. "US Police Have Killed Nearly 600 People in Traffic Stops since 2017, Data Shows." *The Guardian*, April 21, 2022. www.theguardian.com /us-news/2022/apr/21/us-police-violence-traffic-stop-data.

Levine, Kate. "Police Prosecutions and Punitive Instincts." *Washington University Law Review* 98, no. 4 (2021): 997–1057.

Levinson-Waldman, Rachel. "Hiding in Plain Sight: A Fourth Amendment Framework for Analyzing Government Surveillance in Public." *Emory Law Journal* 66, no. 3 (2017): 527–615.

Liederbach, John, and James Frank. "Policing Mayberry: The Work Routines of Small-Town and Rural Officers." *American Journal of Criminal Justice* 28, no. 1 (2003): 53–72.

Loor, Karen Pita. "Tear Gas + Water Hoses + Dispersal Orders: The Fourth Amendment Endorses Brutality in Protest Policing." *Boston University Law Review* 100, no. 5 (2020): 817–48.

Lopez, German. "The Evidence for Violence Interrupters Doesn't Support the Hype." *Vox*, September 3, 2021. www.vox.com/22622363/police-violence-interrupters-cure-violence-research-study.

Lopez, German. "He Helped His Overdosing Friend by Calling 911. Police Slapped Him with a Manslaughter Charge." *Vox*, May 24, 2017. www.vox .com/policy-and-politics/2017/5/24/15684664/opioid-epidemic-manslaughter-overdose-charge.

Lopez Segoviano, Maria G. "The Criminal Justice Standard for Determining Whether Police Officers Used Excessive Force: A Validation of White Supremacy." *Hastings Race and Poverty Law Journal* 16, no. 2 (2019): 233–62.

Lowery, Wesley. "Aren't More White People Than Black People Killed by Police? Yes, but No." *Washington Post*, July 11, 2016. www.washingtonpost.com /news/post-nation/wp/2016/07/11/arent-more-white-people-than-black-people-killed-by-police-yes-but-no/.

Lowery, Wesley, Kimberly Kindy, Keith L. Alexander, Julie Tate, Jennifer Jenkins, and Steven Rich, "Distraught People, Deadly Results." *Washington Post*, June 30, 2015. www.washingtonpost.com/sf/investigative/2015/06 /30/distraught-people-deadly-results/?utm_term=.a263183cf8bc.

Lowrey-Kingberg, Belén, and Grace Sullivan Buker. "'I'm Giving You a Lawful Order': Dialogic Legitimacy in Sandra Bland's Traffic Stop." *Law and Society Review* 51, no. 2 (2017): 379–412.

Luden, Jennifer. "Homelessness in the U.S. Hit a Record High Last Year as Pandemic Aid Ran Out." *NPR*, December 15, 2023. www.npr.org /homelessness-affordable-housing-crisis-rent-assistance.

MacDonald, John, Jonathan Klick, and Ben Grunwald. "The Effect of Privately Provided Police Services on Crime: Evidence from a Geographic Regression Discontinuity Design." *Journal of the Royal Statistical Society* 179, no. 3 (2016): 831–46.

Maclin, Tracey. "Is Obtaining an Arrestee's DNA a Valid Special Needs Search under the Fourth Amendment?" *Journal of Law, Medicine and Ethics* 33, no. 1 (2005): 102–24.

Maclin, Tracey. "Race and the Fourth Amendment." *Vanderbilt Law Review* 51, no. 2 (1998): 355–67.

MacNeill, Arianna. "'Unarmed Response Teams' May Be Coming to a Massachusetts City Near You, and Soon." *Boston.com*, August 3, 2021. www.boston.com /news/local-news/2021/08/03/massachusetts-communities-unarmed-response-teams/.

Magid, Laurie. "The *Miranda* Debate: Questions Past, Present, and Future." Review of *The* Miranda *Debate: Law, Justice, and Policing*, ed. Richard A. Leo and George C. Thomas III. *Houston Law Review* 36, no. 3 (1999): 1251–1314.

Maiarechi, Kia. "What the Data Really Says about Police and Racial Bias." *Vanity Fair*, July 14, 2016. www.vanityfair.com/news/2016/07/data-police-racial-bias.

Martinsburg Initiative. "Martinsburg Police." Accessed January 18, 2024. www .martinsburgpd.org/martinsburg-initiative.

Mathiesen, Thomas. *Prison on Trial*. 3rd ed. Winchester, UK: Waterside Press, 2006.

Matthiesen, Wickert, & Lehrer, SCc. "Municipal/County/Local Governmental Immunity and Tort Liability in All 50 States." Accessed November 30, 2024. www.mwl-law.com/resources/municipal-county-local-governmental-immunity-tort-liability-50-states/.

Maxted, David. "The Qualified Immunity Litigation Machine." *Denver Law Review* 98, no. 3 (2021): 629–82.

Mays, Jeffery C. "New York Adopts Record $99 Billion Budget to Aid Pandemic Recovery." *New York Times*, June 30, 2021. www.nytimes.com/2021/06/30 /nyregion/nyc-budget-covid.html.

McAffee, Thomas. "The Federal System as Bill of Rights: Original Understandings, Modern Misreadings." *Villanova Law Review* 43, no. 1 (1998): 90.

McCarthy, Niall. "U.S. Civilians Own 393 Million Firearms." Statista, June 28, 2018. www.statista.com/chart/14468/us-civilians-own-393-million-firearms/#:~:text=The%202018%20Small%20Arms%20Survey%20 analyzed%20the%20number,are%20owned%20by%20civilians%20in%20 the%20United%20States.

McCord, Eva. "The Fourteen Lost Clinics." *Chicago Maroon*, October 9, 2022. https://chicagomaroon.com/36921/grey-city/the-fourteen-lost-clinics/.

McDowell, Megha G., and Luis A. Fernandez. "'Disband, Disempower, Disarm': Amplifying the Theory and Practice of Police Abolition." *Critical Criminology* 26, no. 3 (2018): 373–91.

McLeod, Allegra M. "Beyond the Carceral State." Review of *Caught: The Prison State and the Lockdown of American Politics*, by Marie Gottschalk. *University of Texas Law Review* 95, no. 3 (2017): 651–706.

McWhinney, Jakob. "La Mesa Taps Outreach Workers, Not Cops, to Reach Homeless Population." *Voice of San Diego*, April 19, 2022. https://voiceofsandiego.org/2022/04/19/la-mesa-taps-outreach-workers-not-cops-to-reach-homeless-population/.

MehChu, Nduoh. "Policing as Assault." *California Law Review* 111, no. 3 (2023): 865–925.

Meko, Hurubie, and Brittany Kriegstein. "He Was Mentally Ill and Armed. The Police Shot Him within 28 Seconds." *New York Times*, March 30, 2023. www.nytimes.com/2023/03/30/nyregion/nypd-shooting-mental-health.html.

Mello-Klein, Cody. "How Do Videos of Police Brutality Affect Us, and How Should We Engage with Them?" *Northeastern Global News*, February 6, 2023. https://news.northeastern.edu/2023/02/06/police-brutality-videos-impact/.

Méndez, Juan. *Report of the Special Rapporteur on Torture and Other Cruel, Inhuman or Degrading Treatment or Punishment*. Human Rights Council. UN Doc. A/HRC/22/53 (2013). https://documents.un.org/doc/undoc/gen/g13/105/77/pdf/g1310577.pdf.

Mental Health Center of Denver. "Support Team Assisted Response." January 27, 2022. https://mhcd.org/star-program/.

Merker, Irene. "A Modest Proposal for the Abolition of Custodial Confessions." *North Carolina Law Review* 68, no. 1 (1989): 69–115.

Miller, Leila. "Reformers Want Police to Step Back from Mental Health Calls. The LAPD Says It's Been Trying." *Los Angeles Times*, June 24, 2020. www.latimes.com/california/story/2020-06-24/protests-spur-bid-for-lapd-to-move-back-from-mental-health-calls.

Milligan, Luke. "Congressional End-Run: The Ignored Constraint on Judicial Review." *Georgia Law Review* 45, no. 1 (2010): 211–73.

Milligan, Luke. "The Forgotten Right to Be Secure." *Hastings Law Journal* 65, no. 3 (2014): 713–60.

Mind Freedom International. "Fighting Back against Human Rights Abuses in the Mental Health System." https://mindfreedom.org/image-view-fullscreen-d159/.

Morgan, Jamelia. "Policing under Disability Law." *Stanford Law Review* 73, no. 6 (2021): 1401–69.

Morgan, Jamelia. "Psychiatric Holds and the Fourth Amendment." *Columbia Law Review* 124, no. 5 (2023): 1363–1442.

Mundell, Ernie. "Most Homeless Americans Are Battling Mental Illness." *U.S. News*, April 17, 2024. www.usnews.com/news/health-news/articles/2024-04-17/most-homeless-americans-are-battling-mental-illness#:~:text= The%20mental%20health%20of%20participants,least%20sometime%20 during%20their%20lives.

Nakaso, Dan. "Social Service Workers and Police Join Forces to Aid Homeless." *Star Advertiser*, August 11, 2017. www.staradvertiser.com/2017/08/11 /hawaii-news/social-service-workers-and-police-join-forces-to-aid-homeless.

National Alliance on Mental Illness. "Crisis Intervention Team Programs." January 27, 2022. www.nami.org/Advocacy/Crisis-Intervention/Crisis-Intervention-Team-(CIT)-Programs.

National Association of Emergency Medical Technicians. "Code of Ethics." January 24, 2024. www.naemt.org/about-ems/code-of-ethics.

National Association of Social Workers. "Code of Ethics." 2008. www .socialworkers.org/LinkClick.aspx?fileticket=KZmmbz15evc%3D&.

National Committee on Law Observance and Law Enforcement. "Report on Lawlessness in Law Enforcement." 1931. Office of Justice Programs. www .ojp.gov/ncjrs/virtual-library/abstracts/us-national-commission-law-observance-and-enforcement-report-no-11.

National Institutes of Justice. "Perceptions of Treatment by Police: Impacts of Personal Interactions and the Media." March 17, 2014. https://nij.ojp.gov /topics/articles/perceptions-treatment-police-impacts-personal-interactions-and-media.

National Law Enforcement Officers Memorial Fund. "Slave Patrols: An Early Form of American Policing." Accessed October 18, 2023. https://nleomf.org /slave-patrols-an-early-form-of-american-policing/.

National Safety Council. "Preventable Deaths: Odds of Dying." Accessed 2022. https://injuryfacts.nsc.org/all-injuries/preventable-death-overview/odds-of-dying/.

Nawaz, Anna. "Study Shows First Words from Police during Traffic Stops Affect Outcome for Black Drivers." *PBS*, June 7, 2023. www.pbs.org/newshour /show/study-shows-first-words-from-police-during-traffic-stops-affect-outcome-for-black-drivers.

NBC 5 Chicago. "City of Chicago Paying up to $1.2 Million to Private Security Firms to Deter Looting." June 6, 2020. www.nbcchicago.com/news/local /city-of-chicago-paying-up-to-1-2-million-to-private-security-firms -to-deter-looting/2285718/.

Nelson, Blake. "Move-Ins Are Underway at Newest Safe Sleeping Site as San Diego Enforces Homeless Camping Ban." *San Diego Union Tribune*, October

23, 2023. www.sandiegouniontribune.com/news/homelessness/story/2023
-10-23/san-diego-safe-sleeping-site-homeless-camping-ban.

Neusteter, Rebecca. "Every Three Seconds: Unlocking Police Data on Arrests."
Vera Institute of Justice, 2019. www.vera.org/publications/arrest-trends
-every-three-seconds-landing/arrest-trends-every-three-seconds/overview.

Newman, Andy, and Emma G. Fitzsimmons. "New York City to Involuntarily
Remove Mentally Ill People from Streets." *New York Times*, June 20, 2023.
www.nytimes.com/2022/11/29/nyregion/nyc-mentally-ill-involuntary
-custody.html.

Newman, Benjamin J., Tyler T. Reny, and Jennifer L. Merolla. "Race, Prejudice,
and Support for Racial Justice Countermovements: The Case of 'Blue Lives
Matter.'" *Political Behavior* 46, no. 3 (2023): 1491–1510.

Newsom, Gavin. "Governor Newsom Orders State Agencies to Address
Encampments in Their Communities with Urgency and Dignity." July 25,
2024. www.gov.ca.gov/2024/07/25/governor-newsom-orders-state-
agencies-to-address-encampments-in-their-communities-with-urgency
-and-dignity/.

Nir, Sarah Maslin. "On City Streets, Fear and Hope as Mayor Pushes to Remove
Mentally Ill." *New York Times*, November 30, 2022. http://narpa.org
/conferences/narpa-2022/round-up-the-usual-suspects/NYT-On-City
-Streets-12-01-2022.pdf.

Nordberg, Maya. "Jails Not Homes: Quality of Life on the Streets of San
Francisco." *Hastings Women's Law Journal* 13, no. 2 (2002): 261–305.

Nowell, Cecelia. "Adora Perez Is Free." *The Cut*, May 12, 2022. www.thecut
.com/2022/05/adora-perezs-murder-charges-over-stillbirth-are-dropped.html.

Oakland POWER Projects. "Abolitionist." Brochure. Accessed January 15,
2025. https://static1.squarespace.com/static/59ead8f9692ebee25b72f17f
/t/5b6ab5f7352f535083505c5a/1533720057821/TheOakPowerProj
_HEALTHreport.pdf.

Obasogie, Osagie. "Excited Delirium and Police Use of Force." *Virginia Law
Review* 107, no. 8 (2021): 1545–1620.

Obasogie, Osagie, and Zachary Newman. "The Endogenous Fourth Amendment: An Empirical Assessment of How Police Understandings of Excessive
Force Become Constitutional Law." *Cornell Law Review* 104, no. 5 (2019):
1281–1336.

Obasogie, Osagie, and Anna Zaret. "Medical Professionals, Excessive Force,
and the Fourth Amendment." *California Law Review* 109, no. 1 (2021):
1–61.

Ocen, Priscilla A. "The New Racially Restrictive Covenant: Race, Welfare, and
the Policing of Black Women in Subsidized Housing." *University of California, Los Angeles Law Review* 59, no. 6 (2012): 1541–82.

O'Connor, Meg. "Los Angeles Is Locking Up More People with Mental Illness Than Ever Before. Why?" Center for Health Journalism, October 14, 2022. https://centerforhealthjournalism.org/our-work/insights/los-angeles-locking-more-people-mental-illness-ever-why.

Oppel, Richard. "Minneapolis Police Use Force against Black People at 7 Times the Rate of Whites." *New York Times*, June 3, 2020. www.nytimes.com /interactive/2020/06/03/us/minneapolis-police-use-of-force.html.

Orange County EMS. "Paramedics Are Clearly Prohibited from 'Hog-Tying' Patients, in Contrast with Police. Compare Application of Restraints by EMS Personnel." April 1, 2019. www.ochealthinfo.com/sites/hca/files/import /data/files/38654.pdf.

Ortiz, Erik. "Inside 100 Million Police Traffic Stops: New Evidence of Racial Bias." *NBC News*, March 13, 2019.

Ostrowsky, Jonathan. "#MeToo's Unseen Frontier: Law Enforcement's Sexual Misconduct and the Fourth Amendment Response." *University of California Los Angeles Law Review* 67, no. 1 (2020): 258.

Paradis, Renée. "Carpe Demonstratores: Towards a Bright-Line Rule Governing Seizure in Excessive Force Claims Brought by Demonstrators." *Columbia Law Review* 103, no. 2 (2003): 316–49.

Parafiniuk-Talesnick, Tatiana. "In Cahoots: How the Unlikely Pairing of Cops and Hippies Became a National Model." *Register Guard*, October 20, 2019. www.registerguard.com/story/news/2021/12/10/cahoots-eugene-oregon-unlikely-pairing-cops-and-hippies-became-national-model-crisis-response /6472369001/.

Paulas, Rick. "Encampment Sweeps Take Away Homeless People's Most Important Belongings." *VICE*, March 4, 2020. www.vice.com/en/article /encampment-sweeps-take-away-homeless-peoples-most-important-belongings/#:~:text=%E2%80%9CPeople%20are%20only%20given%20 a,Department%20of%20Transportation%20for%20destroying.

PBS News. "U.S. Homelessness Up 12 Percent to Highest Reported Level as Rents Soar and Pandemic Aid Lapses." December 15, 2023. www.pbs.org /newshour/economy/u-s-homelessness-up-12-percent-to-highest-reported-level-as-rents-soar-and-pandemic-aid-lapses.

Pearson, Jake. "Actors, Mentally Ill, Aid NYC Police Training Meant to Calm." *Associated Press*, September 13, 2015. https://apnews.com/article/8977d364 6c6d4ffb9e0f423e295e20a7.

Peha, Joseph. "Councilmember Lewis Announces Proposal to Lower Costs and Fast Track Construction of Permanent Supportive Housing." *Seattle City Council Blog*, November 30, 2020. https://council.seattle.gov/2020/11/30 /councilmember-lewis-announces-proposal-to-lower-costs-and-fast -track-construction-of-permanent-supportive-housing/.

Peha, Joseph. "Lewis Proposes New Public Health-Informed 911 Response Service." *Seattle City Council Blog*, July 6, 2020. https://council.seattle.gov /2020/07/06/lewis-proposes-new-public-health-informed-911-response-service/.

Perkins, Jane. "Ask a Firefighter: Why Do Firetrucks and Police Respond to 911 Medical Calls?" *Westerly Sun*, May 4, 2019. www.thewesterlysun.com /opinion/guest-columns/ask-a-firefighter-why-do-firetrucks-and-police -respond-to-911-medical-calls/article_bc9cd518-6ddd-11e9-982c -87378d5cfaed.html.

Peterson, Jillian. "Presence of Armed School Officials and Fatal and Nonfatal Gunshot Injuries during Mass School Shootings, United States, 1980–2019." *JAMA Network Open*, February 16, 2021. https://jamanetwork.com /journals/jamanetworkopen/fullarticle/2776515.

Pierrotti, Andy. "'I Was a Cash Cow'—Georgia Cities Accused of Using Police as Revenue Generators." *Atlanta News First*, August 5, 2024. www .atlantanewsfirst.com/2024/08/05/i-was-cash-cow-i-georgia-cities-accused-using-police-revenue-generators/.

Pierson, Emma, Camelia Simoiu, Jan Overgoor, Sam Corbett-Davies, Daniel Jenson, Amy Shoemaker, Vignesh Ramachandran, et al. "A Large-Scale Analysis of Racial Disparities in Police Stops across the United States." *Nature Human Behavior* 4, no. 7 (2020): 736–45. https://5harad.com /papers/100M-stops.pdf.

Pittman, Ashton, and William Pittman. "How Brett Favre Got $6 Million in Welfare Funds for a Volleyball Stadium." *Mississippi Free Press*, September 16, 2022. www.mississippifreepress.org/in-depth-how-brett-favre-secured-6-million-in-welfare-funds-for-a-volleyball-stadium/.

Plant-Chirlin, Jeanine. "Saddled with Debt, Indigent Defendants Face New Paths Back to Prison." Brennan Center for Justice, October 4, 2010. www .brennancenter.org/our-work/analysis-opinion/saddled-debt-indigent-defendants-face-new-paths-back-prison.

Police Accountability Task Force. "Recommendations for Reform: Restoring Trust between the Chicago Police and the Communities They Serve. Executive Summary." 2016. https://chicagopatf.org/wp-content/uploads/2016/04 /PATF_Final_Report_Executive_Summary_4_13_16–1.pdf.

Police Executive Research Forum (PERF). "Use of Force: Taking Policing to a Higher Standard, at Policy 2." January 29, 2016. www.policeforum.org /assets/30guidingprinciples.pdf.

Primus, Eve Breniske. "Disentangling Administrative Searches." *Columbia Law Review* 111, no. 2 (2011): 254–312.

Radiolab. "Mr. Graham and the Reasonable Man." *More Perfect* podcast, Season 2, November 30, 2017. https://radiolab.org/podcast/radiolab-presents-more-perfect-mr-graham-reasonable-man.

Rahman, Khaleda. "Overwhelming Support for Non-police First Responder Agency: Poll." *Newsweek*, June 17, 2020. www.newsweek.com/overwhelming-support-non-police-first-responder-agency-1511362.

Ramirez, Rachel. "Obama Said "Defund the Police" Is a Bad Slogan. This Shouldn't Come as a Surprise." *Vox*, December 3, 2020. www.vox.com /2020/12/3/22150452/obama-defund-the-police-snappy-slogan.

Rao, Maya. "Between Defund and Defend, L.A. Tries New Tactics, Bigger Budget for Cops." *PBS Frontline*, August 28, 2021. www.pbs.org/wgbh /frontline/article/between-defund-and-defend-l-a-tries-new-tactics-bigger-budget-for-cops/.

Reamey, Gerald. "When 'Special Needs' Meet Probable Cause: Denying the Devil Benefit of Law." *Hastings Law Constitutional Quarterly* 19, no. 1 (1992): 295–342.

Regions Hospital Emergency Medical Services. "'Patient Restraint': Regions Hospital Emergency Medical Services. Year 2000 EMS Guidelines." January 25, 2024. http://wearcam.org/decon/full_body_restraint.htm.

Reinart, Alexander. "New Federalism and Civil Rights Enforcement." *Northwestern University Law Review* 116, no. 3 (2021): 737–816.

Reiss, Albert. *The Police and the Public.* New Haven, CT: Yale University Press, 1972.

Renan, Daphna. "The Fourth Amendment as Administrative Governance." *Stanford Law Review* 68, no. 5 (2016): 1039–1129.

Reuters. "Minneapolis Restores Police Budget after 'Defund' Cuts." December 12, 2021. www.rt.com/usa/542973-minneapolis-police-budget/.

Rhoden, Giselle. "The Jayland Walker Shooting Revives Debate about How Police Interact with Black People. Here Are Other High-Profile Cases." *CNN*, July 7, 2022. www.cnn.com/2022/04/16/us/police-shootings-outcomes -controversies/index.html.

Riga, Kate. "City Officials Weigh Police Department Budget Cuts amid Nationwide Protests." *Talking Points Memo*, June 4, 2020. https://talkingpointsmemo.com /news/police-department-budget-cut-los-angeles-protest.

Riski, Tess. "A Portland Program Intended to Reduce Police Interactions with People in Crisis Is Off to a Slow Start." *Willamette Week*, April 14, 2021. www.wweek.com/news/2021/04/14/a-portland-program-intended-to-reduce-police-interactions-with-people-in-crisis-is-off-to-a-slow-start/.

Ritchie, Andrea. *Invisible No More: Police Violence against Black Women and Women of Color.* Boston: Beacon Press, 2017.

Roberts, Dorothy. "Abolition Constitutionalism." *Harvard Law Review* 133, no. 1 (2019): 1–122.

Rogers, Michael S., Dale E. McNeil, and Renee L. Binder. "Effectiveness of Police Crisis Intervention Training Programs." *Journal of the American Academy of Psychiatry and the Law* 52, no. 3 (2024): 414–21.

Rosenthal, Lawrence. "Good and Bad Ways to Address Police Violence." *Urban Law* 48, no. 4 (2016): 675–736.

Ross, Cody T. "A Multi-level Bayesian Analysis of Racial Bias in Police Shootings at the County-Level in the United States, 2011–2014." *PLoS One* 10, no. 11 (2015): e0141854.

Ross, Josephine. "Blaming the Victim: 'Consent' within the Fourth Amendment and Rape Law." *Harvard Journal on Racial and Ethnic Justice* 26, no. 1 (2010): 1–61.

Roth, Alisa. "The Truth about Deinstitutionalization." *The Atlantic*, May 25, 2021. www.theatlantic.com/health/archive/2021/05/truth-about-deinstitutionalization/618986/.

RT. "Minneapolis Restores Police Budget after 'Defund' Cuts." December 12, 2021. www.rt.com/usa/542973-minneapolis-police-budget/.

Ruderman Family Foundation. "Media Missing the Story: Half of All Recent High Profile Police-Related Killings Are People with Disabilities." Ruderman Foundation, The Ruderman White Paper, March 8, 2016. https://rudermanfoundation.org/media-missing-the-story-half-of-all-recent-high-profile-police-related-killings-are-people-with-disabilities/.

Rudovsky, David, and Lawrence Rosenthal. "Debate: The Constitutionality of Stop-and-Frisk in New York City." *University of Pennsylvania Law Review* 117 (2013). https://scholarship.law.upenn.edu/cgi/viewcontent.cgi?params=/context/faculty_scholarship/article/1589/&path_info=162_U_Pa_L_Rev_Online_117.pdf.

Rush, Claire. "From San Francisco to New York City, Cities Are Cracking Down on Homeless Encampments." *Mercury News*, November 28, 2023. www.mercurynews.com/2023/11/28/cities-crack-down-on-homeless-encampments-advocates-say-thats-not-the-answer/#:~:text=Cities%20across%20the%20U.S.%20are%20struggling%20with%20and,there%20aren%E2%80%99t%20enough%20homes%20or%20beds%20for%20everyone.

Rushin, Stephen. "An Empirical Assessment of Pretextual Stops and Racial Profiling." *Stanford Law Review* 73, no. 3 (2021): 675–90.

Sabalow, Ryan. "Bill Would Let Therapists and Social Workers Decide When to Confine Mentally Ill Californians for Treatment." *KQED*, January 30, 2024. www.kqed.org/news/11974214/bill-would-let-therapists-and-social-workers-decide-when-to-confine-mentally-ill-californians-for-treatment.

Saletan, William. "'Defund the Police' Is a Self-Destructive Slogan." *Slate*, November 18, 2020. https://slate.com/news-and-politics/2020/11/defund-police-slogan-election-polls-democrats.html.

Sanchez, Rosa. "Minneapolis City Council Approves Police Budget Cuts 7 Months after George Floyd's Death." *ABC News*, December 10, 2020. https://

abcnews.go.com/US/minneapolis-city-council-approves-police-budget-cuts-months/story?id=74643667.

Sanders, Kindaka. "The New Dread, Part II: The Judicial Overthrow of the Reasonableness Standard in Police Shooting." *Cleveland State Law Review* 71, no. 4 (2023): 1029–1146.

San Diego County. "P.E.R.T. Psychiatric Emergency Response Team." January 27, 2022. www.sandiegocounty.gov/content/dam/sdc/hhsa/programs/bhs/documents/pert_flyer.pdf.

Sato, Mia. "Social Workers Are Rejecting Calls for Them to Replace Police." *The Appeal*, August 20, 2020. https://theappeal.org/social-workers-are-rejecting-calls-for-them-to-replace-police/.

Schuppe, Jon. "Biden Wants to Give Anti-violence Groups $5 Billion. Here's How It Could Be Spent." *NBC News*, April 14, 2021. www.nbcnews.com/news/us-news/biden-wants-give-anti-violence-groups-5-billion-here-s-n1263990.

Schwartz, Joanna. "After Qualified Immunity." *Columbia Law Review* 120, no. 2 (2020): 309–88.

Schwartz, Joanna. "The Case against Qualified Immunity." *Notre Dame Law Review* 93, no. 5 (2018): 1797–1852.

Schwartz, Joanna. *Shielded: How the Police Became Untouchable*. New York: Viking, 2023.

Schwartzapfel, Beth, and Cary Aspinwall. "'Using Medication as a Weapon': What's the Consequence When a Paramedic Is Involved in a Deadly Police Encounter?" *USA Today*, September 22, 2021. www.usatoday.com/story/news/investigations/2021/09/22/paramedics-charged-manslaughter-elijah-mcclain-case-its-rare/5799209001/.

Scott, A. O. "*Everything Everywhere All at Once* Review: It's Messy, and Glorious." *New York Times*, March 24, 2022. www.nytimes.com/2022/03/24/movies/everything-everywhere-all-at-once-review.html.

Searcy, Dionne. "What Would Efforts to Defund or Disband Police Departments Really Mean?" *New York Times*, June 8, 2020. www.nytimes.com/2020/06/08/us/what-does-defund-police-mean.html.

Sekhon, Nirej. "Police and the Limit of Law." *Columbia Law Review* 119, no. 6 (2019): 1711–72.

Selsky, Andrew. "How Some Encounters between Police and People with Mental Illness Can Turn Tragic." *PBS*, September 2, 2022. www.pbs.org/newshour/health/how-some-encounters-between-police-and-people-with-mental-illness-can-turn-tragic.

Selsky, Andrew, and Leah Willingham. "'Tragic Outcomes': Mentally Ill Face Fatal Risk with Police." *Los Angeles Times*, September 1, 2022. www.latimes.com/world-nation/story/2022-09-01/mentally-ill-face-fatal-risk-with-police.

Settembre, Jeanette. "Small Businesses, Retailers Hire Private Security to Protect Stores." *Fox Business*, June 5, 2020. www.foxbusiness.com/retail /small-businesses-retailers-private-security-protect-against-looting.

Shapiro, Ari, Mia Venkat, and Patrick Jarenwattananon. "New Report Tracks Criminal Prosecutions of Self-Managed Abortions." *NPR*, August 9, 2022. www.npr.org/2022/08/09/1116590982/new-report-tracks-criminal-prose-cutions-of-self-managed-abortions#:~:text=Preliminary%20research %20from%20this%20report,compared%20to%20the%20larger%20 population.

Sharkey, Patrick. "Why Do We Need the Police?" *Washington Post*, June 12, 2020. www.washingtonpost.com/outlook/2020/06/12/defund-police-violent-crime/?arc404=true.

Shaver, Elizabeth. "Handcuffing a Third Grader? Interactions between School Resource Officers and Students with Disabilities." *Utah Law Review* 2017, no. 2 (2017): 229–82.

Shourd, Sarah. "They Called for Help. They'd Always Regret It." *The Atlantic*, January 30, 2021. www.theatlantic.com/health/archive/2021/01/when-mental-health-crisis-lands-you-jail/617599/.

Shults, Joel. "What Officers and the Public Are Thinking about Mental Health Crisis Response." *Police 1*, May 14, 2021. www.police1.com/chiefs-sheriffs /articles/what-officers-and-the-public-are-thinking-about-mental-health-crisis-response-CNCSlABMEV5aHt7q/.

Sifuentes, Edward, and Alison Ross. "The 21-Year Fight to Bring Down Project 100%." ACLU, December 21, 2021. www.aclu-sdic.org/en/publications /the-21-year-fight-to-bring-down-project100.

Simmons, Ric. "Constitutional Double Standards: The Unintended Conse-quences of Reducing Police Presence." *George Washington Law Review* 91, no. 4 (2023): 817–63.

Simonson, Jocelyn. "Police Reform through a Power Lens." *Yale Law Journal* 130, no. 4 (2017): 778–860.

Slevin, Colleen, and Matthew Brown. "Two Paramedics Found Guilty in the Death of Elijah McClain." *Time*, December 23, 2023. https://time.com /6550708/elijah-mcclain-verdict-paramedics-guilty-fatal-ketamine/.

Slobogin, Christopher. "Testilying: Police Perjury and What to Do about It." *University of Colorado Law Review* 67, no. 1 (1996): 1037–60.

Smith, Greg B. "What Happens When Police Show Up for Mental Health Calls?" *The City* (NYC), December 12, 2022. www.thecity.nyc/2022/12/12/what-happens-police-respond-mental-health-calls-edp/.

Social Service Workers United–Chicago. "The NASW Is Failing Us. Either It Changes, or We Will Change It Ourselves." January 28, 2022. https:// socialserviceworkersunited.medium.com/the-nasw-is-failing-us-either-it-changes-or-we-will-change-it-ourselves-b1da4c8a0096.

Solove, Daniel J. "Digital Dossiers and the Dissipation of Fourth Amendment Privacy." *Southern California Law Review* 75, no. 10 (2002): 1084–1168.

Song, Ji Seon. "Policing the Emergency Room." *Harvard Law Review* 134, no. 8 (2021): 2646–2720.

Song Richardson, L. "Arrest Efficiency and the Fourth Amendment." *Minnesota Law Review* 95, no. 6 (2011): 2035–98.

Sow, Marissa Jackson. "Protect and Serve." *California Law Review* 110 (2022): 743–93.

Spoerre, Anna. "Missouri Republicans Push Bill to Defund Planned Parenthood after Years of Legal Fights." *KBIA*, January 26, 2024. www.kbia.org/missouri -news/2024-01-26/missouri-republicans-push-bill-to-defund-planned- parenthood-after-years-of-legal-fights.

Stamper, Norm. *To Protect and Serve: How to Fix America's Police.* New York: Nation Books, 2016.

Statista. "Rate of Civilians Killed by the Police Annually in Selected Countries, as of 2019." www.statista.com/statistics/1124039/police-killings-rate-selected- countries/.

Statista Research Department. "Number of Arrests for All Offenses in the United States from 1990 to 2022." October 20, 2023. www.statista.com/statistics /191261/number-of-arrests-for-all-offenses-in-the-us-since-1990/.

Stefkovich, Jacqueline. "Law Enforcement Officers in Public Schools: Student Citizens in Safe Havens?" *Brigham Young University Education and Law Journal* 1999, no. 2 (1999): 25–69.

Steiker, Carol. "Second Thoughts about First Principles." *Harvard Law Review* 107, no. 4 (1994): 820–57.

Stein, Robin. "Before the Final Frame: When Police Missteps Create Danger." *New York Times*, February 1, 2024. www.nytimes.com/interactive/2021 /10/30/video/police-traffic-stops-danger-video.html.

Stephens, Alain. "The 'Warrior Cop' Is a Toxic Mentality. And a Lucrative Industry." *Slate*, June 19, 2020. https://slate.com/news-and-politics/2020/06 /warrior-cop-trainings-industry.html.

Stoughton, Seth. "Commentary: Law Enforcement's 'Warrior' Problem." *Harvard Law Review* 128, no. 6 (2015): 226–29.

Stoughton, Seth. "How the Fourth Amendment Frustrates the Regulation of Police Violence." *Emory Law Journal* 70, no. 3 (2021): 521–85.

Stuntz, William. "Implicit Bargains, Government Power, and the Fourth Amendment." *Stanford Law Review* 44, no. 3 (1992): 553–91.

Subramanian, Ram, Jackie Fielding, Lauren-Brooke Eisen, Hernandez D. Stroude, and Taylor King. *Revenue over Public Safety: How Perverse Financial Incentives Warp the Criminal Justice System.* Brennan Center for Justice, July 6, 2022. www.brennancenter.org/our-work/research-reports /revenue-over-public-safety.

Sundby, Scott. "A Return to Fourth Amendment Basics: Undoing the Mischief of *Camara* and *Terry*." *Minnesota Law Review* 72, no. 2312 (1988): 383–448.

Sutherland, Arthur E., Jr. "Crime and Confession." *Harvard Law Review* 79, no. 1 (1965): 21–41.

Swan, Sarah. "Discriminatory Dualism." *Georgia Law Review* 54, no. 1 (2020): 869–926.

Sweeney, Annie. "Police De-escalation Training—How It Could Help Chicago." *Chicago Tribune*, March 25, 2016. www.chicagotribune.com/news/ct-police-training-las-vegas-chicago-met-20160324-story.html.

Swenson, Kyle. "Teens Tied Down and Shot Up with Drugs at Pembroke Pines Facility." *Miami New Times*, February 20, 2014. www.miaminewtimes.com /news/teens-tied-down-and-shot-up-with-drugs-at-pembroke-pines-facility-6394901.

Thompson, Christie. "Sending Unarmed Responders Instead of Police: What We've Learned." *MindSite News*, August 6, 2024. https://mindsitenews .org/2024/08/06/sending-unarmed-responders-instead-of-police-what-weve-learned/.

Thompson, Derek. "Unbundle the Police." *The Atlantic*, June 11, 2020. www .theatlantic.com/ideas/archive/2020/06/unbundle-police/612913/.

Toronto Sun. "Social Worker Accused of Sex Assault, Indecent Act at Brampton Shelter." January 17, 2024. www.msn.com/en-ca/news/world/social-worker -accused-of-sex-assault-indecent-act-at-brampton-shelter/ar-AA1mTnmT.

Torralva, Krista. "New Video Shows Dallas Paramedic Kicking Homeless Man at Least Nine Times before Police Arrived." *Dallas News*, October 20, 2021. www.dallasnews.com/news/investigations/2021/10/20/new-video-shows-dallas-paramedic-kick-homeless-man-at-least-nine-times-before-police -arrive/.

Tran, Mark. "FBI Chief: 'Unacceptable' That Guardian Has Better Data on Police Violence." *The Guardian*, October 8, 2015. www.theguardian.com /us-news/2015/oct/08/fbi-chief-says-ridiculous-guardian-washington-post-better-information-police-shootings.

Treatment Advocacy Center. "Grading the States: An Analysis of Involuntary Psychiatric Treatment Laws." 2020. www.tac.org/reports_publications /grading-the-states-an-analysis-of-involuntary-psychiatric-treatment -laws-2020/.

Treger, Harvey. "Police Social Work." In *The Encyclopedia of Social Work*, edited by Terry Mizrahi and Larry E. Davis. New York: Oxford University Press, 2008.

Tuerkheimer, Deborah. "Underenforcement as Unequal Protection." *Boston College Law Review* 57, no. 4 (2026): 1287–1335.

UC Center for Police Research and Policy. "Assessing the Impact of Co-responder Team Programs: A Review of Research." www.theiacp.org/sites

/default/files/IDD/Review%20of%20Co-Responder%20Team%
20Evaluations.pdf.

Uetricht, Micah. "Policing Is Fundamentally a Tool of Social Control to Facilitate Our Exploitation." *Jacobin*, June 8, 2020. https://jacobinmag.com
/2020/06/alex-vitale-police-reform-defund-protests.

Urbonya, Kathryn. "Public School Officials' Use of Physical Force as a Fourth
Amendment Seizure: Protecting Students from the Constitutional Chasm
between the Fourth and Fourteenth Amendments." *George Washington Law
Review* 69, no. 1 (2000): 1–56.

US Census Bureau. "U.S. and World Population Clock." January 14, 2024.
www.census.gov/popclock/.

US Department of Justice. "What Is a School Resource Officer?" January 24,
2024. https://cops.usdoj.gov/supportingsafeschools#:~:text=SROs%20
are%20sworn%20law%20enforcement%20officers%20responsible%20
for,in%20an%20effort%20to%20create%20a%20safer%20environment.

US Department of Housing and Urban Development. "2022 Annual Homelessness Assessment Report (AHAR) to Congress—December 2022." January 24,
2024. www.huduser.gov/portal/sites/default/files/pdf/2022-ahar-part-1.pdf.

U.S. News & World Report. "Most Expensive Places to Live in the U.S. in 2023–
2024." January 14, 2024. https://realestate.usnews.com/places/rankings
/most-expensive-places-to-live.

Vera Institute. "Redefining Public Safety Initiative." Accessed January 20, 2025.
www.vera.org/ending-mass-incarceration/criminalization-racial-disparities
/public-safety/redefining-public-safety-initiative.

Viscusi, W. Kip, and Scott Jeffrey. "Damages to Deter Police Shootings."
University of Illinois Law Review 741, no. 1 (2021): 741–802.

Vitale, Alex. *The End of Policing.* London: Verso, 2017.

Wald, Johanna, and Nat Kendall-Taylor. "Keep the Ideas behind 'Defund the
Police,' but Forget the Slogan." *The Hill*, January 28, 2021. https://thehill
.com/opinion/criminal-justice/535895-keep-the-ideas-behind-defund-
the-police-but-forget-the-slogan/.

Washington Post. "Fatal Force: Police Shooting Database 2015–2023." www
.washingtonpost.com/graphics/investigations/police-shootings-database/.

Washington Post Editorial Board. "Opinion: Sending Armed Police Officers
Isn't the Right Answer for Every Emergency." *Washington Post*, October 16,
2020. www.washingtonpost.com/opinions/sending-armed-police-officers
-isnt-the-right-answer-for-every-emergency/2020/10/16/606b0cd0-0cae
-11eb-b1e8-16b59b92b36d_story.html.

Waters, Rob. "Calling Mental Health Workers, Not Police, to Deal with Mental
Health Crises." *Washington Post*, June 20, 2021. www.washingtonpost.com
/health/mental-health-workers-not-police/2021/06/18/bf250938-c937
-11eb-a11b-6c6191ccd599_story.html.

Watson, Amy, Melissa Schaefer Morabito, Jeffrey Draine, and Victor Ottati. "Improving Police Response to Persons with Mental Illness: A Multi-level Conceptualization of CIT." *International Journal of Law and Psychiatry* 31, no. 4 (2008): 359–68.

WBUR. "'Happy Hunting': Documents Reveals Close Ties between ICE and Boston Police." November 6, 2019. www.wbur.org/news/2019/10/25/boston-police-immigration-officers-relationship-documents.

Weatherspoon, Floyd. "Ending Racial Profiling of African-Americans in the Selective Enforcement of Laws: In Search of Viable Remedies." *University of Pittsburgh Law Review* 65, no. 4 (2004): 721–61.

Websdale, Neil. *Policing the Poor: From Slave Plantation to Public Housing.* Boston: Northeastern University Press, 2001.

Wells, Michael. "Scott v. Harris and the Role of the Jury in Constitutional Litigation." *Review of Litigation* 29, no. 9 (2009): 65–119.

Western, Bruce. *Homeward: Life in the Year after Prison.* New York: Russell Sage, 2018.

White, Welsh S. "What Is an Involuntary Confession Now?" *Rutgers Law Review* 50, no. 1 (1998): 2001–57.

White House. "Remarks of President Joe Biden—State of the Union Address as Prepared for Delivery." March 1, 2022. www.whitehouse.gov/briefing-room/speeches-remarks/2022/03/01/remarks-of-president-joe-biden-state-of-the-union-address-as-delivered/.

Williams, Timothy. "Study Supports Suspicion That Police Are More Likely to Use Force on Blacks." *New York Times*, July 7, 2016. www.nytimes.com/2016/07/08/us/study-supports-suspicion-that-police-use-of-force-is-more-likely-for-blacks.html#:~:text=For%20those%20who%20were%20arrested,36%20per%201%2C000%20for%20whites.

Wilson, James Q., and George L. Kelling. "Broken Windows: The Police and Neighborhood Safety." *The Atlantic*, March 1982. www.theatlantic.com/magazine/archive/1982/03/broken-windows/304465/.

Woods, Jordan Blair. "Policing, Danger Narratives, and Routine Traffic Stops." *Michigan Law Review* 117, no. 4 (2019): 635–712.

Woods, Jordan Blair. "Traffic Enforcement Would Be Safer without Police." *Washington Post*, April 21, 2021. www.washingtonpost.com/outlook/2021/04/21/traffic-enforcement-without-police/.

Woods, Jordan Blair. "Traffic without the Police." *Stanford Law Review* 73, no. 3 (2021): 1471–1549.

Yang, Tiffany. "'Send Freedom House!': A Study in Police Abolition." *Washington Law Review* 96, no. 3 (2021): 1067–1112.

Yee, Michelle. "Yes, U.S. Locks People Up at a Higher Rate Than Any Other Country." *Washington Post*, July 7, 2015. www.washingtonpost.com/news

/fact-checker/wp/2015/07/07/yes-u-s-locks-people-up-at-a-higher-rate
-than-any-other-country/.

Yglesias, Matthew. "*The End of Policing* Left Me Convinced We Still Need
Policing." *Vox*, June 18, 2020. www.vox.com/2020/6/18/21293784/alex-
vitale-end-of-policing-review.

Yglesias, Matthew. "Growing Calls to 'Defund the Police,' Explained." *Vox*, June
3, 2020. www.vox.com/2020/6/3/21276824/defund-police-divest-explainer.

YouTube. "Audio, Video of Fatal Little Rock Police Shooting Released." February
1, 2024. www.youtube.com/watch?v=46s8JDzT_9E.

YouTube. "Police Chase Shootout in Rock Falls." January 26, 2018. www.youtube
.com/watch?v=G7l1IBjsIMY.

Zick, Timothy. *Managed Dissent: The Law of Public Protest*. Cambridge:
Cambridge University Press, 2023.

Zimring, Frank. *When Police Kill*. Cambridge, MA: Harvard University Press,
2017.

Index

abolitionists, 8–9, 26–28, 48–49, 108, 149. *See also* Defund the Police movement

abortion, 62–63

Adams, Mayor Eric, 37, 41, 70

adult protective service agencies, 147

Advance Peace, 45

affirmative regulation, 105. *See also* public safety

African Americans, 3, 23–27, 116. *See also* poorer communities

Akbar, Amna: "An Abolitionist Horizon for (Police) Reform," 26

Alabama, 20

alcoholism, 17, 22, 40. *See also* drug addiction

Alexander v. DeAngelo, 95

alternative dispatch infrastructure, 40

alternative response services, 35, 38, 46–81, 84–87, 103, 112, 122–24, 132, 136, 147–49; administrative searches by, 64, 140; of co-responders, 37–39, 42–43, 45, 47, 77, 141–43, 153; entanglement with police of, 140–44, 147, 153–55, 158, 183n45; government, 94, 131–32; "mixed motives" of, 73–76; private, 96–97, 101; regulating, 154–56, 158; relative legal impunity enjoyed by, 51, 84–86, 99, 127, 157; restrictions (or lack of restrictions) placed on, 126–29, 130–33, 135–37, 156–57; Supreme Court's elimination of protections for vulnerable citizens when involved in, 130–31, 135–36, 157; three models of, 35–36. *See also* civilian traffic enforcement; community caretaking; crisis interventionists; de-escalation; drug treatment; medical professionals; mental health responders; nonpolice alternate responders; psychiatrists; public safety; qualified immunity; violence interruption

Amara Lamin, Sylvester, 14

American College of Obstetricians and Gynecologists, 62

American Medical Association, 62

antipsychotic medications, 87, 89–90; as restraining sedatives, 90–91, 107, 156. *See also* drugs; involuntary psychiatric treatment

assault and battery claims, 97, 101

Baltimore, 16

Behavioral Health Emergency Assistance Response Division (B-HEARD), 41, 48

Bell, Monica, 30

Berkeley, 143

Biden, President Joe, 46

219

Founded in 1893,
UNIVERSITY OF CALIFORNIA PRESS
publishes bold, progressive books and journals
on topics in the arts, humanities, social sciences,
and natural sciences—with a focus on social
justice issues—that inspire thought and action
among readers worldwide.

The UC PRESS FOUNDATION
raises funds to uphold the press's vital role
as an independent, nonprofit publisher, and
receives philanthropic support from a wide
range of individuals and institutions—and from
committed readers like you. To learn more, visit
ucpress.edu/supportus.